Get the eBook FREE!

(PDF, ePub, Kindle, and liveBook all included)

We believe that once you buy a book from us, you should be able to read it in any format we have available. To get electronic versions of this book at no additional cost to you, purchase and then register this book at the Manning website.

Go to https://www.manning.com/freebook and follow the instructions to complete your pBook registration.

That's it!
Thanks from Manning!

Programming
with Types

WITH EXAMPLES IN TYPESCRIPT

VLAD RISCUTIA

MANNING
SHELTER ISLAND

For online information and ordering of this and other Manning books, please visit
www.manning.com. The publisher offers discounts on this book when ordered in quantity.
For more information, please contact

Special Sales Department
Manning Publications Co.
20 Baldwin Road
PO Box 761
Shelter Island, NY 11964
Email: orders@manning.com

Manning Publications Co.
20 Baldwin Road
PO Box 761
Shelter Island, NY 11964

Development editor:	Elesha Hyde
Technical development editor:	Mike Shepard
Review editor:	Aleksandar Dragosavljević
Project manager:	Lori Weidert
Copy editor:	Kathy Simpson
Proofreader:	Melody Dolab
Technical proofreader:	German Gonzalez-Morris
Typesetter and cover designer:	Marija Tudor

ISBN 9781617296413
Printed in the United States of America

To my wife, Diana, for her infinite patience

contents

preface

Programming with Types is the culmination of multiple years of learning about type systems and software correctness, distilled into a practical book with real-world applications.

I've always liked learning how to write better code, but if I were to point out exactly when I started down this path, I'd say it was 2015. I was switching teams at that point and wanted to get up to speed on modern C++. I started watching C++ conference videos, picked up Alexander Stepanov's books on generic programming, and gained a completely different perspective on how to write code.

In parallel, I was learning Haskell in my spare time and working my way through the advanced features of its type system. Programming in a functional language makes it obvious how some of the features taken for granted in such languages get adopted by more mainstream languages as time goes by.

I read several books on the topic, from Stepanov's *Elements of Programming* and *From Mathematics to Generic Programming* to Bartosz Milewski's *Category Theory for Programmers* and Benjamin Pierce's *Types and Programming Languages*. As you might be able to tell from the titles, these books are more on the theoretical/mathematical side. While learning more about type systems, I could tell that the code I was writing at work became better. There is a direct link between the more theoretical realm of type system design and the day-to-day production software. This isn't a revolutionary discovery: fancy type system features exist to address real-world problems.

I realized that not every practicing programmer has the time and patience to read dense books with mathematical proofs. On the other hand, my time wasn't wasted reading such books: they made me a better software engineer. I figured there is room for a book that covers type systems and the benefits they provide more informally, focusing on practical applications anyone can use in their day job.

Programming with Types aims to provide a walk-through of type system features start-ing from basic types, covering function types and subtyping, OOP, generic program-ming, and higher kinded types such as functors and monads. Instead of focusing on the theory behind these features, I describe each one of them in terms of practical applications. The book shows how and when to use each of these features to improve your code.

The code samples were originally supposed to be in C++. The C++ type system is powerful and more feature-rich than languages such as Java and C#. On the other hand, C++ is a complex language, and I didn't want to limit the audience of the book, so I decided to use TypeScript instead. TypeScript has a powerful type system too, but its syntax is more accessible, so it should be easy to work through most examples even if you're coming from another language. Appendix B provides a quick cheat sheet for the subset of TypeScript used in this book.

I hope you enjoy reading this book and learn some new techniques that you can apply to your projects right away.

acknowledgments

First, I want to thank my family for their support and understanding. My wife, Diana, and my daughter, Ada, were with me every step of the way, giving me all the encouragement and space I needed to complete this book.

Writing a book is most definitely a team effort. I'm grateful for Michael Stephens' initial feedback, which helped shape the book into what you are reading today. I want to thank my editor, Elesha Hyde, for all her help, advice, and feedback. Thanks to Mike Shepard for reviewing every chapter and keeping me honest. Also, thanks to German Gonzales for going through each and every code sample and making sure that everything works as described. I want to thank all reviewers for taking their time and providing invaluable feedback. Thanks to Viktor Bek, Roberto Casadei, Ahmed Chicktay, John Corley, Justin Coulston, Theo Despoudis, David DiMaria, Christopher Fry, German Gonzalez-Morris, Vipul Gupta, Peter Hampton, Clive Harber, Fred Heath, Ryan Huber, Des Horsley, Kevin Norman D. Kapchan, Jose San Leandro, James Liu, Wayne Mather, Arnaldo Gabriel Ayala Meyer, Riccardo Noviello, Marco Perone, Jermal Prestwood, Borja Quevedo, Domingo Sebastián Sastre, Rohit Sharm, and Greg Wright.

I want to thank my colleagues and mentors for everything they taught me. As I was learning about leveraging types to improve our codebase, I was lucky to have some great, supportive managers. Thanks to Mike Navarro, David Hansen, and Ben Ross for your trust.

Thanks to the whole C++ community from which I learned so much and especially to Sean Parent for his inspiring talks and his great advice.

about this book

Programming with Types aims to show how you can use type systems to write better, safer code. Although most books discussing type systems focus on more formal aspects, this book takes a pragmatic approach. It contains numerous examples, applications, and scenarios that you will encounter in your day job.

Who should read this book

This book is for practicing programmers who want to learn more about how type systems work and how to use them to improve code quality. You should have some experience using an object-oriented language such as Java, C#, C++, or JavaScript/TypeScript. You should also have some minimum software design experience. Although the book will provide various techniques for writing robust, composable, and better-encapsulated code, it assumes that you know why these properties are desirable.

How this book is organized: a road map

This book has 11 chapters covering various aspects of programming with types:

- Chapter 1 introduces types and type systems, discussing why they exist and how they are useful. We go over types of type systems and talk about typing strength, static typing, and dynamic typing.
- Chapter 2 covers basic types common across most languages and gotchas to be aware of when using them. Common basic types are the empty and unit types, Booleans, numbers, strings, arrays, and references.
- Chapter 3 is about composition: various ways in which types can be combined to define new types. The chapter also shows different ways to implement the visitor design pattern and defines algebraic data types.

- Chapter 4 talks about type safety—how we can use types to reduce ambiguity and prevent errors. The chapter also shows how we can add or remove typing information from our code by using type casting.
- Chapter 5 introduces function types and what we can do when we have the ability to create function variables. The chapter shows alternative ways to implement the strategy pattern and state machines, and introduces the fundamental `map()`, `filter()`, and `reduce()` algorithms.
- Chapter 6 builds on the preceding chapter and shows a few advanced applications of function types, from a simplified decorator pattern to resumable functions and asynchronous functions.
- Chapter 7 introduces subtyping and discusses type compatibility. We look at applications of top and bottom types and then see how sum types, collections, and function types relate to one another from a subtyping perspective.
- Chapter 8 talks about the key elements of object-oriented programming and when to use each one. The chapter covers interfaces, inheritance, composition, and mix-ins.
- Chapter 9 introduces generic programming and its first application: generic data structures. Generic data structures separate the layout of the data from the data itself; iterators enable traversal of these data structures.
- Chapter 10 continues the topic of generic programming and discusses generic algorithms and iterator categories. Generic algorithms are algorithms we can reuse across different types of data. Iterators act as an interface between data structures and algorithms, and depending on their capabilities, they enable different algorithms.
- Chapter 11, the final chapter, introduces higher kinded types and explains what functors and monads are and how they can be used. The chapter ends with some pointers for further study.
- The chapters in the book build on concepts introduced in earlier chapters, so you should read them in order. That being said, there are four major topics in the book that are fairly independent. The first four chapters cover fundamentals; chapters 5 and 6 cover function types; chapters 7 and 8 cover subtyping; and chapters 9, 10, and 11 are about generic programming.

About the code

This book contains many examples of source code both in numbered listings and inline with normal text. In both cases, source code is formatted in a `fixed-width font like this` to separate it from ordinary text. Sometimes, code is also **in bold** to highlight code that has changed from previous steps in the chapter, such as when a new feature adds to an existing line of code.

In many cases, the original source code has been reformatted; I've added line breaks and reworked indentation to accommodate the available page space in the book. In rare cases, even this was not enough, and listings include line-continuation markers (➥). Additionally, comments in the source code have often been removed from the listings when the code is described in the text. Code annotations accompany many of the listings, highlighting important concepts.

All the code samples in this book are available on GitHub at https://github.com/vladris/programming-with-types/. The code was built with version 3.3 of TypeScript, targeting the ES6 standard, with strict settings.

About the author

Vlad Riscutia is a software engineer at Microsoft with more than a decade of experience. During this time, he has led several major software projects and mentored many junior engineers.

Book forum

Purchase of *Programming with Types* includes free access to a private web forum run by Manning Publications where you can make comments about the book, ask technical questions, and receive help from the author and from other users. To access the forum, go to https://forums.manning.com/forums/programming-with-types. You can also learn more about Manning's forums and the rules of conduct at https://forums.manning.com/forums/about.

Manning's commitment to our readers is to provide a venue where a meaningful dialogue between individual readers and between readers and the author can take place. It is not a commitment to any specific amount of participation on the part of the author, whose contribution to the forum remains voluntary (and unpaid). We suggest you try asking the author some challenging questions lest his interest stray! The forum and the archives of previous discussions will be accessible from the publisher's website as long as the book is in print.

about the cover illustration

Saint-Sauver

The figure on the cover of *Programming with Types* is captioned "Fille Lipporette en habit de Noce," or "Liporette girl in wedding dress." The illustration is taken from a collection of dress costumes from various countries by Jacques Grasset de Saint-Sauveur (1757–1810), titled *Costumes de Différents Pays,* published in France in 1797. Each illustration is finely drawn and colored by hand. The rich variety of Grasset de Saint-Sauveur's collection reminds us vividly of how culturally apart the world's towns and regions were just 200 years ago. Isolated from each other, people spoke different dialects and languages. In the streets or in the countryside, it was easy to identify where they lived and what their trade or station in life was just by their dress.

The way we dress has changed since then and the diversity by region, so rich at the time, has faded away. It is now hard to tell apart the inhabitants of different continents, let alone different towns, regions, or countries. Perhaps we have traded cultural diversity for a more varied personal life—certainly for a more varied and fast-paced technological life.

At a time when it is hard to tell one computer book from another, Manning celebrates the inventiveness and initiative of the computer business with book covers based on the rich diversity of regional life of two centuries ago, brought back to life by Grasset de Saint-Sauveur's pictures.

Introduction to typing

This chapter covers

- Why type systems exist
- Benefits of strongly typed code
- Types of type systems
- Common features of type systems

The Mars Climate Orbiter disintegrated in the planet's atmosphere because a component developed by Lockheed produced momentum measurements in pound-force seconds (U.S. units), whereas another component developed by NASA expected momentum to be measured in Newton seconds (metric units). Using different types for the two measures would have prevented the catastrophe.

As we will see throughout this book, type checkers provide powerful ways to eliminate whole classes of errors, provided they are given enough information. As software complexity increases, so does the need to provide better correctness guarantees. Monitoring and testing can show that the software is behaving according to spec at a given point in time, given specific input. Types give us more general proofs that the code will behave according to spec regardless of input.

Programming language research is coming up with ever-more-powerful type systems. (See, for example, languages like Elm and Idris.) Haskell is gaining in popularity. At the same time, there are ongoing efforts to bring compile-time type checking to dynamically typed languages: Python added support for type hints, and TypeScript is a language created for the sole purpose of providing compile-time type checking to JavaScript.

There clearly is value in typing code, and leveraging the features of the type systems that your programming languages provide will help you write better, safer code.

1.1 Whom this book is for

This is a book for practicing programmers. You should be comfortable writing code in a mainstream programming language like Java, C#, C++, or JavaScript/TypeScript. The code examples in this book are in TypeScript, but most of the content is language-agnostic. In fact, the examples don't always use idiomatic TypeScript. Where possible, code examples are written to be accessible to programmers coming from other languages. See appendix A for how to build the code samples in this book and appendix B for a short TypeScript cheat sheet.

If you are developing object-oriented code at your day job, you might have heard of algebraic data types (ADTs), lambdas, generics, functors, or monads, and would like to better understand what these are and how they are relevant to your work.

This book will teach you how to rely on the type system of your programming language to design code that is less error-prone, better componentized, and easier to understand. We'll see how errors which could happen at run time and cause an entire system to malfunction can be transformed into compilation errors and caught before they can cause any damage.

A lot of the literature on type systems is formal. This book focuses on practical applications of type systems; thus, math is kept to a minimum. That being said, you should be familiar with basic algebra concepts like functions and sets. We will rely on these to explain some of the relevant concepts.

1.2 Why types exist

At the low level of hardware and machine code, the program logic (the *code*) and the data it operates on are both represented as bits. At this level, there is no difference between the code and the data, so errors can easily happen when the system mistakes one for the other. These errors range from program crashes to severe security vulnerabilities in which an attacker "tricks" the system into executing their input data as code.

An example of this kind of loose interpretation is the JavaScript `eval()` function, which evaluates a string as code. It works well when the string provided is valid JavaScript code but causes a run-time error when it isn't, as shown in the next listing.

Listing 1.1 Trying to interpret data as code

```
console.log(eval("40+2"));          ◁──┐ Prints "42" to
                                       │ the console
console.log(eval("Hello world!"));  ◁──┘
                                       Raises "SyntaxError:
                                       unexpected token: identifier"
```

1.2.1 0s and 1s

Beyond distinguishing between code and data, we need to know how to interpret a piece of data. The 16-bit sequence 1100001010100011 can represent the unsigned 16-bit integer 49827, the signed 16-bit integer -15709, the UTF-8 encoded character '£', or something completely different, as we can see in figure 1.1. The hardware our programs run on stores everything as sequences of bits, so we need an extra layer to give meaning to this data.

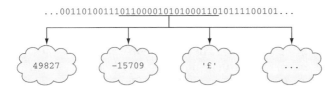

Figure 1.1   A sequence of bits can be interpreted in multiple ways.

Types give meaning to this data and tell our software how to interpret a given sequence of bits in a given context so that it preserves the intended meaning.

Types also constrain the set of valid values a variable can take. A signed 16-bit integer can represent any integer value from -32768 to 32767 but nothing else. The ability to restrict the range of allowed values helps eliminate whole classes of errors by not allowing invalid values to appear at run time, as shown in figure 1.2. Viewing types as sets of possible values is important to understanding many of the concepts covered in this book.

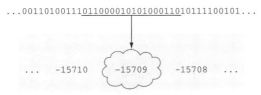

Type: signed 16-bit integer

Figure 1.2   The sequence of bits typed as a signed 16-bit integer. The type information (16-bit signed integer) tells the compiler and/or run time that the sequence of bits represents an integer value between -32768 and 32767, ensuring the correct interpretation as -15709.

As we will see in section 1.3, many other safety properties are enforced by the system when we add properties to our code, such as marking a value as const or a member as private.

1.2.2 *What are types and type systems?*

Because this book talks about types and type systems, let's define these terms before moving forward.

> **TYPE** A *type* is a classification of data that defines the operations that can be done on that data, the meaning of the data, and the set of allowed values. Typing is checked by the compiler and/or run time to ensure the integrity of the data, enforce access restrictions, and interpret the data as meant by the developer.

In some cases, we will simplify our discussion and ignore the operations part, so we'll look at types simply as sets, which represent all the possible values an instance of that type can take.

> **TYPE SYSTEM** A *type system* is a set of rules that assigns and enforces types to elements of a programming language. These elements can be variables, functions, and other higher-level constructs. Type systems assign types through notation you provide in the code or implicitly by deducing the type of a certain element based on context. They allow various conversions between types and disallow others.

Now that we've defined types and type systems, let's see how the rules of a type system are enforced. Figure 1.3 shows, at a high-level, how source code gets executed.

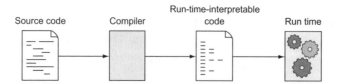

Figure 1.3   Source code is transformed by a compiler or interpreter into code that can be executed by a run time. The run time is a physical computer or a virtual machine, such as Java's JVM, or a browser's JavaScript engine.

At a very high level, the source code we write gets transformed by a compiler or interpreter into instructions for a machine, or *run time*. This run time can be a physical computer, in which case the instructions are CPU instructions, or it can be a virtual machine, with its own instruction set and facilities.

TYPE CHECKING   The process of *type checking* ensures that the rules of the type system are respected by the program. This type checking is done by the compiler when converting the code or by the run time while executing the code. The component of the compiler that handles enforcement of the typing rules is called a *type checker*.

If type checking fails, meaning that the rules of the type system are not respected by the program, we end up with a failure to compile or with a run-time error. We will go over the difference between compile-time type checking versus execution-time (or run-time) type checking in more detail in section 1.4.

Type checking and proofs

There is a lot of formal theory behind type systems. The remarkable Curry-Howard correspondence, also known as *proofs-as-programs*, shows the close connection between logic and type theory. It shows that we can view a type as a logic proposition, and a function from one type to another as a logic implication. A value of a type is equivalent to evidence that the proposition is true.

Take a function that receives as argument a `boolean` and returns a `string`.

Boolean to string

```
function booleanToString(b: boolean): string {
    if (b) {
        return "true";
    } else {
        return "false";
    }
}
```

This function can also be interpreted as "`boolean` implies `string`." Given evidence of the proposition `boolean`, this function (implication) can produce evidence of the proposition `string`. Evidence of `boolean` is a value of that type, `true` or `false`. When we have that, this function (implication) will give us evidence of `string` as either the string `"true"` or the string `"false"`.

The close relationship between logic and type theory shows that a program that respects the type system rules is equivalent to a logic proof. In other words, the type system is the language in which we write these proofs. The Curry-Howard correspondence is important because it brings logic rigor to the guarantees that a program will behave correctly.

1.3   *Benefits of type systems*

Because ultimately data is all 0s and 1s, properties of the data, such as how to interpret it, whether it is immutable, and its visibility, are type-level properties. We declare a variable as a number, and the type checker ensures that we don't interpret its data as a string. We declare a variable as private or read-only, and although the data itself in memory is no different from public mutable data, the type checker can make sure we do not refer to a private variable outside its scope or try to change read-only data.

The main benefits of typing are *correctness, immutability, encapsulation, composability,* and *readability.* All five are fundamental features of good software design and behavior. Systems evolve over time. These features counterbalance the entropy that inevitably tries to creep into the system.

1.3.1   *Correctness*

Correct code means code that behaves according to its specification, producing expected results without creating run-time errors or crashes. Types help us add more strictness to the code to ensure that it behaves correctly.

As an example, let's say we want to find the index of the string `"Script"` within another string. Without providing enough type information, we can allow a value of any type to be passed as an argument to our function. We are going to hit run-time errors if the argument is not a string, as the next listing shows.

Listing 1.2   Insufficient type information

```
function scriptAt(s: any): number {
    return s.indexOf("Script");
}

console.log(scriptAt("TypeScript"));
console.log(scriptAt(42));
```

Argument s has type any, which allows a value of any type.

This line correctly prints "4" to the console.

Passing a number as an argument causes a run-time TypeError.

The program is incorrect, as `42` is not a valid argument to the `scriptAt` function, but the compiler did not reject it because we hadn't provided enough type information. Let's refine the code by constraining the argument to a value of type `string` in the next listing.

Listing 1.3   Refined type information

```
function scriptAt(s: string): number {
    return s.indexOf("Script");
}
console.log(scriptAt("TypeScript"));
console.log(scriptAt(42));
```

Argument s now has type string.

Code fails to compile at this line due to type mismatch.

Now the incorrect program is rejected by the compiler with this error message:

```
Argument of type '42' is not assignable to parameter of type 'string'
```

Leveraging the type system, we transformed what used to be a run-time issue that could have been hit in production, affecting our customers, into a harmless compile-time issue that we must fix before deploying our code. The type checker makes sure we never try to pass apples as oranges; thus, our code becomes more robust.

Errors occur when a program gets into a *bad state*, which means that the current combination of all its live variables is invalid for whatever reason. One technique for eliminating some of these bad states is reducing the state space by constraining the number of possible values that variables can take, like in figure 1.4.

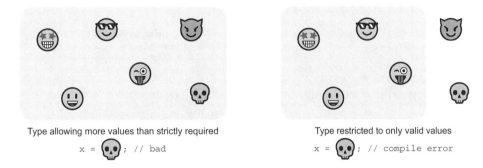

Type allowing more values than strictly required
x = 💀; // bad

Type restricted to only valid values
x = 💀; // compile error

Figure 1.4 Declaring a type correctly, we can disallow invalid values. The first type is too loose and allows for values we don't want. The second, more restrictive type won't compile if the code tries to assign an unwanted value to a variable.

We can define the *state space* of a running program as the combination of all possible values of all its live variables. That is, the Cartesian product of the type of each variable. Remember, a type can be viewed as a set of possible values for a variable. The Cartesian product of two sets is the set comprised of all ordered pairs from the two sets.

> **Security**
>
> An important byproduct of disallowing potential bad states is more secure code. Many attacks rely on executing user-provided data, buffer overruns, and other such techniques, which can often be mitigated with a strong-enough type system and good type definitions.
>
> Code correctness goes beyond eliminating innocent bugs in the code to preventing malicious attacks.

1.3.2 *Immutability*

Immutability is another property closely related to viewing our running system as moving through its state space. When we are in a known-good state, if we can keep parts of that state from changing, we reduce the possibility of errors.

Let's take a simple example in which we attempt to prevent division by 0 by checking the value of our divisor and throwing an error if the divisor is 0, as shown in the following listing. If the value can change after we inspect it, the check is not very valuable.

Listing 1.4   Bad mutation

```
function safeDivide(): number {
    let x: number = 42;

    if (x == 0) throw new Error("x should not be 0");    ⊲──┘  Check if x
                                                                is valid.

    x = x - 42;    ⊲──┐  Bug: x becomes 0
                       │  after the check.
    return 42 / x;               ⊲──┐  Division by 0 results
}                                   │  in Infinity.
```

This happens all the time in real programs, in subtle ways: a variable gets changed concurrently by a different thread or obscurely by another called function. Just as in this example, as soon as a value changes, we lose any guarantees we were hoping to get from the checks we performed. Making x a constant, we get a compilation error when we try to mutate it in the next listing.

Listing 1.5   Immutability

```
function safeDivide(): number {
    const x: number = 42;                         ⊲──────────────┐  x is declared using the
                                                                    keyword const instead
    if (x == 0) throw new Error("x should not be 0");  │  of the keyword let.

    x = x - 42;    ⊲──┐  This line no longer compiles
                       │  as x is immutable and
    return 42 / x;     │  cannot be reassigned.
}
```

The bug is rejected by the compiler with the following error message:

```
Cannot assign to 'x' because it is a constant.
```

In terms of in-memory representation, there is no difference between a mutable and an immutable x. The constness property is meaningful only for the compiler. It is a property enabled by the type system.

Marking state that shouldn't change as such by adding the const notation to our type prevents the kind of mutations with which we lose guarantees we previously checked for. Immutability is especially useful when concurrency is involved, as data races become impossible if data is immutable.

Optimizing compilers can emit more-efficient code when dealing with immutable variables, as their values can be inlined. Some functional programming languages make all data immutable: a function takes some data as input and returns other data without ever changing its input. In such cases, when we validate a variable and confirm that it is in a good state, we are guaranteed it will be in a good state for its whole lifetime. The trade-off, of course, is that we end up copying data when we could have operated on it in-place, which is not always desirable.

Making everything immutable might not always be feasible. That being said, making as much of the data immutable as you reasonably can will tremendously reduce the opportunity for issues such as preconditions not being met and data races.

1.3.3 Encapsulation

Encapsulation is the ability to hide some of the internals of our code, be it a function, a class, or a module. As you probably know, encapsulation is desirable, as it helps us deal with complexity: we split the code into smaller components, and each component exposes only what is strictly needed to the outside world, while its implementation details are kept hidden and isolated.

In the next listing, let's extend our safe division example to a class that tries to ensure that division by 0 never happens.

Listing 1.6 Not enough encapsulation

```
class SafeDivisor {
    divisor: number = 1;                                      Ensure that divisor does
                                                              not become 0 by checking
    setDivisor(value: number) {                               value before assigning
        if (value == 0) throw new Error("Value should not be 0");  ◁

        this.divisor = value;
    }

    divide(x: number): number {          Division by 0 should
        return x / this.divisor;    ◁┘   never happen.
    }
}

function exploit(): number {          Because the divisor
    let sd = new SafeDivisor();        member is public, the
                                       check can be bypassed.
    sd.divisor = 0;             ◁┘
    return sd.divide(42);        ◁   Division by 0
}                                     returns Infinity.
```

In this case we can no longer make the divisor immutable, as we do want to give callers of our API the ability to update it. The problem is that callers can bypass the 0 check and directly set `divisor` to any value because it is visible to them. The fix in this case is to mark it as `private` and scope it to the class, as the following listing shows.

Listing 1.7 Encapsulation

```
class SafeDivisor {
    private divisor: number = 1;        ◁   Member is now
                                             marked as private.
    setDivisor(value: number) {
        if (value == 0) throw new Error("Value should not be 0");
```

```
        this.divisor = value;
    }

    divide(x: number): number {
        return x / this.divisor;
    }
}

function exploit() {
    let sd = new SafeDivisor();

    sd.divisor = 0;
    sd.divide(42);
}
```

> This line fails to compile as divisor can no longer be referenced outside the class.

A `public` and a `private` member have the same in-memory representation; the fact that the problematic code no longer compiles in the second example is simply due to the type notations we provided. In fact, `public`, `private`, and other visibility kinds are properties of the type in which they appear.

Encapsulation, or information hiding, enables us to split logic and data across a public interface and a nonpublic implementation. This is extremely helpful in large systems, as working against interfaces (or abstractions) reduces the mental effort it takes to understand what a particular piece of code does. We need to understand and reason about only the interfaces of components, not all their implementation details. It also helps by scoping nonpublic information within a boundary and guarantees that external code cannot modify it, as it simply does not have access to it.

Encapsulation appears at multiple layers: a service exposes its API as an interface, a module exports its interface and hides implementation details, a class exposes only its public members, and so on. Like nesting dolls, the weaker the relationship between two parts of the code, the less information they share. This strengthens the guarantees a component can make about the data it manages internally, as no outside code can be allowed to modify it without going through the component's interface.

1.3.4 Composability

Let's say we want to find the first negative number in an array of numbers and the first one-character string in an array of strings. Without thinking about how we can break down this problem into composable pieces and put them back together into a composable system, we could end up with two functions: `findFirstNegativeNumber()` and `findFirstOneCharacterString()`, as shown in the following listing.

Listing 1.8   Noncomposable system

```
function findFirstNegativeNumber(numbers: number[])
    : number | undefined {
    for (let i of numbers) {
        if (i < 0) return i;
    }
}
```

```
function findFirstOneCharacterString(strings: string[])
    : string | undefined {
    for (let str of strings) {
        if (str.length == 1) return str;
    }
}
```

The two functions search for the first negative number and for the first one-character string, respectively. If no such element is found, the functions return `undefined` (implicitly, by exiting the function without a `return` statement).

If a new requirement comes in that we should also log an error whenever we fail to find an element, we need to update both functions, as shown in the next listing.

Listing 1.9   Noncomposable system update

```
function findFirstNegativeNumber(numbers: number[])
    : number | undefined {
    for (let i of numbers) {
        if (i < 0) return i;
    }
    console.error("No matching value found");
}

function findFirstOneCharacterString(strings: string[])
    : string | undefined {
    for (let str of strings) {
        if (str.length == 1) return str;
    }
    console.error("No matching value found");
}
```

This is already less than ideal. What if we forget to apply the update everywhere? Such issues compound in large systems. Looking more closely at what each function does, we can tell that the algorithm is the same; but in one case, we operate on numbers with one condition, and in the other, we operate on strings with a different condition. We can provide a generic algorithm parameterized on the type it operates on and the condition it checks for, as shown in the following listing. Such an algorithm does not depend on the other parts of the system, and we can reason about it in isolation.

Listing 1.10   Composable system

```
function first<T>(range: T[], p: (elem: T) => boolean)
    : T | undefined {
    for (let elem of range) {
        if (p (elem)) return elem;
    }
}

function findFirstNegativeNumber(numbers: number[])
    : number | undefined {
    return first(numbers, n => n < 0);
}
```

```
function findFirstOneCharacterString(strings: string[])
    : string | undefined {
    return first(strings, str => str.length == 1);
}
```

Don't worry if the syntax of this looks a bit strange; we'll cover inline functions such as n => n < 0 in chapter 5 and generics in chapters 9 and 10.

If we want to add logging to this implementation, we need only to update the implementation of first. Better still, if we figure out a more efficient algorithm, simply updating the implementation benefits all callers.

As we'll learn in chapter 10 when we discuss generic algorithms and iterators, we can make this function even more general. Currently, it only operates on an array of some type T. It can be extended to traverse any data structure.

If the code is not composable, we need a different function for each data type, data structure, and condition, even though they all fundamentally implement the same abstraction. Having the ability to abstract and then mix and match components reduces a lot of duplication. Generic types enable us to express these kinds of abstractions.

Having the ability to combine independent components yields a modular system and less code to maintain. Composability becomes important as the size of the code and the number of components increase. In a composable system, the parts are loosely coupled; at the same time, code does not get duplicated in each subsystem. New requirements can usually be incorporated by updating a single component instead of making large changes across the whole system, at the same time understanding that such a system requires less thought, as we can reason about its parts in isolation.

1.3.5   *Readability*

Code is read many more times than it is written. Typing makes it clear what a function expects from its arguments, what the prerequisites for a generic algorithm are, what interfaces a class implements, and so on. This information is valuable because we can reason about readable code in isolation: just by looking at a definition, we should be able to easily understand how the code is supposed to work without having to navigate the sources to find callers and callees.

Naming and comments are important parts of this, too, but typing adds another layer of information, as it allows us to name constraints. Let's look at an untyped find() function declaration in the following listing.

> **Listing 1.11   Untyped find()**

```
declare function find(range: any, pred: any): any;
```

Just looking at this function, it's hard to tell what kind of arguments it expects. We need to read the implementation, pass in our best guess, and see whether we get a run-time error or hope that the documentation covers this.

Contrast the following code with the previous declaration.

> **Listing 1.12 Typed `find()`**

```
declare function first<T>(range: T[],
    p: (elem: T) => boolean): T | undefined;
```

Reading this declaration, we see that for any type T, we need to provide an array T[] as the range argument and a function that takes a T and returns a boolean as the p argument. We can also immediately see that the function is going to return a T or undefined.

Instead of having to find the implementation or look up the documentation, just reading this declaration tells us exactly what type of arguments to pass and reduces our cognitive load, as we can treat it as a self-contained, separate entity. Having such type information explicit, available not only to the compiler but also to the developer, makes understanding the code a lot easier.

Most modern languages provide some level of *type inference*, which means deducing the type of a variable based on context. This is useful, as it saves us redundant typing, but becomes a problem when the compiler can understand the code easily while it becomes too effortful for people to do so. A spelled-out type is much more valuable than a comment, as it is enforced by the compiler.

1.4 Types of type systems

Nowadays, most languages and run times provide some form of typing. We realized long ago that being able to interpret code as data and data as code can lead to catastrophic results. The main distinction between contemporary type systems lies in when types get checked and how strict the checks are.

With static typing, type checking is performed at compile time, so when compilation is done, the run-time values are guaranteed to have correct types. Dynamic typing, on the other hand, defers type checking to the run time, so type mismatches become run-time errors.

Strong typing does few if any implicit type conversions, whereas weaker type systems allow more implicit type conversions.

1.4.1 Dynamic and static typing

JavaScript is dynamically typed, and TypeScript is statically typed. In fact, TypeScript was created to add static type checking to JavaScript. Converting what would otherwise be run-time errors to compilation errors, especially in large applications, makes code more maintainable and resilient. This book focuses on static typing and statically typed languages, but it's good to understand the alternative.

Dynamic typing does not impose any typing constraints at compile time. The colloquial name *duck typing* comes from the phrase "If it waddles like a duck and it quacks like a duck, it must be a duck." Code can attempt to freely use a variable in any way it wants, and typing is applied by the run time. We can simulate dynamic typing in Type-Script by using the any keyword, which allows untyped variables.

We can implement a quacker() function that takes a duck argument of type any and calls quack() on it. As long as we pass it an object that has a quack() method, everything works. If, on the other hand, we pass something that can't quack(), we get a run-time TypeError, as shown in the following listing.

Listing 1.13   Dynamic typing

```
function quacker(duck: any) {
    duck.quack();
}

quacker({ quack: function () { console.log("quack"); } });
quacker(42);
```

The function takes an argument of type any, so it bypasses compile-time type checking.

We pass an object with a quack() method, so the call prints "quack."

This causes a run-time error: TypeError: duck.quack is not a function.

Static typing, on the other hand, performs type checks at compile time, so attempting to pass an argument of the wrong type causes a compilation error. To leverage the static typing features of TypeScript, we can update the code by declaring a Duck interface and properly typing the function's argument, as shown in listing 1.14. Note that in TypeScript, we do not have to explicitly declare that we are implementing the Duck interface. As long as we provide a quack() function, the compiler considers the interface to be implemented. In other languages, we would have to be explicit by declaring a class as implementing the interface.

Listing 1.14   Static typing

```
interface Duck {
    quack(): void;
}

function quacker(duck: Duck) {
    duck.quack();
}

quacker({ quack: function () { console.log("quack"); } });
quacker(42);
```

Interface declaration for an object we expect has a quack() method

Updated function now requires an argument of type Duck.

Compile error: Argument of type '42' is not assignable to parameter of type 'Duck'.

Catching these types of errors at compile time, before they can cause a running program to malfunction, is the key benefit of static typing.

1.4.2 Weak and strong typing

We often hear the terms *strong typing* and *weak typing* to describe a type system. The strength of a type system describes how strict the system is with regard to enforcing type constraints. A weak type system implicitly tries to convert values from their actual types to the types expected when the value is used.

Consider this question: Does milk equal white? In a strongly typed world, no, milk is a liquid, and it makes no sense to compare it to a color. In a weakly typed world, we can say, "Well, milk's color is white, so yes, it does equal white." In the strongly typed world, we can explicitly convert milk to a color by making the question more explicit: Does the color of milk equal white? In the weakly typed world, we don't need this refinement.

JavaScript is weakly typed. We can see this by using the any type in TypeScript and deferring to JavaScript to handle typing at run time. JavaScript provides two equality operators: ==, which checks whether two values are equal, and ===, which checks both that the values and the type of the values are equal, as shown in the next listing. Because JavaScript is weakly typed, an expression such as "42" == 42 evaluates to true. This is surprising, because "42" is text, whereas 42 is a number.

Listing 1.15 Weak typing

```
const a: any = "hello world";
const b: any = 42;

console.log(a == b);          // Prints "false," though comparing a string to a number is allowed.

console.log("42" == b);       // Prints "true"; the JavaScript run time implicitly converts the values to the same type.

console.log("42" === b);      // Prints "false"; the === operator also compares the types.
```

Implicit type conversions are handy in that we don't have to write more code to explicitly convert between types, but they are dangerous because in many cases we do not want conversions to happen and are surprised by the results. TypeScript, being strongly typed, doesn't compile any of the preceding comparisons when we properly declare a to be a string and b to be a number, as the following listing shows.

Listing 1.16 Strong typing

```
const a: string =c"hello world";   // a and b are no longer declared as any, so they get type checked.
const b: number = 42;

console.log(a == b);

console.log("42" == b);            // All three comparisons fail to compile, as TypeScript doesn't allow comparing different types.

console.log("42" === b);
```

All the comparisons now cause the error `"This condition will always return 'false' since the types 'string' and 'number' have no overlap"`. The type checker determines that we are trying to compare values of different types and rejects the code.

Although a weak type system is easier to work with in the short term, as it doesn't force programmers to explicitly convert values between types, it does not provide the same guarantees we get from a stronger type system. Most of the benefits described in this chapter and the techniques employed in the rest of this book lose their effectiveness if they are not properly enforced.

Note that although a type system is either dynamic (type checking at run time) or static (type checking at compile time), its strength lies on a spectrum: the more implicit conversions it performs, the weaker it is. Most type systems, even strong ones, do provide some limited implicit casting for conversions that are deemed safe. A common example is conversions to `boolean`: `if (a)` in most languages would compile even if a is a `number` or a reference type. Another example is *widening casts*, which we'll cover in detail in chapter 4. TypeScript uses only the `number` type to represent numeric values, but in languages in which, for example, we need a 16-bit integer but pass in an 8-bit integer, the conversion is usually done automatically, as there is no risk of data corruption. (A 16-bit integer can represent any value that an 8-bit integer can, and more.)

1.4.3   *Type inference*

In some cases, the compiler can infer the type of a variable or a function without us having to specify it explicitly. If we assign the value `42` to a variable, for example, the TypeScript compiler can infer that its type is `number`, so we don't need to provide the type notations. We can do so if we want to be explicit and make the type clear to readers of the code, but the notation is not strictly required.

Similarly, if a function returns a value of the same type on each `return` statement, we don't need to spell out its return type explicitly in the function definition. The compiler can infer it from the code, as shown in the next listing.

Listing 1.17   Type inference

```
function add(x: number, y: number) {          The function does not have an
    return x + y;                             explicit return type, but the
}                                             compiler infers it as number.

let sum = add(40, 2);                         The type of the variable sum is
                                              not explicitly declared as
                                              number; rather, it is inferred.
```

Unlike dynamic typing, in which typing is performed only at run time, in these cases the typing is still determined and checked at compile time, but we don't have to supply it explicitly. If typing is ambiguous, the compiler will issue an error and ask us to be more explicit by providing type notations.

1.5   *In this book*

A strong, static type system enables us to write code that is more correct, more composable, and more readable. This book will cover common features of such modern type systems with a focus on practical applications of these features.

We'll start with *primitive types*, the out-of-the-box types available in most languages. We'll cover using them correctly and avoiding some common pitfalls. In some cases, we show how to implement some of these types if your particular language does not provide them natively.

Next, we'll look at composition and how primitive types can be put together to build a large universe of types supporting your particular problem domain. There are multiple ways to combine types, so you'll learn how to pick the right tool for the job depending on the particular problem you are trying to solve.

Then we will cover *function types* and the new implementations that open to us when a type system can type functions and treat them as regular values. Functional programming is a very deep topic, so instead of attempting to explain it fully, we'll borrow a set of useful concepts and apply them to a nonfunctional language to solve real-world problems.

The next step in the evolution of type systems, after being able to type values, compose types, and type functions, is *subtyping*. We'll go over what makes a type a subtype of another type and see how we can apply some object-oriented programming concepts to our code. We'll discuss inheritance, composition, and the less-traditional mix-ins.

We'll continue with *generics*, which enable type variables and allow us to parameterize code on types. Generics open a whole new level of abstraction and composability, decoupling data from data structures, data structures from algorithms, and enabling adaptive algorithms.

Last, we'll cover *higher kinded types*, which are the next level of abstraction, parameterizing generic types. Higher kinded types formalize data structures such as monoids and monads. Many programming languages do not support higher kinded types today, but their extensive use in languages such as Haskell and increasing popularity will eventually lead to their adoption across more established languages.

Summary

- A *type* is a classification of data that defines the operations that can be done on that data, the meaning of the data, and the set of allowed values.
- A *type system* is a set of rules that assigns and enforces types to elements of a programming language.
- Types restrict the range of values a variable can take, so in some cases, what would've been a run-time error becomes a compile-time error.
- *Immutability* is a property of the data enabled by typing, which ensures that values don't change when they're not supposed to.
- *Visibility* is another type-level property that determines which components are allowed to access which data.

- Generic programming enables powerful decoupling and code reuse.
- Type notations make code easier to understand for readers of the code.
- Dynamic typing (or duck typing) determines types at run time.
- Static typing checks types at compile time, catching type errors that otherwise would've become run-time errors.
- The strength of a type system is a measure of how many implicit conversions between types are allowed.
- Modern type checkers have powerful type inference algorithms that enable them to determine the types of variables, functions, and so on without your having to write them out explicitly.

In chapter 2, we will look at primitive types, which are the building blocks of the type system. We'll learn how to avoid some common mistakes that arise when using these types and see how we can build almost any data structure from arrays and references.

Basic types

2

This chapter covers

- Common primitive types and their uses
- How Boolean expressions are evaluated
- Pitfalls of numerical types and text encoding
- Fundamental types for building data structures

Computers represent data internally as sequences of bits. Types give meaning to these sequences. At the same time, types restrict the range of possible values any piece of data can take. Type systems provide a set of primitive or built-in types and a set of rules for combining these types.

In this chapter we will look at some of the commonly available primitive types (empty, unit, Booleans, numbers, strings, arrays, and references), their uses, and common pitfalls to be aware of. Although we use primitive types every day, each comes with subtle nuances we must be aware of to use them effectively. Boolean expressions can be short-circuited, for example, and numerical expressions can overflow.

We'll start with some of the simplest types, which carry little or no information, and move on to types that represent data via various encodings. Finally, we'll look at

19

arrays and references, which are building blocks for all other more-complex data structures.

2.1 *Designing functions that don't return values*

Viewing types as sets of possible values, you may wonder whether there is a type to represent the empty set. The empty set has no elements, so this would be a type for which we can never create an instance. Would such a type be useful?

2.1.1 *The empty type*

As part of a utility library, let's see how we would define a function that, given a message, logs the fact that an error occurred, including a timestamp and the message, and then throws an exception, as shown in the next listing. Such a function is a wrapper over `throw`, so it is not meant to return a value.

Listing 2.1   Raising and logging an error if a config file is not found

```
const fs = require("fs");                          The function never returns (always
                                                   throws), so its return type is never.
function raise(message: string): never {    ◄──────┘
    console.error(`Error "${message}" raised at ${new Date()}`);
    throw new Error(message);
}

function readConfig(configFile: string): string {
    if (!fs.existsSync(configFile))
        raise(`Configuration file ${configFile} missing`);

    return fs.readFileSync(configFile, "utf-8");       Example use: if a config
}                                                      file is not found, we want
                                                       to log and throw an error.
```

Note that the return type of the function in the example is `never`. This makes it clear to readers of the code that `raise()` is never meant to return. Even better, if someone accidentally updates the function later and makes it return, the code no longer compiles. Absolutely no value can be assigned to `never`, so the compiler ensures that the function keeps behaving as designed and never returns.

Such a type is named an *uninhabitable type* or *empty type* because no instance of it can be created.

> **EMPTY TYPE** An *empty type* is a type that cannot have any value: its set of possible values is the empty set. We can never instantiate a variable of such a type. We use an empty type to denote impossibility, such as by using it as the return type of a function that never returns (throws or loops forever).

An uninhabitable type is used to declare a function that never returns. A function might not return for several reasons: it might throw an exception on all code paths, it might loop forever, or it might crash the program. All these scenarios are valid. We might want to implement a function that does some logging or sends some telemetry before throwing an exception or crashing in case of unrecoverable error. We can have code that we want to run continuously on a loop until the whole system is shut down, such as the event-processing loop of the system.

Declaring such a function as returning `void`, which is the type used by most programming languages to indicate the absence of a meaningful value, is misleading. Our function not only doesn't return a meaningful value, but also doesn't return at all!

> ## Nonterminating functions
>
> The empty type might seem trivial, but it shows a fundamental difference between mathematics and computer science: in mathematics, we cannot define a function from a nonempty set to an empty set. This simply doesn't make sense. Functions in mathematics are not "evaluated"; they simply "are."
>
> Computers, on the other hand, evaluate programs; they execute instructions step by step. Computers can end up evaluating an infinite loop, which means that they would never stop their execution. For this reason, a computer program *can* define a meaningful function to the empty set, as in the preceding examples.

Consider using an empty type whenever you have a nonreturning function or otherwise want to explicitly show that it's impossible to have a value.

DIY EMPTY TYPE

Not all mainstream languages provide a built-in empty type like `never` in TypeScript, but you can implement one in most of them. You can do this by defining an enumeration with no elements or a structure with only a private constructor such that it can never be called.

Listing 2.2 shows how we would implement an empty type in TypeScript as a class that can't be instantiated. Note that TypeScript considers two types to be compatible if they have similar structure, so we need to add a dummy `void` property to ensure that other code cannot end up with a value that can be typed as `Empty`. Other languages, such as Java and C#, would not need this additional property, as they wouldn't consider types to be compatible based on shape. We'll cover this in more detail in chapter 7.

Listing 2.2 Empty type implemented as an uninstantiable class

```
declare const EmptyType: unique symbol;

class Empty {
    [EmptyType]: void;
    private constructor() { }
}
```

A TypeScript-specific way to ensure that other objects with the same shape can't be interpreted as this type

Private constructor ensures that other code cannot instantiate this type

```
function raise(message: string): Empty {
    console.error(`Error "${message}" raised at ${new Date()}`);
    throw new Error(message);
}
```

This function is the same as in the previous example, this time using Empty instead of never.

The code compiles, as the compiler performs control flow analysis and determines no `return` statement is needed. On the other hand, it should be impossible to add a `return` statement, as we cannot create an instance of `Empty`.

2.1.2   *The unit type*

In the previous section, we looked at functions that never return. What about functions that do return but don't return anything useful? There are many functions like this, which we call only for their side effects: they *do* something, change some external state, but don't perform any useful computation to return to us.

Let's take `console.log()` as an example: it outputs its argument to the debug console, but doesn't return anything meaningful. On the other hand, the function *does* return control to the caller when it finishes executing, so its return type can't be `never`.

The classic `"Hello world!"` function shown in the next listing is another good example. We call it to print a greeting (which is a side effect), not to return a value, so we specify its return value as `void`.

Listing 2.3   A "Hello world!" function

```
function greet(): void {
    console.log("Hello world!");
}

greet();
```

The function prints a greeting and doesn't return anything useful.

We usually just ignore the result of such functions.

The return type of such a function is called a *unit type*, a type that allows just one value, and its name in TypeScript and most other languages is `void`. The reason why we usually don't have variables of type `void` and can simply return from a `void` function without providing an actual value is that the value of a unit type is not important.

> **UNIT TYPE** A *unit type* is a type that has only one possible value. If we have a variable of such a type, there is no point in checking its value; it can only be the one value. We use unit types when the result of a function is not meaningful.

Functions that take any number of arguments but don't return any meaningful value are also called *actions* (because they usually perform one or more operations that change the state of the world) or *consumers* (because arguments go in but nothing comes out).

DIY UNIT TYPE

Although a type like `void` is available in most programming languages, some languages treat `void` in a special way and may not allow you to use it exactly the same way as any other type. In such situations, you can create your own unit type by defining an enumeration with a single element or a singleton without state. Because a unit type has only one possible value, it doesn't really matter what that value is; all unit types are equivalent. It's trivial to convert from one unit type to another, as there is no choice to be made: the single value of one type maps to the single value of the other one.

Listing 2.4 shows how we would implement a unit type in TypeScript. As for the DIY empty type, we are using a `void` property to ensure that another type with a compatible structure is not implicitly converted to `Unit`. Other languages, such as Java and C#, would not need this additional property.

Listing 2.4　Unit type implemented as a singleton without state

```
declare const UnitType: unique symbol;        Unique symbol property ensures
                                              that types with similar shape
class Unit {                                   cannot be interpreted as Unit.
    [UnitType]: void;          ◁
    static readonly value: Unit = new Unit();          ◁          Static read-only
    private constructor() { };   ◁                                property of type
}                                   Private constructor ensures   Unit is the only
                                    that other code cannot        possible instance
function greet(): Unit {     ◁      instantiate this type.        of Unit.
    console.log("Hello world!");
    return Unit.value;       ◁      Equivalent to a function
}                                   returning void, this
                                    always returns exactly
                                    the same value.
```

2.1.3　Exercises

1　What should be the return type of a `set()` function that takes a value and assigns it to a global variable?

　　a　`never`

　　b　`undefined`

　　c　`void`

　　d　`any`

2　What should be the return type of a `terminate()` function that immediately stops execution of the program?

　　a　`never`

　　b　`undefined`

　　c　`void`

　　d　`any`

2.2　*Boolean logic and short circuits*

After types with no possible values (empty types such as `never`) and types with one possible value (unit types such as `void`), come types with two possible values. The canonical two-valued type, available in most programming languages, is the *Boolean* type.

Boolean values encode truthiness. The name comes from George Boole, who introduced what is now called Boolean algebra, an algebra consisting of truth (1) and falseness (0) values and logical operations on them such as AND, OR, and NOT.

Some type systems provide Booleans as a built-in type with values `true` and `false`. Other systems rely on numbers, considering 0 to mean `false` and any other number to mean `true` (that is, *whatever is not false is true*). TypeScript has a built-in `boolean` type with possible values `true` and `false`.

Regardless of whether a primitive Boolean type exists or truthiness values are inferred from values of other types, most programming languages use some form of Boolean semantics to enable *conditional branching*. A statement such as `if (condition) { ... }` will execute the part between curly brackets only if the condition evaluates to something true. Loops rely on conditions to determine whether to iterate or finish: `while (condition) { ... }`. Without conditional branching, we wouldn't be able to write very useful code. Think about how you would implement a very simple algorithm, such as finding the first even number in a list of numbers, without any loops or conditional statements.

2.2.1   *Boolean expressions*

Many programming languages use the following symbols for common Boolean operations: `&&` for AND, `||` for OR, and `!` for NOT. Boolean expressions are usually described with truth tables (figure 2.1).

a	b	a && b	a || b	!a
true	true	true	true	false
true	false	false	true	false
false	true	false	true	true
false	false	false	false	true

Figure 2.1 AND, OR, and NOT **truth tables**

2.2.2   *Short circuit evaluation*

Suppose that you must build a gatekeeper for a commenting system as shown in listing 2.5: as users attempt to post comments, the gatekeeper rejects comments posted within 10 seconds of each other (the user is spamming) and comments with empty contents (the user accidentally clicked Comment before typing anything).

The gatekeeper function takes as arguments the comment and the user ID. You have a `secondsSinceLastComment()` function already implemented; this function, given the user ID, queries the database and returns the number of seconds since the last post.

If both conditions are met, post the comment to the database; if not, return `false`.

Listing 2.5 Gatekeeper

secondsSinceLastComment queries the database for the age of the user's last post.

```
declare function secondsSinceLastComment(userId: string): number;
declare function postComment(comment: string, userId: string): void;
```

postComment writes the comment to the database.

```
function commentGatekeeper(comment: string, userId: string): boolean {
    if ((secondsSinceLastComment(userId) < 10) || (comment == ""))
        return false;

    postComment(comment, userId);

    return true;
}
```

If one of the conditions isn't met, return false. Otherwise, post comment and return true.

Listing 2.5 is a possible implementation of the gatekeeper. Note the OR expression where we return `false` if either the age of the last comment in seconds is less than 10 *or* the current comment is empty.

Another way to implement the same logic is to switch the two operands, as shown in the following listing. First check whether the current comment is empty; then check the age of the last posted comment, as in listing 2.5.

Listing 2.6 Alternative gatekeeper implementation

```
declare function secondsSinceLastComment(userId: string): number;
declare function postComment(comment: string, userId: string): void;

function commentGatekeeper(comment: string, userId: string): boolean {
    if ((comment == "") || (secondsSinceLastComment(userId) < 10))
        return false;

    postComment(comment, userId);

    return true;
}
```

The only difference between this version and the previous one is the flipped conditions.

Is one version better in any way than the other? They define the same checks—just in a different order. As it turns out, they are different. Depending on the input received, they behave differently at run time due to the way Boolean expressions are evaluated.

Most compilers and run times perform an optimization called *short circuit* for Boolean expressions. Expressions of the form a AND b are translated to if a then b else false. This respects the truth table for AND: if the first operand is false, then regardless of what the second operand is, the whole expression is false. On the other hand, if the first operand is true, then the whole expression is true if the second operand is also true.

A similar translation happens for a OR b, which becomes if a then true else b. Looking at the truth table for OR, if the first operand is true, then the whole expression is true regardless of what the second operand is; otherwise, if the first operand is false, then the expression is true if the second operand is true.

The reason for this translation and the name *short circuit* come from the fact that if evaluating the first operand provides enough information to evaluate the whole expression, the second operand is not evaluated at all. The gatekeeper function must perform two checks: a relatively inexpensive one, to make sure that the comment it receives is not empty, and a potentially expensive one, which involves querying the comment database. In listing 2.5, the database query happens first. If the last posted comment is more recent than 10 seconds, short-circuiting will not even look at the current comment and will simply return `false`. In listing 2.6, if the current comment is empty, the database doesn't get queried. The second version can potentially skip an expensive check by evaluating a cheap check.

This property of Boolean expression evaluation is important and something to remember when you are combining conditions: short-circuiting can skip evaluation of the expression on the right, depending on the result of evaluating the expression on the left, so prefer ordering conditions from cheapest to most expensive.

2.2.3   *Exercise*

1   What will the following code print?

```
let counter: number = 0;

function condition(value: boolean): boolean {
    counter++;
    return value;
}

if (condition(false) && condition(true)) {
    // ...
}

console.log(counter)
```

  a 0
  b 1
  c 2
  d Nothing; it throws an error.

2.3   *Common pitfalls of numerical types*

Numbers are usually provided as one or more primitive types in most programming languages. There are several gotchas you should be aware of when working with numbers. Take, for example, a simple function that adds up a shopping total. If a user purchases three sticks of bubble gum at 10 cents each, we would expect the total to be 30 cents. Depending on how we use numerical types, we might be in for a surprise.

Listing 2.7   Function adding up item total

```
type Item = { name: string, price: number };

function getTotal(items: Item[]): number {
    let total: number = 0;

    for (let item of items) {
        total += item.price;
    }
```

We represent an item by a name and a price (number).

The getTotal function returns a number as the total.

```
    return total;
}

let total: number = getTotal(
    [{ name: "Cherry bubblegum", price: 0.10 },
     { name: "Mint bubblegum", price: 0.10 },
     { name: "Strawberry bubblegum", price: 0.10 }]
);

console.log(total == 0.30);
```

Compute total for three sticks of bubble gum, 10 cents each.

This prints "false," even though we would expect 0.10 + 0.10 + 0.10 to be 0.30.

Why does adding up 0.10 three times not give us 0.30? To understand this, we need to look at how numerical types are represented by computers. The two defining characteristics of a numerical type are its width and its encoding.

The *width* is the number of bits used to represent a value. This can range from 8 bits (a byte) or even 1 bit up to 64 bits or more. Bit widths have a lot to do with the underlying chip architecture: a 64-bit CPU has 64-bit registers, thus allowing extremely fast operations on 64-bit values. There are three common ways to encode numbers of a given width: *unsigned binary, two's complement,* and *IEEE 754.*

2.3.1 Integer types and overflow

An unsigned binary encoding uses every bit to represent part of the value. A 4-bit unsigned integer, for example, can represent any value from 0 to 15. In general, an N-bit unsigned integer can represent values from 0 (all bits are 0) up to 2^N-1 (all bits are 1). Figure 2.2 shows a few possible values of a 4-bit unsigned integer. You can convert a sequence of N binary digits $(b^{N-1}b^{N-2}...b^1b^0)$ to a decimal number with the formula $b^{N-1} * 2^{N-1} + b^{N-2} * 2^{N-2} + ... + b^1 * 2^1 + b^0 * 2^0$.

Value	4-bit unsigned encoding
0	0000
1	0001
2	0010
10	1010
15	1111

— **Smallest possible value; all bits are 0**

— **Largest possible value; all bits are 1**

Figure 2.2 4-bit unsigned integer encoding. Smallest possible value, when all 4 bits are 0, is 0. Largest possible value, when all bits are 1, is 15 $(1 * 2^3 + 1 * 2^2 + 1 * 2^1 + 1 * 2^0)$.

This encoding is very straightforward but can represent only positive numbers. If we also want to represent negative numbers, we need a different encoding, which is usually two's complement. In two's complement encoding, we reserve a bit to encode the sign. Positive numbers are represented exactly as before, whereas negative numbers

Value	4-bit signed encoding
-8	1000
-3	1101
0	0000
3	0011
7	0111

→ **Smallest possible value; all bits are 0 except the sign bit**

→ **Largest possible value; all bits are 1 except the sign bit**

Figure 2.3   4-bit signed integer encoding. –8 is encoded as $2^4 - 8$ (1000 binary), and –3 is encoded as $2^4 - 3$ (1101 binary). The first bit is always 1 for negative numbers and 0 for positive numbers.

are encoded by subtracting their absolute value from 2^N, where N is the number of bits. Figure 2.3 shows a few possible values of a 4-bit signed integer.

With this encoding, all negative numbers have the first bit 1, and all positive numbers and 0 have the first bit 0. A 4-bit signed integer can represent values from –8 to 7. The more bits we use to represent a value, the larger the value range we can represent.

OVERFLOW AND UNDERFLOW

What happens, though, when the result of an arithmetic operation can't be represented within the given number of bits? What if we are using a 4-bit unsigned encoding and try to add 10 + 10, even though the maximum value we can represent in 4 bits is 15?

Such a situation is called an *arithmetic overflow*. The opposite situation, in which we end up with a number that is too small to represent, is called an *arithmetic underflow*. Different languages treat these situations in different ways (figure 2.4).

An odometer wraps around   A dial knob saturates   A pocket calculator errors out

Figure 2.4   Different ways to handle arithmetic overflow. An odometer wraps around from 999999 back to 0; a dial knob simply stops at the maximum possible value; a pocket calculator prints Error and stops.

The three main ways to handle arithmetic overflow and underflow are to wrap around, saturate, or error out.

Wrap around is what the hardware usually does, as it simply discards the bits that don't fit. For a 4-bit unsigned integer, if the bits are 1111 and we add 1, the result is 10000, but because only 4 bits are allowed, one gets discarded, and we end up with 0000, wrapping back around to 0. This is the most efficient way to handle overflow but also the most dangerous, as it can cause unexpected results. Adding $1 to my $15, I can end up with $0.

Saturation is another way to handle overflow. If the result of an operation exceeds the maximum representable value, we simply stop at the maximum. This maps well to the physical world: if your thermostat only goes up to some temperature, trying to make it warmer won't change that. On the other hand, using saturation, arithmetic operations are no longer always associative. If 7 is our maximum value, $7 + (2 - 2) = 7 + 0 = 7$ but $(7 + 2) - 2 = 7 - 2 = 5$.

The third possibility, *error out*, is to throw an error when an overflow happens. This is the safest approach but has the drawback that every single arithmetic operation needs to be checked, and whenever you perform any arithmetic, your code needs to handle exceptional cases.

DETECTING OVERFLOW AND UNDERFLOW

Depending on the language you are using, arithmetic overflows and underflows could be handled in any one of these ways. If your scenario requires different handling from the language default, you need to check whether an operation would overflow or underflow and handle that scenario separately. The trick is to do this within the range of allowed values.

To check whether adding values a and b would overflow or underflow a [MIN, MAX] range, for example, we need to ensure that we don't have a + b < MIN (when adding two negative numbers) or a + b > MAX.

If b is positive, we can't possibly have a + b < MIN, as we're making a bigger, not smaller. In this case, we only need to check for overflow. We can rewrite a + b > MAX as a > MAX – b (subtract b on both sides). Because we're subtracting a positive number, we are making the value smaller, so there is no risk of overflowing (MAX – b is within the [MIN, MAX] range). So we overflow if b > 0 and a > MAX – b.

If b is negative, we can't possibly have a + b > MAX, as we're making a smaller, not bigger. In this case, we only need to check for underflow. We can rewrite a + b < MIN as a < MIN – b (subtract b on both sides). Because we're subtracting a negative number, we are making the value larger, so there is no risk of underflowing (MIN – b is within the [MIN, MAX] range). So we underflow if b < 0 and a < MIN – b, as shown in the next listing.

Listing 2.8 Checking for addition overflow

```
function addError(a: number, b: number,
    min: number, max: number): boolean {     ◁——  The function takes the numbers
    if (b >= 0) {                                   a and b, and the minimum and
        return a > max - b;                         maximum allowed values.
    } else {                               ◁——┐ If b is positive, we have an
        return a < min - b;                      overflow if a > max – b.
    }                              ◁——┐
}                                       If b is negative, we have an
                                        underflow if a < min – b.
```

We can use similar logic for subtraction.

For multiplication, we check for overflow and underflow by dividing on both sides by b. Here, we need to consider the signs of both numbers, as multiplying two negative numbers yields a positive number, whereas multiplying a positive and a negative number yields a negative number.

We overflow if

- b > 0, a > 0, and a > MAX / b
- b < 0, a < 0, and a < MAX / b

We underflow if

- b > 0, a < 0, and a < MIN / b
- b < 0, a > 0, and a > MIN / b

For integer division, the value of a / b is always an integer whose value is between -a and a. We only need to check for overflow and underflow if [-a, a] is not fully within [MIN, MAX]. Going back to our 4-bit signed integer example, where MIN is −8 and MAX is 7, the only case where division overflows is −8 / −1 (because [−8,8] is not fully within [−8,7]). In fact, for signed integers, the only overflow scenario is when a is the minimum representable value and b is −1. Unsigned integer division can never overflow.

Tables 2.1 and 2.2 summarize the steps necessary to check for overflow and underflow when special handling is required.

Table 2.1   Detecting integer overflow for a and b in a [MIN, MAX] range with MIN = –MAX-1

Addition	Subtraction	Multiplication	Division
b > 0 and a > MAX - b	b < 0 and a > MAX + b	b > 0, a > 0, and a > MAX / b b < 0, a < 0, and a < MAX / b	a == MIN and b == -1

Table 2.2   Detecting integer underflow for a and b in [MIN, MAX] range with MIN = –MAX-1

Addition	Subtraction	Multiplication	Division
b < 0 and a < MIN - b	b > 0 and a < MIN + b	b > 0, a < 0, and a < MIN / b b < 0, a > 0, and a > MIN / b	N/A

2.3.2   *Floating-point types and rounding*

IEEE 754 is the Institute of Electrical and Electronics Engineers standard for representing *floating-point* numbers, or numbers with a fractional part. In TypeScript (and JavaScript), numbers are represented as 64-bit floating-point using the *binary64* encoding. Figure 2.5 details this representation.

The three components of a floating-point number are the sign, the exponent, and the mantissa. The *sign* is a single bit that is 0 for positive numbers or 1 for negative

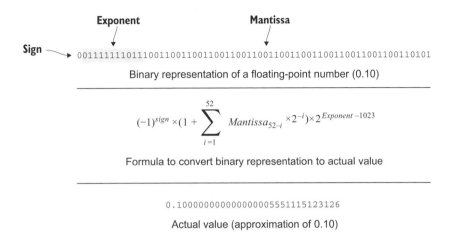

Figure 2.5 **Floating-point representation of 0.10. First, we see the in-memory binary representation of the three components: sign bit, exponent, and mantissa. Below, we have the formula to convert the binary representation to a number. Finally, we see the result of applying the formula: 0.10 is approximated to 0.1000000000000000005551115123126.**

numbers. The *mantissa* is a fraction as described by the formula in figure 2.2. This fraction is multiplied by 2 raised to the *biased exponent*.

The exponent is called *biased* because from the unsigned integer represented by the exponent, we subtract a value so that it can represent both positive and negative numbers. In the binary64 case, the value is 1023. The IEEE 754 standard defines several encodings, some using base 10 instead of base 2, though base 2 appears more often in practice.

The standard also defines special values:

- NaN, which stands for *not a number* and is used to represent the result of invalid operations, such as division by 0.
- Positive and negative infinity (Inf), which are used when operations overflow as saturation values
- Even though 0.10 becomes 0.1000000000000000005551115123126 according to the formula, it is rounded down to 0.1. In fact, 0.10 and 0.1000000000000000005551115123126 compare as equal in JavaScript. The only way floating-point can represent fractional numbers across a huge range of values using a relatively small number of bits is by rounding and approximating.

PRECISION VALUES

If precision is needed—in dealing with currency, for example—avoid using floating-point numbers. The reason why adding 0.10 together three times doesn't equal 0.30 is that although each individual 0.10 representation gets rounded to 0.10, adding them yields a number that rounds to 0.30000000000000004.

Small integer numbers can safely be represented without rounding, so it is a better idea to encode a price as a pair of dollars and cents integers. JavaScript provides

`Number.isSafeInteger()`, which tells us whether an integer value can be represented without rounding, so relying on that, we can design a `Currency` type that encodes two integer values and protects against rounding issues, as the next listing shows.

Listing 2.9   Currency class and currency addition function

```
class Currency {
    private dollars: number;              We store dollars and cents amounts
    private cents: number;                in separate variables.

    constructor(dollars: number, cents: number) {
        if (!Number.isSafeInteger(dollars))
            throw new Error("Cannot safely represent dollar amount");

        if (!Number.isSafeInteger(cents))
            throw new Error("Cannot safely represent cents amount");

        this.dollars = dollars;           Constructor ensures that we store
        this.cents = cents;               only values that can be safely
    }                                     represented without rounding.

    getDollars(): number {
        return this.dollars;              The amounts are accessed
    }                                     via getters, so external code
                                          cannot modify them.
    getCents(): number {
        return this.cents;
    }
}

function add(currency1: Currency, currency2: Currency): Currency {
    return new Currency(
        currency1.getDollars() + currency2.getDollars(),   Adding two Currency values simply
        currency1.getCents() + currency2.getCents());      adds the dollar and cents amounts.
}
```

In another language we would've used two integer types and protected against overflow/underflow. Because JavaScript does not provide an integer primitive type, we rely on `Number.isSafeInteger()` to protect against rounding. When dealing with currency, it's better to error out than to have money mysteriously appear or disappear.

The class in listing 2.9 is still pretty bare-bones. A good exercise is to extend it so that every 100 cents gets automatically converted to a dollar. You must be careful about where to check for safe integers: what if the dollar amount is a safe integer but adding 1 to it (from 100 cents) makes it unsafe?

COMPARING FLOATING-POINT NUMBERS

As we've seen, because of rounding, it's usually not a good idea to compare floating-point numbers for equality. There is a better way to tell whether two values are approximately the same: we can make sure that their difference is within a given threshold.

What should this threshold be? It should be the maximum possible rounding error. This value is called a *machine epsilon* and is encoding-specific. JavaScript provides this value as `Number.EPSILON`. Using this value, we can implement an equality comparison between two numbers, taking the absolute value of their difference and checking whether it is smaller than the machine epsilon. If it is, the values are within rounding error of each other, so we can consider them equal.

Listing 2.10 Floating-point equality within epsilon

```
function epsilonEqual(a: number, b: number): boolean {
    return Math.abs(a - b) <= Number.EPSILON;       ◁─┐  Check whether the two
}                                                        numbers are within rounding
                                                         error of each other.
                                             Prints "false" because 0.1 + 0.1 + 0.1
console.log(0.1 + 0.1 + 0.1 == 0.3);       ◁─┘ rounds to 0.30000000000000004.
console.log(epsilonEqual(0.1 + 0.1 + 0.1, 0.3));  ◁─┐
                                             Prints "true" because 0.3 and
                                             0.30000000000000004 are within
                                             rounding error of each other.
```

It's a good idea in general to use something like `epsilonEqual()` whenever comparing two floating-point numbers, as arithmetic operations can cause rounding errors that lead to unexpected results.

2.3.3 Arbitrarily large numbers

Most languages have libraries that provide arbitrarily large numbers. These types extend their width to as many bits as needed to represent any value. Python provides such a type as the default numerical type, and an arbitrarily large `BigInt` type is currently proposed for standardization for JavaScript. That being said, we won't treat arbitrarily large numbers as primitive types because they can be built out of fixed-width numerical types. They are convenient, but many run times do not provide them natively, as there is no hardware equivalent. (Chips always operate on a fixed number of bits.)

2.3.4 Exercises

1 What will the following code print?

```
let a: number = 0.3;
let b: number = 0.9;

console.log(a * 3 == b);
```

  a Nothing; it throws an error.
  b `true`
  c `false`
  d `0.9`

2 What should be the overflow behavior of a number that tracks unique identifiers?

  a Saturate on overflow.
  b Wrap around on overflow.
  c Error on overflow.
  d Any of them is OK.

2.4   *Encoding text*

Another common primitive type is the *string*, which is used to represent text. A string consists of zero or more characters, which makes it the first primitive type we are covering that can have an infinite set of values.

In the early days of computers, each character was represented by a single byte, so computers had at most 256 characters available to represent text. With the standardization of Unicode, which aims to provide a way to represent all the world's alphabets and other characters (such as emojis), 256 characters obviously are not enough. In fact, Unicode defines more than one million characters!

2.4.1   *Breaking text*

Let's take as an example a simple text-breaking function that takes a string and splits it into multiple strings of a given length so that it can fit within the width of a text-editor control, as shown in the following code.

Listing 2.11   Simple text-breaking function

The lines array will contain the split text.

```
function lineBreak(text: string, lineLength: number): string[] {
    let lines: string[] = [];

    while (text.length > lineLength) {
        lines.push(text.substr(0, lineLength));
        text = text.substr(lineLength);
    }

    lines.push(text);
    return lines;
}
```

Repeat as long as the length of the text is larger than the length of a line.

Add the first lineLength characters of text as a new line; then chop them from the text.

Add the remaining text (smaller than lineLength) to the result as the final line.

At first look, this implementation seems to be correct. For input text such as `"Testing, testing"` and a line length of 5, the resulting lines are `["Testi", "ng, t", "estin", "g"]`. This is what we expect, as the text is divided into multiple lines at every fifth character.

Other symbols have more complex encodings, though. Take, for example, "👮", the woman police-officer emoji. Even though this looks like a single character, JavaScript represents it with five characters. `"👮".length` returns 5. If we try to break a string containing this emoji, depending on where it appears in the text, we can get unexpected results. If we try to break the text "`...👮`" with a line length of 5, we get back the array `["...👮", "♀"]`.

The woman police-officer emoji is composed of two separate emojis: the police-officer emoji and the female-sign emoji. The two emojis are combined with the zero-width joined character `"\ud002"`. This character does not have a graphical representation; rather, it is used for combining other characters.

The police-officer emoji, "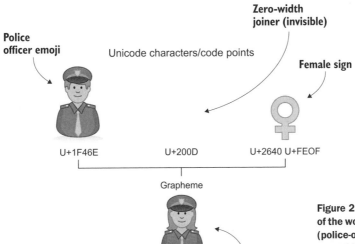", is represented with two adjacent characters, as we can observe if we try to split the longer string "....👮" with a line length of 5. This ends up splitting the police-officer emoji, giving us ["....\ud83d", "\udc6e👮"]. \uXXXX are Unicode escape sequences that represent a character that cannot be printed as is. The woman police-officer emoji, even though it gets rendered as a single symbol, is represented by the five distinct escape sequences \ud83d, \udc6e, \u200d, \u2640, and \ufe0e.

Naïvely breaking text at character boundaries can give results that can't be rendered and can even change the meaning of the text.

2.4.2 Encodings

We need to look at character encodings to better understand how to handle text properly. The Unicode standard works with two similar but distinct concepts: characters and graphemes. *Characters* are the computer representations of text (police-officer emoji, zero-width joiner, and female sign), and *graphemes* are the symbols users see (woman police officer). When rendering text, we work with graphemes, and we don't want to break apart a multiple-character grapheme. When encoding text, we work with characters.

GLYPHS AND GRAPHEMES A *glyph* is a particular representation of a character. "**C**" (bold) and "*C*" (italic) are two different visual renderings of the character "C".

A *grapheme* is an indivisible unit, which would lose its meaning if it were split into components, such as the woman police-officer example. A grapheme can be represented by various glyphs. The Apple emoji for woman police officer looks different from the Microsoft one; they are different glyphs rendering the same grapheme (figure 2.6).

Figure 2.6 Character encoding of the woman police-officer emoji (police-officer emoji character + zero-width joiner + female sign emoji) and resulting grapheme (woman police officer).

Each Unicode character is defined as a code point. This is a value between `0x0` and `0x10FFFF`, so there are 1,114,111 possible code points. These code points represent all the world's alphabets, emojis, and many other symbols, with plenty of room for future additions.

UTF-32

The most straightforward way of encoding these code points is UTF-32, which uses 32 bits for each character. A 32-bit integer can represent values between `0x0` and `0xFFFFFFFF`, so it can fit any code point with room to spare. The problem with UTF-32 is that it's very inefficient, as it wastes a lot of space with unused bits. Because of that, several more compact encodings were developed that use fewer bits for smaller code points and more bits as the values get larger. These are also called *variable-length encodings.*

UTF-16 AND UTF-8

The most commonly used encodings are UTF-16 and UTF-8. UTF-16 is the encoding used by JavaScript. In UTF-16, the unit is 16 bits. Code points that fit in 16 bits (from `0x0` to `0xFFFF`) are represented with a single 16-bit integer, whereas code points that require more than 16 bits (from `0x10000` to `0x10FFFF`) are represented by two 16-bit values.

UTF-8, the most popular encoding, takes this approach a step further: the unit is 8 bits and code points are represented by one, two, three, or four 8-bit values.

2.4.3   *Encoding libraries*

Text encoding and manipulation is a complex topic, with whole books dedicated to it. The good news is that you don't need to learn all the details to effectively work with strings, but you do need to be aware of the complexity and look for opportunities to replace naïve text manipulation, as in our text-breaking example, with calls to libraries that encapsulate this complexity.

`grapheme-splitter`, for example, is a JavaScript text library that works with both characters and graphemes. You can install it by running `npm install grapheme-splitter`. With `grapheme-splitter`, we can implement the `lineBreak()` function to break the text at grapheme level by splitting the text into an array of graphemes and then grouping them in strings of `lineLength` graphemes, as the following listing shows.

Listing 2.12   Text-breaking function using grapheme-splitter library

```
import GraphemeSplitter = require("grapheme-splitter");
const splitter = new GraphemeSplitter();

function lineBreak(text: string, lineLength: number) {
    let graphemes: string[] = splitter.splitGraphemes(text);
    let lines: string[] = [];
```

The splitGraphemes
function splits a string into
an array of graphemes.

```
for (let i = 0; i < graphemes.length; i += lineLength) {
    lines.push(graphemes.slice(i, i + lineLength).join(""));
}

return lines;
}
```

We then get slices of lineLength graphemes and join them into lines of text.

With this implementation, the strings "...👮" and "....👮" for a line length of 5 do not split the string at all, as none of the strings is larger than five graphemes, and the string ".....👮" correctly gets split into [".....", "👮"].

The `grapheme-splitter` library helps prevent one of the three common classes of errors in dealing with strings:

- *Manipulating encoded text at character level instead of grapheme level*—This example was covered in section 2.4.1, where we broke text at character level, even though for rendering purposes we wanted to break it at the grapheme level. Breaking at the fifth character can split a grapheme into multiple graphemes. When displaying text, we also need to be aware of how sequences of characters combine into graphemes.

- *Manipulating encoded text at byte level instead of character level*—This situation happens when we incorrectly handle a sequence of variable-length encoded text without being aware of the encoding, in which case we might split a character into multiple characters by, for example, breaking at the fifth byte even though we meant to break at the fifth character. Depending on the encoding of the actual character, it might take up one or more bytes, so we shouldn't make any assumptions that ignore encoding.

- *Interpreting a sequence of bytes as text with the wrong encoding* (such as trying to interpret UTF-16 encoded text as UTF-8 encoded, or vice-versa)—When receiving text from another component as a sequence of bytes, you must know what encoding the text uses. Different languages have different default encodings for text, so simply interpreting byte sequences as strings may give you wrong interpretations.

Figure 2.7 shows how the woman police-officer grapheme is composed out of two Unicode characters. The figure also shows their UTF-16 encoding and binary representation.

Note that for the same grapheme, the UTF-8 encoding, even though it ends up having the same representation on screen, is different. The UTF-8 encoding is 0xF0 0x9F 0x91 0xAE 0xE2 0x80 0x8D 0xE2 0x99 0x80 0xEF 0xB8 0x8F.

Always make sure you are interpreting byte sequences with the right encoding, and rely on string libraries to manipulate strings at character and grapheme levels.

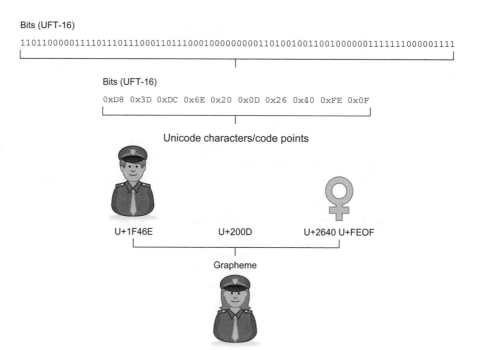

Bits (UFT-16)

1101100000111101110111000110111000100000000011010010011001000000111111000001111

Bits (UFT-16)

0xD8 0x3D 0xDC 0x6E 0x20 0x0D 0x26 0x40 0xFE 0x0F

Unicode characters/code points

U+1F46E   U+200D   U+2640 U+FEOF

Grapheme

Figure 2.7   Woman police-officer emoji viewed as UTF-16 string encoding of bits in memory, UTF-16 byte sequence, sequence of Unicode code points, and grapheme.

2.4.4   Exercises

1   How many bytes are needed to encode a UTF-8 character?

   a   1 byte
   b   2 bytes
   c   4 bytes
   d   It depends on the character.

2   How many bytes are needed to encode a UTF-32 character?

   a   1 byte
   b   2 bytes
   c   4 bytes
   d   It depends on the character.

2.5   *Building data structures with arrays and references*

The last two common primitive types we will discuss are arrays and references. With these, we can build up any of the other more advanced data structures, such as lists and trees. These two primitives offer different trade-offs in implementing data structures. We'll explore how to best leverage them depending on expected access patterns (read versus write frequency) and data density (sparse versus dense).

Fixed-size arrays store several values of a given type one after the other, enabling efficient access. Reference types allow us to split a data structure across multiple locations by having components reference other components.

We will not consider variable-size arrays to be primitive types, because these are implemented with fixed-size arrays and/or references, as we'll see in this section.

2.5.1 *Fixed-size arrays*

Fixed-size arrays represent a contiguous range of memory that contains several values of the same type. An array of five 32-bit integers, for example, is a range of 160 bits (5 * 32) in which the first 32 bits store the first number, the second 32 bits store the next, and so on.

The reason why arrays are a common primitive as opposed to, say, linked lists is efficiency: because the values are stored one after the other, accessing any one of them is a fast operation. If an array of 32-bit integers starts at memory address 101, which is the same as saying that the first integer (at index 0) is stored as the 32 bits between 101 and 132, the integer at index N in the array is at $101 + N * 32$. In general, if the list starts at address *base*, and the size of an element is M, the element at index N can be found at *base* $+ N * M$. Because the memory is contiguous, there is a high chance the array will get paged into memory and cached all at once, which enables very fast access.

By contrast, for a linked list, accessing the Nth element requires us to start from the head of the list and follow the `next` pointers of each node until we reach the Nth one. There is no way to compute the address of a node directly. Nodes are not necessarily

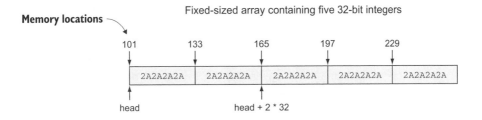

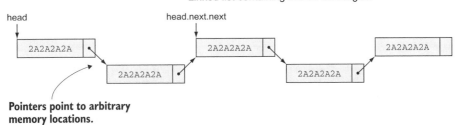

Figure 2.8   Five 32-bit integers stored in a fixed-size array and in a linked list. Finding an element is extremely fast in the fixed-size array, as we can compute its exact location. On the other hand, a linked list requires us to follow the `next` elements until we find the element we are looking for. Elements can be anywhere in memory.

allocated one after the other, so memory might have to be paged in and out until we reach the node we want. Figure 2.8 shows in-memory representations of an array and a linked-list of integers.

The term *fixed-size* comes from the fact that arrays can't be grown or shrunk in place. If we ever want to make our array store six integers instead of five, we would have to allocate a new array that can fit six integers and copy the first five over from the original array. Contrast this with a linked list, in which we can append a node without having to modify any of the existing nodes. Depending on the expected access pattern (more reads or more appends), one representation would work better than the other.

2.5.2   *References*

Reference types hold pointers to objects. The value of a reference type—the actual bits of a variable—do not represent the content of an object, but where the object can be found. Multiple references to a single object do not duplicate the state of the object, so changes made to the object through one of the references are visible through all other references.

Reference types are commonly used in data structure implementations, as they provide a way to connect separate components that can be added to or removed from the data structure at run time.

In the following sections, we will look at a few common data structures and how they can be implemented with arrays, references, or a combination of the two.

2.5.3   *Efficient lists*

Many languages provide a list data structure as part of their library. Note this data structure is not a primitive, but a data structure implemented with primitives. Lists can shrink and grow as items are added or removed.

If lists were implemented as linked lists, we could add and remove nodes without having to copy any data, but traversing the list would be expensive (linear time or `O(n)` complexity, where n is the length of the list). In listing 2.13, `Number-LinkedList` is such a list implementation that provides two functions: `at()`, which retrieves the value at the given index, and `append()`, which adds a value to the end of the list. The implementation keeps two references: one to the beginning of the list, from which we can start a traversal, and one to the end of the list, which allows us to append elements without having to traverse the list.

Listing 2.13   Linked-list implementation

```
class NumberListNode {
    value: number;
    next: NumberListNode | undefined;

    constructor(value: number) {
        this.value = value;
        this.next = undefined;
```

A node in the list has a value and a reference to the next node or is undefined if this is the last node.

```
        }
    }
    class NumberLinkedList {
        private tail: NumberListNode = { value: 0, next: undefined };
        private head: NumberListNode = this.tail;

        at(index: number): number {
            let result: NumberListNode | undefined = this.head.next;
            while (index > 0 && result != undefined) {
                result = result.next;
                index--;
            }

            if (result == undefined) throw new RangeError();

            return result.value;
        }

        append(value: number) {
            this.tail.next = { value: value, next: undefined };
            this.tail = this.tail.next;
        }
    }
}
```

> The list starts as empty, with both head and tail pointing to a dummy node.

> To get the node at a given index, we must start from the head and follow the next references.

> Appending a node is efficient: we just add it to the tail and then update the tail property.

As we can see, append() is very efficient in this case, as it only needs to add a node to the tail and then make that new node the tail. On the other hand, at() requires us to start from the head and move along next references until we reach the node we were looking for.

In the next listing, let's contrast this with an array-based implementation, in which accessing an element can be done efficiently, but appending an element is the expensive operation.

Listing 2.14 Array-based list implementation

```
class NumberArrayList {
    private numbers: number[] = [];
    private length: number = 0;

    at(index: number): number {
        if (index >= this.length) throw new RangeError();
        return this.numbers[index];
    }

    append(value: number) {
        let newNumbers: number[] = new Array(this.length + 1);
        for (let i = 0; i < this.length; i++) {
            newNumbers[i] = this.numbers[i];
        }
        newNumbers[this.length] = value;
        this.numbers = newNumbers;
        this.length++;
    }
}
```

> We store the values in a number array, originally of 0 length.

> Accessing an element simply means indexing in the array.

> Appending a number requires us to allocate a new array and copy the old elements.

> Finally, the last element is added to the end of the new array.

Here, accessing the element at a given index simply means indexing in the underlying numbers array. On the other hand, appending a value becomes an involved operation:

1 We must allocate a new array one element larger than the current array.
2 Then we must copy over all the elements from the current array to the newly allocated one.
3 We append the value as the last element in the new array.
4 We replace the current array with the new one.

Copying all the elements of the array whenever we need to append a new value is, again, not very efficient.

In practice, most libraries implement lists as an array with extra capacity. The array has a larger size than initially needed, so new elements can be appended without having to create a new array and copy data. When the array gets filled up, a new array is allocated, and elements do get copied over, but the new array has double the capacity (figure 2.9).

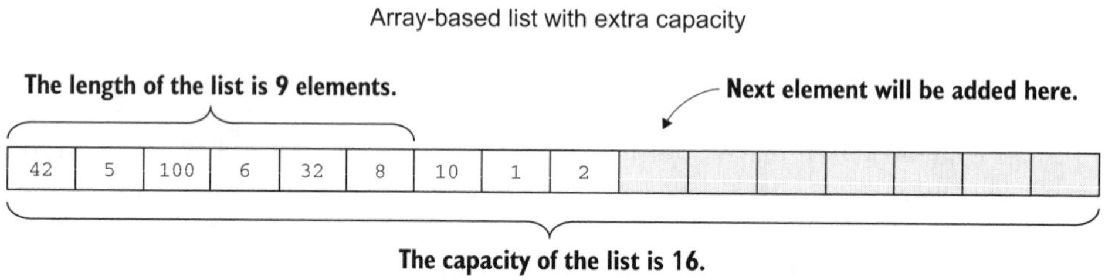

Array-based list with extra capacity

Figure 2.9 An array-based list with 9 elements and capacity for 16. Seven more elements can be appended before the data has to be moved to a larger array.

With this heuristic, the array capacity grows exponentially, so data doesn't get copied as much as it would if the array grew by only one element every time.

Listing 2.15 Array-based list implementation with additional capacity

```
class NumberList {
    private numbers: number[] = new Array(1);
    private length: number = 0;
    private capacity: number = 1;

    at(index: number): number {
        if (index >= this.length) throw new RangeError();
        return this.numbers[index];
    }

    append(value: number) {
        if (this.length < this.capacity) {
            this.numbers[length] = value;
            this.length++;
```

Even though the list is empty, we start with a capacity of 1.

Accessing an element is identical to the previous implementation.

If the array is not filled to capacity, we can simply add the element and update the length.

```
        return;
    }

    this.capacity = this.capacity * 2;
    let newNumbers: number[] = new Array(this.capacity);
    for (let i = 0; i < this.length; i++) {
        newNumbers[i] = this.numbers[i];
    }
    newNumbers[this.length] = value;
    this.numbers = newNumbers;
    this.length++;
    }
}
```

> If we're at capacity, we need to allocate a new array and copy elements, but we do this by doubling the capacity so that future appends do not require a reallocation.

Other linear data structures, such as stacks and heaps, can be implemented in a similar way. These data structures are optimized for read access, which is always extremely efficient. Using the extra capacity makes most writes efficient, but some writes, when the data structure is filled to capacity, require moving all elements to a new array, which is inefficient. There is also memory overhead, as the list allocates more elements than there are in use to make room for future appends.

2.5.4 Binary trees

Let's look at another type of data structure: a data structure in which we can append items in multiple places. An example of such a data structure is a binary tree, in which nodes can be appended to any node that doesn't have two children.

One option is to represent a binary tree as an array. The first level of the tree, the root, has at most one node. The second level of the tree has at most two nodes: the children of the root. The third level has at most four nodes: the children of the previous two nodes and so on. In general, for a tree with N levels, a binary tree can have at most $1 + 2 + \ldots + 2^{N-1}$ nodes, which is 2^N-1.

We can store a binary tree in an array by placing each level after the previous one. If the tree is not complete (not all levels have all the nodes), we mark the missing nodes as undefined. An advantage of this representation is that it's very easy to get from a parent to its children: if the parent is at index i, the left child node is at index 2*i, and the right child node is at index 2*i+1.

Figure 2.10 shows how we can represent a binary tree as a fixed-size array.

Appending a node is also efficient as long as we don't change the number of

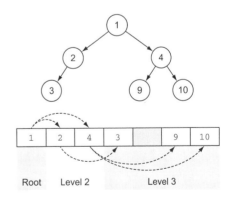

Figure 2.10 Binary tree represented as a fixed-size array. The missing node (right child of 2) is an unused element in the array. The parent–child relation between the nodes is implicit, as the index of a child can be computed from the index of the parent, and vice versa.

levels in the tree. As soon as we increase the level, though, we not only have to copy the whole tree, but also need to double the size of the array to make room for all the new possible nodes, as shown in the following listing. This is similar to the efficient list implementation.

Listing 2.16   Array-based binary tree implementation

```
class Tree {
    nodes: (number | undefined)[] = [];          ◁──── Nodes are stored as an array of number
                                                          values or undefined to represent gaps.
    left_child_index(index: number): number {
        return index * 2;                         ◁────┐
    }                                                    │ Compute the index of left
                                                          │ and right children nodes
    right_child_index(index: number): number {    │ given the index of the parent.
        return index * 2 + 1;                     ◁────┘
    }

    add_level() {
        let newNodes: (number | undefined)[] =
            new Array(this.nodes.length * 2 + 1);  ◁────┐
                                                          │ Adding capacity for a new
        for (let i = 0; i < this.nodes.length; i++) {    │ level doubles the size of the
            newNodes[i] = this.nodes[i];          ◁────┘ array and relocates nodes.
        }
        this.nodes = newNodes;
    }
}
```

The drawback of this implementation is that the amount of additional space required can be unacceptable if the tree is sparse (figure 2.11).

Because of the extra-space overhead, binary trees are usually represented with a more compact representation using references. A node stores a value and references to its children.

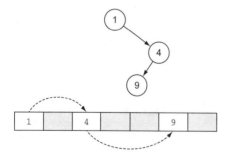

Figure 2.11   A sparse binary tree with only three nodes still requires an array with seven elements to be represented correctly. If node 9 had a child, the array size would become 15.

Listing 2.17 Compact binary tree implementation

```
class TreeNode {
    value: number;                          Each node stores a value.
    left: TreeNode | undefined;
    right: TreeNode | undefined;            Left and right refer to other
                                            nodes or are undefined if the
                                            node doesn't have a child.
    constructor(value: number) {
        this.value = value;
        this.left = undefined;
        this.right = undefined;
    }
}
```

With this implementation, a tree is represented by a reference to its root node. From there, following left and right children, we can access any node in the tree. Appending a node anywhere involves just allocating a new node and setting the left or right property of its parent. Figure 2.12 shows how we can represent a sparse tree using references.

Although the references themselves require some nonzero memory to represent, the amount of space

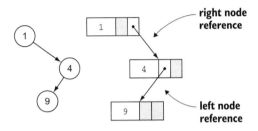

Figure 2.12 Sparse tree represented by using references. The diagram on the right represents the node data structure as value, left reference, right reference.

required is proportional to the number of nodes. For sparse trees, this is much better than the array-based implementation, in which space grows exponentially with the number of levels.

In general, sparse data structures where elements can be added in multiple places and we expect to have a lot of "gaps" are better represented by having elements refer to other elements, as opposed to placing the whole data structure in a fixed-size array that would end up having unacceptable overhead.

2.5.5 Associative arrays

Some programming languages provide other types of data structures as primitives, with built-in syntax support. A common such type is the *associative array*, also known as *dictionary* or *hash table*. This type of data structure represents a set of key-value pairs where, given a key, the value can be retrieved efficiently.

Despite what you may have thought as you followed the previous code examples, JavaScript/TypeScript arrays are associative arrays. The languages do not provide a fixed-size array primitive type. The code examples show how data structures can be implemented over fixed-size arrays. A fixed-size array assumes extremely efficient indexing and immutable size. This is not really the case in JavaScript/TypeScript. The reason we looked at fixed-size arrays instead of associative arrays is that an associative array data structure can be implemented with arrays and references. For illustrative purposes, we treated TypeScript arrays as fixed-size, so the code samples can be directly translated into most other popular programming languages.

Languages such as Java and C# provide dictionaries or hash maps as part of their library, whereas arrays and references are primitives. JavaScript and Python provide associative arrays as primitive types, but their run times also implement them with arrays and references. Arrays and references are lower-level constructs that represent certain memory layouts and access models, whereas associative arrays are higher-level abstractions.

An associative array is often implemented as a fixed-size array of lists. A hash function takes a key of an arbitrary type and returns an index to the fixed-size array. The key-value pair is added to or retrieved from the list at the given index in the array. The list is used because multiple keys can hash to the same index (figure 2.13).

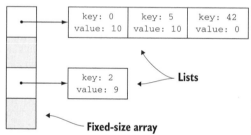

Figure 2.13   Associative array implemented as an array of lists. This instance contains the key-value mappings 0 → 10, 2 → 9, 5 → 10, and 42 → 0.

Looking up a value by key involves finding the list where the key-value pair sits, traversing it until the key is found, and returning the value. If lists become too long, lookup time increases, so efficient associative array implementations rebalance by increasing the size of the array, thus making the lists smaller.

A good hashing function ensures that keys usually get distributed across the lists evenly so that the lists are similar in length.

2.5.6   *Implementation trade-offs*

In the preceding section, we saw how arrays and references are enough to implement other data structures. Depending on the expected access patterns (such as read versus write frequency) and expected shape of the data (dense versus sparse), we can pick the right primitives to represent components of the data structure and combine them to get the most efficient implementation.

Fixed-size arrays have extremely fast read/update capabilities and can easily represent dense data. For variable-size data structures, references perform better on append and can represent sparse data more easily.

2.5.7 *Exercise*

1 Which data structure is best suited for accessing its elements in random order?

a Linked list

b Array

c Dictionary

d Queue

Summary

- Functions that never return (run forever or throw exceptions) should be declared as returning the empty type. An empty type can be implemented as a class that cannot be instantiated or an enum with no elements.

- Functions that finish executing but don't return a meaningful result should be declared as returning the unit type (void in most languages). A unit type can be implemented as a singleton or an enum with a single element.

- Boolean expression evaluation is usually short-circuited, so the order of the operands can affect which of them get evaluated.

- Fixed-width integer types can overflow. The default behavior on overflow is language-specific. The desired behavior depends on the scenario.

- Floating-point numbers are represented approximately, so instead of comparing two values for equality, it's better to check whether they are within EPSILON of each other.

- Text consists of graphemes, which are represented by one or more Unicode code points, each of which is encoded as one or more bytes. String-manipulation libraries shield us from the complexities of encoding and representation, so it's best to rely on them rather than manipulate text directly.

- Fixed-size arrays and references are the building blocks of data structures. Depending on data access patterns and density, we can choose one or the other, or a combination of the two, to implement any data structure efficiently, no matter how complex.

Answers to exercises

DESIGNING FUNCTIONS THAT DON'T RETURN VALUES

1 c—The function doesn't return anything meaningful, so the void unit type is a good return type.

2 a—The function never returns, so the empty type never is a good return type.

Boolean logic and short circuits

1 b—The counter is incremented only once because the function returns `false`, so the Boolean expression is short-circuited.

Common pitfalls of numerical types

1 c—The expression evaluates to `false` because of float rounding.

2 c—Because identifiers need to be unique, erroring out is the preferred behavior.

Encoding text

1 d—UTF-8 is a variable-length encoding.

2 c—UTF-32 is a fixed-length encoding; all characters are encoded in four bytes.

Building data structures with arrays and references

3 b—Arrays are best suited for random access.

Composition

In chapter 2, we looked at some common primitive types that form the building blocks of a type system. In this chapter, we'll look at ways to combine them to define new types.

We'll cover compound types, which group values of several types. We'll look at how naming members gives meaning to data and lowers the chance of misinterpretation, and how we can ensure that values are well-formed when they need to meet certain constraints.

Next, we'll go over either-or types, which contain a single value from one of several types. We will look at some common types such as optional types, either types, and variants, as well as a few applications of these types. We'll see, for example, how returning a result *or* an error is usually safer than returning a result *and* an error.

49

As an application of either-or types, we'll take a look at the visitor design pattern and contrast an implementation that leverages class-hierarchies with an implementation that uses a variant to store and operate on objects.

Finally, we'll provide a description of algebraic data types (ADTs) and see how they relate to the topics discussed in this chapter.

3.1 Compound types

The most obvious way to combine types is to group them to form new types. Let's take a pair of X and Y coordinates on a plane. Both X and Y coordinates have the type number. A point on the plane has both an X and a Y coordinate, so it combines the two types into a new type in which values are pairs of numbers.

In general, combining one or more types this way gives us a new type in which the values are all the possible combinations of the component types (figure 3.1).

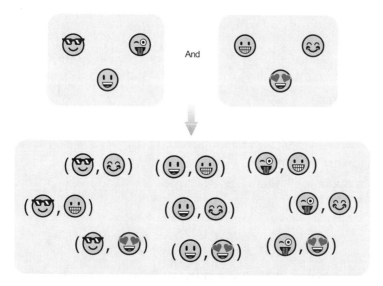

Figure 3.1 Combining two types so that the resulting type contains a value from each of them. Each emoji represents a value from one of the types. The parentheses represent the values of the combined type as pairs of values from the original types.

Note that we're talking about combining values of the types, not their operations. We'll see how operations combine when we look at elements of object-oriented programming in chapter 8. For now, we'll stick to values.

3.1.1 Tuples

Let's say we want to compute the distance between two points defined as pairs of coordinates. We can define a function that takes the X coordinate and Y coordinate of the first point, and the X coordinate and the Y coordinate of the second point, and then computes the distance between the two, as shown in the following listing.

Listing 3.1   Distance between two points

```
function distance(x1: number, y1: number, x2: number, y2: number)
    : number {
    return Math.sqrt((x1 - x2) ** 2 + (y1 - y2) ** 2);
}
```

This works, but it's not ideal: if we are dealing with points, x1 is meaningless without the corresponding Y coordinate. Our application likely needs to manipulate points in multiple places, so instead of passing around independent X and Y coordinates, we could group them in a *tuple*.

> **TUPLE TYPES**   *Tuple types* consist of a set of component types, which we can access by their position in the tuple. Tuples provide a way to group data in an ad hoc way, allowing us to pass around several values of different types as a single variable.

Using tuples, we can pass around pairs of X and Y coordinates together as points. This makes the code both easier to read and easier to write. It's easier to read as it is now clear that we are dealing with points, and it's easier to write as we can simply use point: Point instead of x: number, y: number, as shown in the next listing.

Listing 3.2   Distance between two points defined as tuples

```
                                          ┌─ We define a new type Point
type Point = [number, number];     ◄──────┘  to be a tuple of numbers.

function distance(point1: Point, point2: Point): number {
    return Math.sqrt(
        (point1[0] - point2[0]) ** 2 + (point1[1] - point2[1]) ** 2);
}
```

Tuples are also useful when we need to return multiple values from a function, which we can't easily do without a way to group values. The alternative is to use out parameters, arguments that are updated by the function, but that makes the code harder to follow.

DIY TUPLE

Most languages offer tuples as built-in syntax or as part of their library, but let's look at how we would implement a tuple if it were unavailable. In the following code we'll implement a generic tuple with two component types, also known as a *pair*.

Listing 3.3   Pair type

```
class Pair<T1, T2> {
    m0: T1;               │ The Pair type contains a value of
    m1: T2;               │ type T1 and a value of type T2.

    constructor(m0: T1, m1: T2) {
        this.m0 = m0;
```

```
            this.m1 = m1;
        }
    }

    type Point = Pair<number, number>;

    function distance(point1: Point, point2: Point): number {
        return Math.sqrt(
            (point1.m0 - point2.m0) ** 2 + (point1.m1 - point2.m1) ** 2);
    }
```

Looking at types as sets of possible values, if the X coordinate can be any value in the set defined by number and, similarly, the Y coordinate can be any value in the set defined by number, the Point tuple can be any value in the set defined as the pair <number, number>.

3.1.2   Assigning meaning

Defining points as pairs of numbers works, but we lose some meaning: we can interpret a pair of numbers as either X and Y coordinates or Y and X coordinates (figure 3.2).

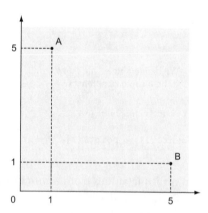

Figure 3.2   **Two ways to interpret the pair (1, 5): as point A with X coordinate 1 and Y coordinate 5, or as point B with X coordinate 5 and Y coordinate 1.**

In our examples so far, we assumed that the first component is the X coordinate and the second the Y coordinate. This works but leaves room for error. It is better if we can encode the meaning within the type system and ensure that there is no room to misinterpret X as Y or Y as X. We can do this by using a *record type*.

RECORD TYPES   *Record types*, similar to tuples, combine multiple other types. Instead of the component values being accessed by their position in the tuple, record types allow us to give their components names and access them by name. Record types are known as record or struct in different languages.

If we define our Point as a record, we can assign the names x and y to the two components and leave no room for ambiguity, as the next listing shows.

Listing 3.4   Distance between two points defined as records

```
class Point {
    x: number;                    | Point defines x and y members, so it is clear which
    y: number;                    | coordinate is encoded by which component.

    constructor(x: number, y: number) {
        this.x = x;
        this.y = y;
    }
}

function distance(point1: Point, point2: Point): number {
    return Math.sqrt(
        (point1.x - point2.x) ** 2 + (point1.y - point2.y) ** 2);
}
```

As a rule of thumb, it's usually best to define records with named components instead of passing tuples around. The fact that tuples do not name their components leaves room for misinterpretation. Tuples don't really provide anything better than records in terms of efficiency or functionality, except that we can usually declare them inline where we are using them, whereas we usually have to provide a separate definition for records. In most cases, the separate definition is worth adding, as it provides extra meaning to our variables.

3.1.3   *Maintaining invariants*

In languages in which record types can have associated methods, there is usually a way to define the visibility of their members. A member can be defined as `public` (accessible from anywhere), `private` (accessible only from within the record), and so on. In TypeScript, members are public by default.

In general, when we define record types, if the members are independent and can vary without causing issues, it's fine to mark them as public. This is the case with points defined as pairs of X and Y coordinates: one of the coordinates can change independently of the other coordinate as a point moves on the plane.

Let's take another example in which the members can't vary independently without causing issues: the currency type we looked at in chapter 2, formed by a `dollar` amount and a `cents` amount. Let's enhance the definition of the type with the following rules that define a well-formed currency amount:

- The dollar amount must be an integer equal to or greater than 0 and safely representable as a `number` type.
- The cent amount must be an integer equal to or greater than 0 and safely representable as a `number` type.
- We shouldn't have more than 99 cents; every 100 cents should be converted to a dollar.

Such rules that ensure a value is well-formed are also called *invariants*, as they shouldn't change even as the values that make up the composite type change. If we make the members public, external code can change them, and we can end up with ill-formed records, as shown in the next listing.

Listing 3.5   Ill-formed currency

```
class Currency {
    dollars: number;
    cents: number;

    constructor(dollars: number, cents: number) {
        if (!Number.isSafeInteger(cents) || cents < 0)
            throw new Error();

        dollars = dollars + Math.floor(cents / 100);
        cents = cents % 100;

        if (!Number.isSafeInteger(dollars) || dollars < 0)
            throw new Error();

        this.dollars = dollars;
        this.cents = cents;
    }
}

let amount: Currency = new Currency(5, 50);
amount.cents = 300;
```

Every 100 cents gets converted to a dollar.

Constructor ensures that we have valid dollars and cents values.

Unfortunately, having the members public still allows external code to make an invalid object.

This situation can be prevented by making the members private and providing methods to update them that ensure the invariants are maintained, as shown in the following listing. If we handle all cases in which invariants would be invalidated, we can ensure that an object is always in a valid state, as changing it would give us another well-formed object or result in an exception.

Listing 3.6   Currency maintaining invariants

```
class Currency {
    private dollars: number = 0;
    private cents: number = 0;

    constructor(dollars: number, cents: number) {
        this.assignDollars(dollars);
        this.assignCents(cents);
    }

    getDollars(): number {
        return this.dollars;
    }

    assignDollars(dollars: number) {
        if (!Number.isSafeInteger(dollars) || dollars < 0)
            throw new Error();

        this.dollars = dollars;
    }
```

Making dollars and cents private ensures that external code can't bypass validation.

If the dollar or cent amount is invalid (negative or nonsafe integer), throw an exception.

```
getCents(): number {
    return this.cents;
}

assignCents(cents: number) {
    if (!Number.isSafeInteger(cents) || cents < 0)
        throw new Error();

    this.assignDollars(this.dollars + Math.floor(cents / 100));
    this.cents = cents % 100;
}
}
```

If the dollar or cent amount is invalid (negative or nonsafe integer), throw an exception.

Normalize the value by converting 100 cents to dollars.

External code now has to go through the `assignDollars()` and `assignCents()` functions, which ensure that all invariants are maintained: if the provided values are invalid, exceptions are thrown. If the number of cents is larger than 100, it is converted to dollars.

In general, we should be fine providing direct access to public members of a record if there are no invariants to be enforced, such as the independent X and Y components of a point on a plane. On the other hand, if we have a set of rules that define what it means for a record to be well-formed, we should use private members and methods to update them to ensure that the rules are enforced.

Another option is to make the members immutable, as shown in the following listing, in which case we can ensure during initialization that the record is well-formed, but then we can allow direct access to the members because they can't be changed by external code.

Listing 3.7 Immutable Currency

```
class Currency {
    readonly dollars: number;
    readonly cents: number;

    constructor(dollars: number, cents: number) {
        if (!Number.isSafeInteger(cents) || cents < 0)
            throw new Error();

        dollars = dollars + Math.floor(cents / 100);
        cents = cents % 100;

        if (!Number.isSafeInteger(dollars) || dollars < 0)
            throw new Error();

        this.dollars = dollars;
        this.cents = cents;
    }
}
```

Dollars and cents are public but read-only and can't be changed after initialization.

All validation takes place in the constructor now.

If the members are immutable, we no longer need functions for them to uphold the invariants. The only time when the members are set is during construction, so we can move all the validation logic there. Immutable data has other advantages: accessing this data concurrently from different threads is guaranteed to be safe, as the data can't change. Mutability can cause data races, when one thread modifies a value while another thread is using it.

The drawback of records with immutable members is that we need to create a new instance whenever we want a new value. Depending on how expensive it is to create new instances, we might opt for a record in which the members can be updated in place by using getter and setter methods, or we might go with an implementation in which each update requires creating a new object.

The goal is to prevent external code from making changes that bypass our validation rules, either by making members private and routing all access through methods or by making the members immutable and applying validation in the constructor.

3.1.4   *Exercise*

1   What is the preferred way of defining a point in 3D space?

    a `type Point = [number, number, number];`
    b `type Point = number | number | number;`
    c `type Point = { x: number, y: number, z: number };`
    d `type Point = any;`

3.2   *Expressing either-or with types*

So far, we've looked at combining types by grouping them such that values are composed of one value from each of the member types. Another fundamental way in which we can combine types is either-or, in which a value is any one of a possible set of values of one or more underlying types (figure 3.3).

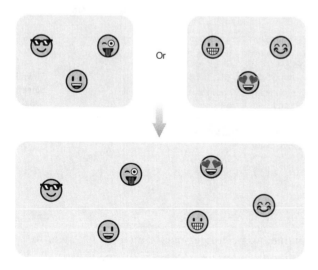

Figure 3.3   **Combining two types so that the resulting type allows values from either of the two types.**

3.2.1 *Enumerations*

Let's start with a very simple task: encoding a day of the week in the type systems. We could say the day of the week is a number between 0 and 6, 0 being the first day of the week and 6 being the last one. This is less than ideal, because multiple engineers working on the code might have different opinions of what the first day of the week is. Countries such as the United States, Canada, and Japan consider Sunday to be the first day of the week, whereas the ISO 8601 standard and most European countries consider Monday to be the first day of the week.

Listing 3.8 Encoding day of week as a number

```
function isWeekend(dayOfWeek: number): boolean {
    return dayOfWeek == 5 || dayOfWeek == 6;
}

function isWeekday(dayOfWeek: number): boolean {
    return dayOfWeek >= 1 && dayOfWeek <= 5;
}
```

A European developer would consider days 5 and 6 to be the weekend (Saturday and Sunday).

An American developer would consider days 1 to 5 to be weekdays (Monday through Friday).

It should be obvious from this code example that the two functions can't both be correct. If 0 represents Sunday, isWeekend() is incorrect; if 0 represents Monday, isWeekday() is incorrect. Unfortunately, because the meaning of 0 is not enforced but determined by convention, there is no automatic way to prevent this error.

An alternative is to declare a set of constant values to represent the days of the week and make sure that these constants are used whenever a day of the week is expected.

Listing 3.9 Encoding day of week with constants

```
const Sunday: number = 0;
const Monday: number = 1;
const Tuesday: number = 2;
const Wednesday: number = 3;
const Thursday: number = 4;
const Friday: number = 5;
const Saturday: number = 6;

function isWeekend(dayOfWeek: number): boolean {
    return dayOfWeek == Saturday || dayOfWeek == Sunday;
}

function isWeekday(dayOfWeek: number): boolean {
    return dayOfWeek >= Monday && dayOfWeek <= Friday;
}
```

Instead of numbers, we now use named constants to ensure consistency.

This implementation is slightly better than the previous implementation, but there's still a problem: looking at the declaration of a function, it's not clear what the expected values are for an argument of type number. How is someone who's new to the code supposed to know that whenever they see a dayOfWeek: number, they should use one of the constants? They may not be aware that these constants exist somewhere in some module, and instead, they could interpret the number themselves, as in our first example in listing 3.8. Someone can also call the function with completely invalid values, such as -1 or 10. An even better solution is to declare an enumeration for the days of the week.

Listing 3.10   Encoding day of week as an enum

```
enum DayOfWeek {                          ◁──┐  An enum replaces
    Sunday,                                   │  the constants.
    Monday,
    Tuesday,
    Wednesday,
    Thursday,
    Friday,
    Saturday
}

function isWeekend(dayOfWeek: DayOfWeek): boolean {   ◁──┐
    return dayOfWeek == DayOfWeek.Saturday                │
        || dayOfWeek == DayOfWeek.Sunday;                 │  We now have a distinct
}                                                         │  type that represents a
                                                          │  day of the week.
function isWeekday(dayOfWeek: DayOfWeek): boolean {   ◁──┘
    return dayOfWeek >= DayOfWeek.Monday
        && dayOfWeek <= DayOfWeek.Friday;
}
```

With this approach, we directly encode the days of the week in an enumeration that has two big advantages: there is no ambiguity about what is Monday and what is Sunday, as they are spelled out in the code. Also, it's very clear, when looking at a function declaration expecting a dayOfWeek: DayOfWeek argument, that we should pass in a member of DayOfWeek, such as DayOfWeek.Tuesday, not a number.

This is a basic example of combining a set of values into a new type. A variable of that type can be one of the provided values. We would use enumerations whenever we have a small set of possible values and want to represent them in an unambiguous manner. Next, let's see how we apply this concept to types instead of values.

3.2.2 *Optional types*

Let's say we want to convert a string, provided as user input, to a DayOfWeek. If we can interpret the string as a day of week, we want to return a DayOfWeek value, but if we can't interpret it, we want to explicitly say that the day of the week is undefined. We can implement this in TypeScript by using the | type operator, which allows us to combine types, as shown in the following code.

Listing 3.11   Parsing input into a DayOfWeek or undefined

```
function parseDayOfWeek(input: string): DayOfWeek | undefined {   ◁──┐
    switch (input.toLowerCase()) {                                    │
        case "sunday": return DayOfWeek.Sunday;        The function returns a
                                                       DayOfWeek or undefined.
```

```
        case "monday": return DayOfWeek.Monday;
        case "tuesday": return DayOfWeek.Tuesday;
        case "wednesday": return DayOfWeek.Wednesday;
        case "thursday": return DayOfWeek.Thursday;
        case "friday": return DayOfWeek.Friday;
        case "saturday": return DayOfWeek.Saturday;
        default: return undefined;
    }
}
```

⟵ **If neither case matches, we return undefined to signal that we couldn't parse the input.**

```
function useInput(input: string) {
    let result: DayOfWeek | undefined = parseDayOfWeek(input);

    if (result === undefined) {
        console.log(`Failed to parse "${input}"`);
    } else {
        let dayOfWeek: DayOfWeek = result;
        /* Use dayOfWeek */
    }
}
```

⟵ **Check whether we failed to parse, in which case we log an error.**

⟵ **If result is not undefined, we can extract a DayOfWeek value from it and use it going forward.**

This `parseDayOfWeek()` function returns a `DayOfWeek` or `undefined`. The use-
`Input()` function calls this function and then tries to unwrap the result, logging an
error or ending up with a `DayOfWeek` value that it can use.

> **OPTIONAL TYPES** *An optional type*, also known as a maybe type, represents an
> optional value of another type `T`. An instance of the optional type can hold a
> value (any value) of type `T` or a special value indicating the absence of a value
> of type `T`.

DIY OPTIONAL

Some mainstream programming languages do not have syntax-level support for combining types this way, but a set of common constructs is available as libraries. Our
`DayOfWeek` or `undefined` example is an *optional type*. An optional contains either a
value of its underlying type or no value.

An optional type usually wraps another type provided as a generic type argument
and provides a couple of methods: a `hasValue()` method, which tells us whether we
have an actual value, and a `getValue()`, which returns that value. Attempting to call
`getValue()` when no value is set causes an exception to be thrown, as shown in the
next listing.

Listing 3.12 Optional type

```
class Optional<T> {
    private value: T | undefined;
    private assigned: boolean;

    constructor(value?: T) {
        if (value) {
            this.value = value;
            this.assigned = true;
```

⟵ **Optional wraps a generic type T.**

⟵ **value is an optional argument, because TypeScript doesn't support constructor overloads.**

```
        } else {
            this.value = undefined;
            this.assigned = false;
        }
    }

    hasValue(): boolean {
        return this.assigned;
    }

    getValue(): T {
        if (!this.assigned) throw Error();

        return <T>this.value;
    }
}
```

If this Optional is not assigned, attempting to get a value throws an exception.

In other languages that don't have a | type operator that allows us to define a T | undefined type, we would use a nullable type instead. A *nullable type* allows for any value of the type or null, which represents the absence of a value.

You might wonder why this optional type is useful, considering that in most languages, reference types are allowed to be null, so there is already a way to encode "no value available" without needing such a type.

The difference is that using null is error-prone (see the sidebar "A billion-dollar mistake"), as it's hard to tell when a variable can or can't be null. We must add null checks all over the code or risk dereferencing a null variable, which results in a run-time error. The idea behind an optional type is to decouple the null from the range of allowed values. Whenever we see an optional, we *know* that it can have no value. After we check that we indeed have a value, we unwrap it from the optional and get a variable of the underlying type. From here on, we *know* that the variable cannot be null. This distinction is captured in the type system, as the "might be null" variable has a different type (DayOfWeek | undefined or Optional<DayOfWeek>) from the unwrapped value, which we know can't be null (DayOfWeek). It helps that an optional type and its underlying type are incompatible, so we can't accidentally use an optional (which may not have a value) instead of its underlying type without explicitly unwrapping the value.

A billion-dollar mistake

Famous computer scientist and Turing Award winner Sir Tony Hoare calls null references his "billion-dollar mistake." He is quoted as saying:

"I call it my billion-dollar mistake. It was the invention of the null reference in 1965. At that time, I was designing the first comprehensive type system for references in an object oriented language. My goal was to ensure that all use of references should be absolutely safe, with checking performed automatically by the compiler. But I couldn't resist the temptation to put in a null reference, simply because it was so easy to implement. This has led to innumerable errors, vulnerabilities, and system crashes, which have probably caused a billion dollars of pain and damage in the last forty years."

After decades of `null` dereference errors, it's becoming clear that it is better if `null`, or the absence of the value, is not itself a valid value of a type.

3.2.3 Result or error

Let's extend our `DayOfWeek` string conversion example so that instead of simply returning no value when we cannot determine the `DayOfWeek` value, we return more detailed error information. We want to distinguish between when the string is empty and when we are unable to parse it. This is useful if we run this code behind a text input control, as we want to show different error messages to the user, depending on the error (`Please enter a day of week` versus `Invalid day of week`).

A common antipattern returns *both* a `DayOfWeek` and an error code, as shown in the next listing. If the error code indicates success, we use the `DayOfWeek` value. If the error code indicates an error, the `DayOfWeek` value is invalid, and we shouldn't use it.

Listing 3.13 Returning result and error from a function

```
enum InputError {            ◁─────┐  InputError represents
    OK,                             │  the error code.
    NoInput,
    Invalid
}

class Result {       #B
    error: InputError;
    value: DayOfWeek;

    constructor(error: InputError, value: DayOfWeek) {
        this.error = error;
        this.value = value;
    }                                       Result combines the error code
}                                             and the DayOfWeek value.

function parseDayOfWeek(input: string): Result {              ◁─────
    if (input == "")
        return new Result(InputError.NoInput, DayOfWeek.Sunday);   ◁───

    switch (input.toLowerCase()) {                    We return NoInput if the string is
        case "sunday":                                  empty and a default DayOfWeek.
            return new Result(InputError.OK, DayOfWeek.Sunday);
        case "monday":
            return new Result(InputError.OK, DayOfWeek.Monday);
        case "tuesday":
            return new Result(InputError.OK, DayOfWeek.Tuesday);
        case "wednesday":
            return new Result(InputError.OK, DayOfWeek.Wednesday);
```

We return OK and the parsed DayOfWeek if we can successfully parse the input.

```
        case "thursday":
            return new Result(InputError.OK, DayOfWeek.Thursday);
        case "friday":
            return new Result(InputError.OK, DayOfWeek.Friday);
        case "saturday":
            return new Result(InputError.OK, DayOfWeek.Saturday);
        default:
            return new Result(InputError.Invalid, DayOfWeek.Sunday);   ◁──┐
    }
}
```

Otherwise, we return Invalid and a default DayOfWeek if we fail to parse.

This is not ideal because if we accidentally forget to check the error code, nothing prevents us from using the `DayOfWeek` member. Now the value can be a default, and we aren't necessarily able to tell that it is invalid. We might propagate the error through the system, such as writing it to a database, without realizing that we shouldn't have used the value at all.

Looking at this from the lens of types as sets, our result contains the combination of all possible error codes *and* all possible results (figure 3.4).

Figure 3.4   All possible values of the `Result` type as combinations of `InputError` and `DayOfWeek`. That's 21 values (3 InputError x 7 DayOfWeek).

Instead, we should try to return *either* an error *or* a valid value. If we manage to do that, the set of possible values is drastically decreased, and we eliminate the possibility of using the `DayOfWeek` component of a `Result` in which the `InputError` component is `NoInput` or `Invalid` (figure 3.5).

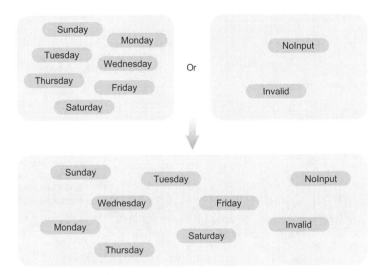

Figure 3.5 All possible values of `Result` **type as a combination of** `InputError` *or* `DayOfWeek`. **That's 9 values (2 InputError + 7 DayOfWeek). We no longer need an OK InputError, as the absence of an error is indicated by the fact that we have a** `DayOfWeek` **value.**

DIY EITHER

An `Either` type wraps two types, `TLeft` and `TRight`, the convention being that `TLeft` stores the error type and `TRight` stores the valid value type. (If there's no error, the value is "right".) Again, some programming languages provide this as part of their library, but if necessary, we can easily implement such a type.

Listing 3.14 `Either` type

```
class Either<TLeft, TRight> {
    private readonly value: TLeft | TRight;      The type wraps a value of TLeft or TRight and
    private readonly left: boolean;              a flag to keep track of which type is used.

    private constructor(value: TLeft | TRight, left: boolean) {
        this.value = value;
        this.left = left;                        Private constructor, as we need
    }                                            to make sure that the value and
                                                 boolean flag are in sync
    isLeft(): boolean {
        return this.left;
    }

    getLeft(): TLeft {
        if (!this.isLeft()) throw new Error();   Attempting to get a TLeft
                                                 when we have a TRight or
        return <TLeft>this.value;                vice versa throws an error.
    }
```

```
isRight(): boolean {
    return !this.left;
}

getRight(): TRight {
    if (!this.isRight()) throw new Error();

    return <TRight>this.value;
}

static makeLeft<TLeft, TRight>(value: TLeft) {
    return new Either<TLeft, TRight>(value, true);
}

static makeRight<TLeft, TRight>(value: TRight) {
    return new Either<TLeft, TRight>(value, false);
}
}
```

> Attempting to get a TLeft when we have a TRight or vice versa throws an error.

> Factory functions call the constructor and ensure that the boolean flag is consistent with the value.

In a language that's missing the type operator |, we could simply make the value a common type, such as Object in Java and C#. The getLeft() and getRight() methods handle conversion back to the TLeft and TRight types.

With such a type, we can update our parseDayOfWeek() implementation to return an Either<InputError, DayOfWeek> result and make it impossible to propagate an invalid or default DayOfWeek value. If the function returns an InputError, there is no DayOfWeek in the result, and attempting to unwrap one via a call to getLeft() throws an error.

Again, we have to be explicit about unpacking the value. When we know that we have a valid value (isLeft() returns true), and we extract it with getLeft(), we are guaranteed to have valid data.

Listing 3.15   Returning result or error from a function

```
enum InputError {
    NoInput,
    Invalid
}

type Result = Either<InputError, DayOfWeek>;

function parseDayOfWeek(input: string): Result {
    if (input == "")
        return Either.makeLeft(InputError.NoInput);

    switch (input.toLowerCase()) {
        case "sunday":
            return Either.makeRight(DayOfWeek.Sunday);
        case "monday":
            return Either.makeRight(DayOfWeek.Monday);
        case "tuesday":
            return Either.makeRight(DayOfWeek.Tuesday);
```

> We no longer need an OK InputError. If we don't have an error, we have a value.

> We update Result to be an InputError or a DayOfWeek instead of a combination of the two.

> We return a result or an error by Either.makeRight and Either.makeLeft.

```
        case "wednesday":
            return Either.makeRight(DayOfWeek.Wednesday);
        case "thursday":
            return Either.makeRight(DayOfWeek.Thursday);
        case "friday":
            return Either.makeRight(DayOfWeek.Friday);
        case "saturday":
            return Either.makeRight(DayOfWeek.Saturday);
        default:
            return Either.makeLeft(InputError.Invalid);  ◁──┐  We return a result or an
    }                                                        │  error by Either.makeRight
}                                                            │  and Either.makeLeft.
```

The updated implementation leverages the type system to eliminate invalid states such as (NoInput, Sunday) from which we could've accidentally used the Sunday value. Also, there's no need for an OK value for InputError because we don't have an error if parsing succeeds.

EXCEPTIONS

Throwing an exception on error is a perfectly valid example of result or error: the function either returns a result or throws an exception. In several situations, exceptions cannot be used and an Either type is preferred, such as when propagating errors across processes or across threads; as a design principle, when the error itself is not exceptional (often the case when we deal with user input); when calling operating system APIs that use error codes; and so on. In these situations, when we can't or don't want to throw an exception but need to communicate that we got a value or failed, it's best to encode this as an *either value or error* as opposed to *value and error.*

When throwing exceptions is acceptable, we can use them as another way to ensure that we don't end up with an invalid result *and* an error. When an exception is thrown, the function no longer returns the "normal" way, by passing back a value to the caller with a return statement. Rather, it propagates the exception object until a matching catch is found. This way, we get a result or an exception. We won't cover throwing exceptions in depth, because although many languages provide facilities for exceptions to be thrown and caught, from a type perspective, exceptions aren't very special.

3.2.4 Variants

We've looked at optional types, which contain a value of the underlying type or no value. Then we looked at either types, which contain a TLeft or a TRight value. The generalizations of these types are the *variant types.*

> **VARIANT TYPES** *Variant types*, also known as *tagged union types*, contain a value of any number of underlying types. *Tagged* comes from the fact that even if the underlying types have overlapping values, we are still able to tell exactly which type the value comes from.

Let's look at an example of a collection of geometric shapes in listing 3.16. Each shape has a different set of properties and a tag (implemented as a kind property). We can define a type that is the union of all these shapes. Then, when we want to (for example) render these shapes, we can use their kind property to determine which of the possible shapes an instance is, then cast it to that shape. This process is the same as the unwrapping in previous examples.

Listing 3.16 Tagged union of shapes

```
class Point {
    readonly kind: string = "Point";
    x: number = 0;
    y: number = 0;
}

class Circle {
    readonly kind: string = "Circle";
    x: number = 0;
    y: number = 0;
    radius: number = 0;
}

class Rectangle {
    readonly kind: string = "Rectangle";
    x: number = 0;
    y: number = 0;
    width: number = 0;
    height: number = 0;
}

type Shape = Point | Circle | Rectangle;

let shapes: Shape[] = [new Circle(), new Rectangle()];

for (let shape of shapes) {                    We iterate over the shapes and
    switch (shape.kind) {                      check the kind property of each.
        case "Point":
            let point: Point = <Point>shape;
            console.log(`Point ${JSON.stringify(point)}`);
            break;                                                  If the kind is "Point",
        case "Circle":                                             we can safely use the
            let circle: Circle = <Circle>shape;                    shape as a Point. The
            console.log(`Circle ${JSON.stringify(circle)}`);       same is true for
            break;                                                 Circle and Rectangle.
        case "Rectangle":
            let rectangle: Rectangle = <Rectangle>shape;
            console.log(`Rectangle ${JSON.stringify(rectangle)}`);
            break;
        default:                                        We throw an error if the kind is
            throw new Error();                           unknown. This means that some other
    }                                                    type somehow made its way into the
}                                                        union, which should never be the case.
```

In the preceding example, the kind member of each class represents the tag which tells us the actual type of a value. The value of shape.kind tells us whether the Shape instance is a `Point`, `Circle`, or `Rectangle`. We can also implement a general-purpose variant that keeps track of the types without requiring the types themselves to store a tag.

Let's implement a simple variant that can store a value of up to three types and keep track of the actual type stored based on a type index.

DIY VARIANT

Different programming languages provide different generic and type-checking features. Some languages allow a variable number of generic arguments, for example (so we can have variants of any number of types); others provide different ways to determine whether a value is of a certain type at both compile and run time.

The following TypeScript implementation has some trade-offs that don't necessarily translate to other programming languages. It's a starting point for a general-purpose variant, but it would be implemented differently in, say, Java or C#. TypeScript doesn't support method overloads, for example, but in other languages, we could get away with a single `make()` function overloaded on each generic type.

Listing 3.17 Variant type

```
class Variant<T1, T2, T3> {
    readonly value: T1 | T2 | T3;
    readonly index: number;

    private constructor(value: T1 | T2 | T3, index: number) {
        this.value = value;
        this.index = index;
    }

    static make1<T1, T2, T3>(value: T1): Variant<T1, T2, T3> {
        return new Variant<T1, T2, T3>(value, 0);
    }

    static make2<T1, T2, T3>(value: T2): Variant<T1, T2, T3> {
        return new Variant<T1, T2, T3>(value, 1);
    }

    static make3<T1, T2, T3>(value: T3): Variant<T1, T2, T3> {
        return new Variant<T1, T2, T3>(value, 2);
    }
}
```

This implementation takes on the responsibility of maintaining the tags, so now we can remove them from our geometric shapes.

Listing 3.18 Union of shapes as variant

```
class Point {
    x: number = 0;
    y: number = 0;
}
```
Shapes no longer need to store tags themselves.

```
class Circle {
    x: number = 0;
    y: number = 0;
    radius: number = 0;
}

class Rectangle {
    x: number = 0;
    y: number = 0;
    width: number = 0;
    height: number = 0;
}

type Shape = Variant<Point, Circle, Rectangle>;

let shapes: Shape[] = [
    Variant.make2(new Circle()),
    Variant.make3(new Rectangle())
];

for (let shape of shapes) {
    switch (shape.index) {
        case 0:
            let point: Point = <Point>shape.value;
            console.log(`Point ${JSON.stringify(point)}`);
            break;
        case 1:
            let circle: Circle = <Circle>shape.value;
            console.log(`Circle ${JSON.stringify(circle)}`);
            break;
        case 2:
            let rectangle: Rectangle = <Rectangle>shape.value;
            console.log(`Rectangle ${JSON.stringify(rectangle)}`);
            break;
        default:
            throw new Error();
    }
}
```

Shapes no longer need to store tags themselves.

Shape is now a Variant of these three types.

We look at the index property to find the tag and the value property to get the actual object.

This implementation might not look as though it adds a lot of benefit; we ended up using numeric tags and arbitrarily decided that 0 is a Point and 1 is a Circle. You might also wonder why we didn't use a class hierarchy for our shapes, where we have a base method that each type implements instead of switching on tags.

For that task, we need to take a look at the visitor design pattern and the ways in which it can be implemented.

3.2.5 Exercises

1 Users can provide a selection among the colors red, green, and blue. What should be the type of this selection?

a number with Red = 0, Green = 1, Blue = 2

b string with Red = "Red", Green = "Green", Blue = "Blue"

    c `enum Colors { Red, Green, Blue }`

    d `type Colors = Red | Green | Blue` where the colors are classes

2 What should be the return type of a function that takes a string as input and parses it into a number? The function does not throw.

    a `number`

    b `number | undefined`

    c `Optional<number>`

    d Either b or c

3 Operating systems usually use numbers to represent error codes. What should be the return type of a function that can return either a numerical value or a numerical error code?

    a `number`

    b `{ value: number, error: number }`

    c `number | number`

    d `Either<number, number>`

3.3 *The visitor pattern*

Let's go over the visitor design pattern and look at traversing the items that make up a document—first through an object-oriented lens and then with the generic tagged union type we implemented. Don't worry if you aren't very familiar with the visitor design pattern; we'll review how it works as we're working through our example.

We'll start with a naïve implementation, show how the visitor design pattern improves the design, and then show an alternative implementation that removes the need for class hierarchies.

We start with three document items: paragraph, picture, and table. We want to either render them onscreen or have a screen reader read them aloud for visually impaired users.

3.3.1 *A naïve implementation*

One approach we can take is to provide a common interface to ensure that each item knows how to draw itself on a screen and read itself, as shown in the next listing.

Listing 3.19   Naïve implementation

```
class Renderer { /* Rendering methods */ }
class ScreenReader { /* Screen reading methods */ }

interface IDocumentItem {
    render(renderer: Renderer): void;
    read(screenReader: ScreenReader): void;
}
```

The two classes provide methods to render and read, omitted here for brevity.

The IDocumentItem interface specifies that each item can render itself and read itself.

```
class Paragraph implements IDocumentItem {
    /* Paragraph members omitted */
    render(renderer: Renderer) {
        /* Uses renderer to draw itself on screen */
    }

    read(screenReader: ScreenReader) {
        /* Uses screenReader to read itself */
    }
}

class Picture implements IDocumentItem {
    /* Picture members omitted */
    render(renderer: Renderer) {
        /* Uses renderer to draw itself on screen */
    }

    read(screenReader: ScreenReader) {
        /* Uses screenReader to read itself */
    }
}

class Table implements IDocumentItem {
    /* Table members omitted */
    render(renderer: Renderer) {
        /* Uses renderer to draw itself on screen */
    }

    read(screenReader: ScreenReader) {
        /* Uses screenReader to read itself */
    }
}

let doc: IDocumentItem[] = [new Paragraph(), new Table()];
let renderer: Renderer = new Renderer();

for (let item of doc) {
    item.render(renderer);
}
```

Document elements implement IDocumentItem and, given a renderer or screen reader, draw themselves or read themselves aloud.

This approach is not great from a design point of view. The document items store information that describes document content, such as text or an image, and should not be responsible for other things, such as rendering and accessibility. Having rendering and accessibility code in each document item class bloats the code. Worse, if we need to add a new capability—say, for printing—we need to update the interface and all implementing classes to implement the new capability.

3.3.2   *Using the visitor pattern*

The visitor pattern is an operation to be performed on elements of an object structure. This pattern lets you define a new operation without changing the classes of the elements on which it operates.

In our example shown in listing 3.20, the pattern should allow us to add a new capability without having to touch the code of the document items. We can achieve

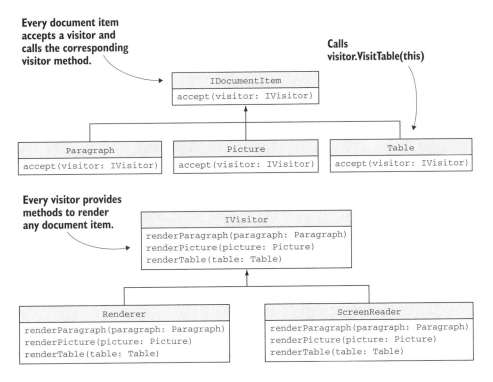

Figure 3.6 A visitor pattern. The `IDocumentItem` interface ensures that every document item has an `accept()` method that takes an `IVisitor`. `IVisitor` ensures that every visitor can handle all possible document item types. Each document item implements `accept()` to send itself to the visitor. With this pattern, we can separate responsibilities, such as screen rendering and accessibility, to individual components (visitors) and abstract them away from the document items.

this task with the *double-dispatch mechanism,* in which document items accept any visitor and then pass themselves to it. The visitor knows how to process each individual item (by rendering it, reading it aloud, and so on), so given an instance of the item, it performs the right operation (figure 3.6).

Double dispatch comes from the fact that, given an `IDocumentItem`, the right `accept()` method is called first; then, given the `IVisitor` argument, the right operation is performed.

Listing 3.20 Processing with the visitor pattern

```
interface IVisitor {
    visitParagraph(paragraph: Paragraph): void;
    visitPicture(picture: Picture): void;
    visitTable(table: Table): void;
}
```

The IVisitor interface specifies that each visitor should be able to process all shapes.

```
class Renderer implements IVisitor {
    visitParagraph(paragraph: Paragraph) { /* ... */ }
    visitPicture(picture: Picture) { /* ... */ }
    visitTable(table: Table) { /* ... */ }
}

class ScreenReader implements IVisitor {
    visitParagraph(paragraph: Paragraph) { /* ... */ }
    visitPicture(picture: Picture) { /* ... */ }
    visitTable(table: Table) { /* ... */ }
}

interface IDocumentItem {
    accept(visitor: IVisitor): void;
}

class Paragraph implements IDocumentItem {
    /* Paragraph members omitted */
    accept(visitor: IVisitor) {
        visitor.visitParagraph(this);
    }
}

class Picture implements IDocumentItem {
    /* Picture members omitted */
    accept(visitor: IVisitor) {
        visitor.visitPicture(this);
    }
}

class Table implements IDocumentItem {
    /* Table members omitted */
    accept(visitor: IVisitor) {
        visitor.visitTable(this);
    }
}

let doc: IDocumentItem[] = [new Paragraph(), new Table()];
let renderer: IVisitor = new Renderer();

for (let item of doc) {
    item.accept(renderer);
}
```

The concrete Renderer and ScreenReader implement this interface.

Now document items need only implement an accept() method that takes any visitor.

Items call the appropriate method on the visitor and pass themselves as arguments.

Now a visitor can go over a collection of IDocumentItem objects and process them by calling accept() on each. The responsibility of processing is moved from the items themselves to the visitors. Adding a new visitor does not affect the document items; the new visitor just needs to implement the IVisitor interface, and document items would accept it as they would any other.

A new Printer visitor class would implement logic to print a paragraph, a picture, and a table in the visitParagraph(), visitPicture(), and visitTable() methods. The document items themselves would become printable without having to change.

This example is a classical implementation of the visitor pattern. Next, let's look at how we could achieve something similar by using a variant instead.

3.3.3 Visiting a variant

First, let's go back to our generic variant type and implement a `visit()` function that takes a variant and a set of functions, one for each type, and (depending on the value stored in the variant) applies the right function to it.

Listing 3.21 Variant visitor

```
function visit<T1, T2, T3>(
    variant: Variant<T1, T2, T3>,
    func1: (value: T1) => void,
    func2: (value: T2) => void,
    func3: (value: T3) => void
): void {
    switch (variant.index) {
        case 0: func1(<T1>variant.value); break;
        case 1: func2(<T2>variant.value); break;
        case 2: func3(<T3>variant.value); break;
        default: throw new Error();
    }
}
```

> The visit function takes as arguments a function for each type that makes up the variant.

> Based on index, the function matching the type of the stored value is called.

If we place our document items in a variant, we can use this function to select the appropriate visitor method. If we do this, we no longer have to force any of our classes to implement certain interfaces: responsibility for matching the right document item with the right processing method is moved to this generic `visit()` function.

Document items no longer need to know anything about visitors and don't need to "accept" them, as the following listing shows.

Listing 3.22 Alternative processing with variant visitor

```
class Renderer {
    renderParagraph(paragraph: Paragraph) { /* ... */ }
    renderPicture(picture: Picture) { /* ... */ }
    renderTable(table: Table) { /* ... */ }
}

class ScreenReader {
    readParagraph(paragraph: Paragraph) { /* ... */ }
    readPicture(picture: Picture) { /* ... */ }
    readTable(table: Table) { /* ... */ }
}

class Paragraph {
    /* Paragraph members omitted */
}

class Picture {
```

> Document items no longer need a common interface.

```
    /* Picture members omitted */
}

class Table {
    /* Table members omitted */          Document items no longer
}                                         need a common interface.

let doc: Variant<Paragraph, Picture, Table>[] = [      We store document items in
    Variant.make1(new Paragraph()),                    a variant that can hold any
    Variant.make3(new Table())                         of the available items.
];

let renderer: Renderer = new Renderer();

                                          The visit function matches the item
for (let item of doc) {                   with the right processing method.
    visit(item,
        (paragraph: Paragraph) => renderer.renderParagraph(paragraph),
        (picture: Picture) => renderer.renderPicture(picture),
        (table: Table) => renderer.renderTable(table)
    );
}
```

With this approach, we decouple the double-dispatch mechanism from the types we are using and move it to the variant/visitor. The variant and visitor are generic types that can be reused across different problem domains. The advantage of this approach is that it lets visitors be responsible only for processing and document items be responsible only for storing domain data (figure 3.7).

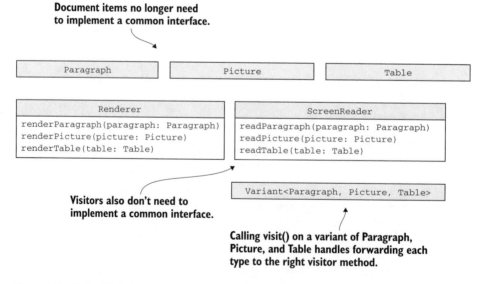

Figure 3.7 A simplified visitor pattern: now the document items and visitors don't need to implement any interfaces. Contrast this figure with figure 3.6. Responsibility for matching a document item with the right visitor method is encapsulated in the `visit()` method. As we can see from the figure, the types are not related, which is a good thing: it makes our program more flexible.

The visit() function we introduced is also the expected way to use a variant type. Performing a switch on the index of the variant when we want to figure out exactly which type it contains could be error-prone. But usually, once we have a variant, we don't want to extract the value; instead, we apply functions to it by using visit(). This way, the error-prone switch is handled in the visit() implementation, and we don't have to worry about it. Encapsulating error-prone code in a reusable component is good practice for reducing risk, because when the implementation is stable and tested, we can rely on it in multiple scenarios.

Using a variant-based visitor instead of the classical OOP implementation has the advantage that it fully separates our domain objects from the visitors. Now we don't even need an accept() method, and document items don't need to know anything about what is processing them. They also don't have to conform to any particular interface, such as IDocumentItem in our example. That's because the glue code that matches visitors with shapes is encapsulated in Variant and its visit() function.

3.3.4 Exercise

1 Our visit() implementation returns void. Extend it so that given a Variant<T1, T2, T3>, it returns a Variant<U1, U2, U3> by applying one of three functions: (value: T1) => U1, or (value: T2) => U2, or (value: T3) => U3.

3.4 *Algebraic data types*

You might have heard the term *algebraic data types* (ADTs). ADTs are ways to combine types within a type system. In fact, this is exactly what we covered during this chapter. ADTs provide two ways to combine types: product types and sum types.

3.4.1 *Product types*

Product types are what we called *compound types* in this chapter. Tuples and records are product types because their values are products of their composing types. The types A = {a1, a2} (type A with possible values a1 and a2) and B = {b1, b2} (type B with possible values b1 and b2) combine into the tuple type <A, B> as A x B = { (a1, b1), (a1, b2), (a2, b1), (a2, b2) }.

> **PRODUCT TYPES** Product types combine multiple other types into a new type that stores a value from each of the combined types. The product type of types A, B, and C—which we can write as A x B x C—contains a value from A, a value from B, *and* a value from C. Tuple and record types are examples of product types. Additionally, records allow us to assign meaningful names to each of their components.

Record types should be very familiar, as they are usually the first composition method that new programmers learn. Recently, tuples have made their way into mainstream programming languages, but they shouldn't be particularly hard to understand.

Tuples are very similar to record types except that we can't name their members and usually can define them inline by specifying the types that make up the tuple. In TypeScript, for example, [number, number] defines the tuple type composed of two number values.

We covered product types before sum types, as they should be more familiar. Almost all programming languages provide ways to define record types. Fewer mainstream languages provide syntactic support for sum types.

3.4.2 Sum types

Sum types are what we called *either-or* types earlier in this chapter. They combine types by allowing a value from any one of the types, but only one of them. The types A = {a1, a2} and B = {b1, b2} combine into the sum type A | B as A + B = {a1, a2, b1, b2}.

> **SUM TYPES** Sum types combine multiple other types into a new type that stores a value from any one of the combined types. The sum type of types A, B, and C—which we can write as A + B + C—contains a value from A, *or* a value from B, *or* a value from C. Optional and variant types are examples of sum types.

As we saw, TypeScript has the | type operator, but common sum types such as Optional, Either, and Variant can be implemented without it. These types provide powerful ways for representing result or error and closed sets of types, and enable different ways to implement the common visitor pattern.

In general, sum types allow us to store values from unrelated types in a single variable. As in the visitor pattern example, an object-oriented alternative would be to use a common base class or interface, but that doesn't scale as well. If we mix and match different types in different places of our application, we end up with a lot of interfaces or base classes that aren't particularly reusable. Sum types provide a simple, clean way to compose types for such scenarios.

3.4.3 Exercises

1 What kind of type does the following statement declare?

```
let x: [number, string] = [42, "Hello"];
```

a A primitive type
b A sum type
c A product type
d Both a sum and a product type

2 What kind of type does the following statement declare?

```
let y: number | string = "Hello";
```

a A primitive type
b A sum type

    c A product type

    d Both a sum and a product type

3 Given an enum Two { A, B } and an enum Three { C, D, E }, how many possible values does the tuple type [Two, Three] have?

    a 2

    b 5

    c 6

    d 8

4 Given an enum Two { A, B } and an enum Three { C, D, E }, how many possible values does the type Two | Three have?

    a 2

    b 5

    c 6

    d 8

Summary

- Product types are tuples and records that group values from multiple types.
- Records allow us to name members, thus giving them meaning. Records leave less room for ambiguity than tuples.
- Invariants are rules that a well-formed record must obey. If a type has invariants, making members private or readonly ensures that the invariants are enforced and that external code cannot break them.
- Sum types group types as either-or, in which values are of one of the component types.
- Functions should return a value *or* an error, not a value *and* an error.
- Optional types hold a value of the underlying type or nothing. It's generally less error-prone when the absence of a value is not itself part of the domain of a variable (null billion-dollar mistake).
- Either types hold a value of the left or the right type. By convention, right is right, so left is error.
- Variants can hold a value of any number of underlying types and enable us to express values of a closed sets of types without requiring any relationship between them (no common interfaces or base type).
- A visitor function that applies the right function to a variant enables an alternative implementation of the visitor pattern, with better division of responsibilities.

In this chapter, we covered various ways to create new types by combining existing types. In chapter 4, we'll see how we can increase the safety of our program by relying on the type system to encode meaning and restricting the range of allowed values for our types. We'll also see how we can add and remove type information and how this can be applied to scenarios such as serialization.

Answers to exercises

COMPOUND TYPES

  1 c—Naming the three components of the coordinates is the preferred approach.

EXPRESSING EITHER-OR WITH TYPES

  1 c—An enum is appropriate in this case. With existing requirements, classes aren't needed.

  2 d—Either a built-in sum type or `Optional` is a valid return type, as both can represent the absence of a value

  3 d—A discriminate union type is best (`number | number` wouldn't be able to distinguish whether the value represents an error.)

THE VISITOR PATTERN

  1 Here is a possible implementation:

```
function visit<T1, T2, T3, U1, U2, U3>(
    variant: Variant<T1, T2, T3>,
    func1: (value: T1) => U1,
    func2: (value: T2) => U2,
    func3: (value: T3) => U3
): Variant<U1, U2, U3> {
    switch (variant.index) {
        case 0:
            return Variant.make1(func1(<T1>variant.value));
        case 1:
            return Variant.make2(func2(<T2>variant.value));
        case 2:
            return Variant.make3(func3(<T3>variant.value));
        default: throw new Error();
    }
}
```

ALGEBRAIC DATA TYPES

  1 c—Tuples are product types.

  2 b—This is a TypeScript sum type.

  3 c—Because tuples are product types, we multiply the possible values of the two enums (2 x 3).

  4 b—Because this is a sum type, we add the possible values of the two enums (2 + 3).

Type safety

Now that we know how to use the basic types provided by our programming language and how to compose them to create new types, let's look at how we can make our programs safer by using types. By *safer*, I mean reducing the opportunity for bugs.

There are a couple of ways to achieve this by creating new types that encode additional information: meanings and guarantees. The former, which we'll cover in the first section, removes the opportunity for us to misinterpret a value, such as mistaking a mile for a kilometer. The latter allows us to encode guarantees such as "an instance of this type will never be less than 0" in the type system. Both techniques make our code safer, as we eliminate invalid values from the set of possible values represented by a type and avoid misunderstandings as soon as we can, preferably at compile time or as soon as we instantiate our types if at run time. When we have an instance of one of our types, from then on we know what it represents and that it is a valid value.

Because we're discussing type safety, we'll also look at how we can add and hide information from the type checker manually. If we somehow know more than the type checker does, we can tell it to trust us and pass our information down to it. On the other hand, if the type checker knows too much and ends up impeding our work, we can make it "forget" some of the typing information, giving us more flexibility at the cost of safety. These techniques are not to be used lightly, as they move the responsibility of proper type checking from the type checker to us as developers, but as we'll see, there are some legitimate scenarios in which these techniques are desired.

4.1 *Avoiding primitive obsession to prevent misinterpretation*

Figure 4.1   The numeric value `1000` could represent **1,000 dollars or 1,000 miles**. Two different developers could interpret it as two very different measures.

In this section, we'll see how using basic types to represent values and implicitly assuming what those values represent can cause problems when two different parts of the code, often written by different developers, make incompatible assumptions (figure 4.1).

We can rely on the type system to make those assumptions explicit by defining types to describe them, in which case the type checker can detect incompatibilities and signal them before anything bad happens.

Let's say we have a function `addToBill()` that takes as its argument a `number`. The function is supposed to add the price of an item to a bill. Because the argument is of type `number`, we could pass it a distance between cities in miles, also represented as a number. We end up adding miles to a price total, and the type checker doesn't suspect anything!

On the other hand, if we make our `addToBill()` function take an argument of type `Currency` and our distance between cities is represented as a type `Miles`, the code will not compile (figure 4.2).

Figure 4.2   Having an explicit `Currency` type makes it clear that the value does not represent 1,000 miles, but rather a dollar amount.

4.1.1 *The Mars Climate Orbiter*

The Mars Climate Orbiter disintegrated because a component developed by Lockheed used a different unit of measure (pound-force seconds) for momentum than a component developed by NASA, which consumed that measure (in metric units). Let's imagine how the code looked for the two components. The `trajectory-Correction()` function consumes a measurement as Newton-seconds, or Ns (the metric unit for momentum), whereas the `provideMomentum()` function produces a measure in pound-force seconds, or lbfs, as shown in the next listing.

Listing 4.1   Sketch of incompatible components

```
function trajectoryCorrection(momentum: number) {
    if (momentum < 2 /* Ns */) {
        disintegrate();
    }

    /* ... */
}

function provideMomentum() {
    trajectoryCorrection(1.5 /* lbfs */);
}
```

trajectoryCorrection takes momentum as an argument of type number.

If momentum is less than 2 Ns, disintegrate.

provideMomentum passes in a measurement of 1.5 lbfs.

Converting to metric, 1 lbfs equals 4.448222 Ns. From the perspective of the `provideMomentum()` function, the value provided is good, because 1.5 lbfs is more than 6 Ns. That's way more than the 2 Ns lower limit. What went wrong? The main issue in this case is that both components treated momentum as a number, implicitly assuming the unit in which it was measured. `trajectoryCorrection()` interpreted the momentum as 1 Ns, less than the 2 Ns lower limit, and inappropriately triggered the disintegration.

Let's see whether we can leverage the type system to prevent such catastrophic misunderstandings. Let's make the unit of measure explicit by defining a `Lbfs` type and a `Ns` type in listing 4.2. Both types wrap a number, as the actual measure is still a value. We will use a unique symbol for each type because TypeScript considers types to be compatible if they have the same shape, as we will see when we discuss subtyping. The unique symbol trick makes it so that one type can't be implicitly interpreted as the other. Not all languages require this additional unique symbol member. We'll explain this trick in chapter 7; for now, we'll focus on the new types defined.

Listing 4.2   Pound-force second and Newton-second types

```
declare const NsType: unique symbol;

class Ns {
    readonly value: number;
    [NsType]: void;
```

TypeScript-specific way to ensure that other objects with the same shape can't be interpreted as this type

Ns effectively just wraps a value of type number.

```
    constructor(value: number) {
        this.value = value;
    }
}

declare const LbfsType: unique symbol;

class Lbfs {
    readonly value: number;
    [LbfsType]: void;

    constructor(value: number) {
        this.value = value;
    }
}
```

Similarly, Lbfs type wraps a number and a unique symbol.

Now that we have our two separate types, we can easily implement a conversion between them because we know the ratio. Let's look at the following listing to see a conversion from lbfs to Ns, which we need in our update `trajectoryCorrection()` code.

Listing 4.3 Converting lbfs to Ns

```
function lbfsToNs(lbfs: Lbfs): Ns {
    return new Ns(lbfs.value * 4.448222);
}
```

Take the lbfs value, multiply by the ratio, and return a Ns value.

Going back to the Mars Climate Orbiter, we can reimplement the two functions to use the new types. `trajectoryCorrection()` expects a Ns momentum (and will still disintegrate if the value is less than 2 Ns), and `provideMomentum()` still produces values as lbfs. But now we can't simply take the value produced by `provideMomentum()` and pass it to `trajectoryCorrection()`, because the returned value and the function argument have different types. We have to explicitly convert from one to the other, using our `lbfsToNs()` function, as the following listing shows.

Listing 4.4 Updated components

```
function trajectoryCorrection(momentum: Ns) {
    if (momentum.value < new Ns(2).value) {
        disintegrate();
    }

    /* ... */
}
function provideMomentum() {
    trajectoryCorrection(lbfsToNs(new Lbfs(1.5)));
}
```

trajectoryCorrection now takes an argument of type Ns and compares it with 2 Ns.

provideMomentum generates a 1.5 lbfs value and has to convert it to Ns.

If we omitted the conversion `lbfsToNs()`, the code would simply not compile, and we would get the following error: Argument of type 'lbfs' is not assignable to parameter of type 'Ns'. Property '[NsType]' is missing in type 'lbfs'.

Let's review what happened: we started with two components that both manipulated momentum values, but even though they used different units when handling those values, they both represented the values simply as `number`. To avoid misinterpretations, we created a couple of new types, one to represent each unit of measure, which effectively left no room for misinterpretation. If a component explicitly deals with `Ns`, it can't accidentally consume a `Lbfs` value.

Also note that the assumptions that showed up in the code as comments in our first example (`1.5 /* lbfs */`) became code in our final implementation (`new Lbfs(1.5)`).

4.1.2 *The primitive obsession antipattern*

In the same way that design patterns capture reusable software designs that are highly reliable and effective, *antipatterns* are common designs that are ineffective and counterproductive when a better alternative exists. The preceding example is an instance of a well-known antipattern called *primitive obsession*. Primitive obsession turns up when we rely on basic types to represent everything: a postal code is a `number`, a phone number is a `string`, and so on.

If we fall into this trap, we leave a lot of room for errors like the one we saw in this section. That's because the meaning of the values is not explicitly captured in the type system. If I consume a momentum value given as a `number`, I, the developer, implicitly assume that it is a Newton-second value. The type checker does not have enough information to detect when two developers make incompatible assumptions. When this assumption is explicitly captured as a type declaration, and I consume a momentum value given as a `Ns` instance, the type checker can verify when someone else is attempting to give me a `Lbfs` instance instead and not allow the code to compile.

Even though a postal code is a number, that doesn't mean we should store it as a value of type `number`. We should never interpret momentum as a postal code.

If the entities you represent are simple values, such as physical measurements and postal codes, consider defining them as new types, even if these types simply wrap a number or a string. This practice gives the type system more information to work with in analyzing our code and eliminates a whole class of errors caused by incompatible assumptions, not to mention that it makes the code more readable. For contrast, compare the first definition of `trajectoryCorrection()`, which is `trajectoryCorrection(momentum: number)`, with the second one, which is `trajectoryCorrection(momentum: Ns)`. The second one gives more information to readers of the code as to what its contract is. (Expected momentum is in `Ns`.)

So far, we've seen how we can wrap primitive types into other types to encode more information. Now let's move on to see how we can provide even more safety by restricting the range of allowed values for a given type.

4.1.3 *Exercise*

1 What is the safest way to represent a weight measurement?

   a As a `number`

   b As a `string`

    c As a custom `Kilograms` type

    d As a custom `Weight` type

4.2   Enforcing constraints

In chapter 3, we talked about composition and how to take basic types and combine them to represent more complex concepts, such as representing a point on a 2D plane as a pair of number values, one for each of the X and Y coordinates. Now let's look at what we can do when the basic types we get out of the box allow for more values than we need.

Let's take, as an example, a measure of temperature. We're going to avoid primitive obsession and declare a `Celsius` type to make it clear which unit of measure we expect the temperature to have. This type will also simply wrap a number.

We have an additional constraint, though: we should never have a temperature less than absolute zero, which is –273.15 degrees Celsius. One option is to check whenever we use an instance of this type that the value is a valid one. This option leaves room for error, though: we always add the check, but a new developer on the team doesn't know the pattern and misses checking. Wouldn't it be better to make sure that we can never get an invalid value?

We can do this in two ways: via the constructor or via a factory.

4.2.1   Enforcing constraints with the constructor

We can implement the constraint in the constructor and handle a value that's too small in one of the two ways we saw when we looked at integer overflow. One option is to throw an exception when the value is invalid and disallow creation of the object.

Listing 4.5   Constructor throwing on invalid value

```
declare const celsiusType: unique symbol;

class Celsius {
    readonly value: number;          ◁── The value is immutable,
    [celsiusType]: void;                  so when it's initialized,
                                          it can't be changed.
    constructor(value: number) {
        if (value < -273.15) throw new Error();    ◁── Constructor throws if
                                                        we attempt to create
        this.value = value;                         an invalid temperature.
    }
}
```

We ensure that the value stays valid after construction by making it `readonly`. Another option would be to make it private and access it with a getter (so that the value can be retrieved but not set).

We can also implement our constructor to coerce the value to be a valid one: anything less than `-273.15` becomes `-273.15`.

```
declare const celsiusType: unique symbol;

class Celsius {
    readonly value: number;
    [celsiusType]: void;

    constructor(value: number) {
        if (value < -273.15) value = -273.15;

        this.value = value;
    }
}
```

Instead of throwing,
we "fix" the value.

Either of the two approaches is valid, depending on the scenario. We can also use a
factory function instead. A *factory* is a class or function whose main job is to create
another object.

4.2.2 Enforcing constraints with a factory

A factory is useful when we don't want to throw an exception, but to return undefined or some other value that is not a temperature and represents failure to create a
valid instance. A constructor can't do this because it doesn't return: it either finishes
initializing its instance or throws. Another reason to use a factory is when the logic
required to construct and validate an object is complex, in which case it might make
sense to implement it outside the constructor. As a rule of thumb, constructors
shouldn't do heavy lifting—just get the object members initialized.

Let's look at how an implementation of a factory works in the following listing. We
will make the constructor private so that only the factory method can call it. The factory will be a static method on our class. It will return either a `Celsius` instance or
undefined.

```
declare const celsiusType: unique symbol;

class Celsius {
    readonly value: number;
    [celsiusType]: void;

    private constructor(value: number) {
        this.value = value;
    }

    static makeCelsius(value: number): Celsius | undefined {
        if (value < -273.15) return undefined;

        return new Celsius(value);
    }
}
```

Constructor is now private
because it doesn't
perform any checks itself.

Factory returns either a valid
Celsius instance or undefined.

Constraint is enforced in the
factory, which is the only way
to create Celsius instances.

In all these cases, we have the additional guarantee that if we have an instance of `Celsius`, its value will never be less than `-273.15`. The advantage of performing the check when an instance of the type is created and ensuring that the type can't be created in other ways is that you are guaranteed a valid value whenever you see an instance of the type being passed around.

Instead of checking whether the instance is valid when using it, which usually means performing the check in multiple places, we perform the check just once and make it impossible for an invalid object of the type to exist.

This technique goes beyond simple value wrappers like `Celsius`, of course. We can ensure that a `Date` object created from a year, a month, and a day is valid and disallow dates like June 31. There are many cases in which the basic types at our disposal don't allow us to impose the restrictions we want directly, in which case we can create types that encapsulate additional constraints and provide the guarantee that they can't exist with invalid values.

Next, let's look at how we can add and hide typing information throughout our code and when this practice is useful.

4.2.3   Exercise

1   Implement a `Percentage` type that represents a value between 0 and 100. Values smaller than 0 should become 0, and values larger than 100 should become 100.

4.3   Adding type information

Although type checking has strong theoretical foundations, all programming languages provide shortcuts that allow us to bypass the type checks and tell the compiler to treat a value as a certain type. We are effectively saying, "Trust us; we know what this type is better than you do." This is called a *type cast*—a term you might have heard before.

TYPE CAST   A type cast converts the type of an expression to another type. Each programming language has its own rules about which conversions are valid and which are not, which can be done automatically by the compiler, and which must be done with additional code (figure 4.3).

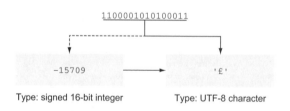

Figure 4.3   With casting, we can turn a value of type 16-bit signed integer into a UTF-8 encoded character.

4.3.1   Type casting

An *explicit type cast* is a cast that allows us to tell the compiler to treat a value as though it had a certain type. In TypeScript, we do a cast to `NewType` by adding `<NewType>` in front of the value or by adding `as NewType` after the value.

This technique can be dangerous when misused: if we bypass the type checker, we get a run-time error if we attempt to use a value as something it is not. I can cast my `Bike`, which I can `ride()`, to a `SportsCar`, for example, but I still won't be able to `drive()` it, as the following listing shows.

Listing 4.8 Type cast causing a run-time error

```
class Bike {
    ride(): void { /* ... */ }
}

class SportsCar {
    drive(): void { /* ... */ }
}

let myBike: Bike = new Bike();        │ myBike is created as type Bike,
                                       │ so we can call ride() on it.
myBike.ride();

let myPretendSportsCar: SportsCar = <SportsCar><unknown>myBike;

myPretendSportsCar.drive();
```

> We can tell the compiler to treat it as a SportsCar, which we assign to myPretendSportsCar.

> Calling drive() on myPretendSportsCar causes a run-time error.

Here, we can tell the type checker to let us pretend that we have a `SportsCar`, but that doesn't mean we actually have one. Calling `drive` results in the following exception being thrown: `TypeError: myPretendSportsCar.drive is not a function`.

We had to cast `myBike` first to the `unknown` type and then to a `SportsCar` because the TypeScript compiler realizes that the `Bike` and `SportsCar` types don't overlap. (A valid value of one of the types can never be a valid value of the other.) So simply calling `<SportsCar>myBike` still causes an error. Instead, we first say `<unknown>myBike`, which tells the compiler to forget the type of `myBike`. Then we can say, "Trust us; it's a `SportsCar`." But as we saw, this still causes a run-time error. In other languages, it can cause a crash. In general, such a situation is not valid. So when would this be useful?

4.3.2 *Tracking types outside the type system*

Sometimes, we know more than the type checker. Let's revisit the `Either` implementation from chapter 3. It stores a value of `TLeft` or `TRight` type, and a `boolean` flag keeps track of whether the value is `TLeft`, as shown in the next listing.

Listing 4.9 Revisiting `Either` implementation

```
class Either<TLeft, TRight> {
    private readonly value: TLeft | TRight;
    private readonly left: boolean;
```

> We store a value of type TLeft or type TRight.

> We keep track of whether it is a TLeft or not by using the left property.

```
    private constructor(value: TLeft | TRight, left: boolean) {
        this.value = value;
        this.left = left;
    }

    isLeft(): boolean {
        return this.left;
    }

    getLeft(): TLeft {
        if (!this.isLeft()) throw new Error();

        return <TLeft>this.value;
    }

    isRight(): boolean {
        return !this.left;
    }

    getRight(): TRight {
        if (!this.isRight()) throw new Error();

        return <TRight>this.value;
    }

    static makeLeft<TLeft, TRight>(value: TLeft) {
        return new Either<TLeft, TRight>(value, true);
    }

    static makeRight<TLeft, TRight>(value: TRight) {
        return new Either<TLeft, TRight>(value, false);
    }
}
```

When we want to get a TLeft, we check whether we are storing the right type; then we cast to TLeft.

The makeLeft factory initializes left to true; makeRight initializes it to false.

This allows us to combine two types into a sum type that can represent a value from either of them. If we look closely, though, the value we are storing has type TLeft | TRight. After we assign it, the type checker no longer knows whether the actual value we stored was a TLeft or a TRight. From now on, it will consider value to be either of the two. This is what we want while storing the value, but at some point, we would like to use it.

The compiler will not allow us to pass a value of type TLeft | TRight to a function that expects a TLeft value, because if our value is in fact TRight, we are going to be in trouble. If we have a triangle or a square, we can't necessarily pass that through a triangular slot. It would work to have a triangle to pass through it. But what if we have a square (figure 4.4)?

Trying to do something like this results in a compiler error, which is good. But we know something the type

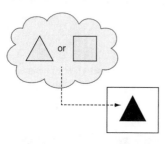

Figure 4.4   If we have a triangle or a square, we can't say for sure whether the actual shape we have will pass through a triangular slot. It will if it's a triangle, but it won't if it's a square.

checker doesn't: we know from when we set the value whether it came from a TLeft or a TRight. If we created our object by using makeLeft(), we set left to true. If we created our object by using makeRight(), we set left to false, as shown in the next listing. We are keeping track of this fact even if the type checker forgets.

Listing 4.10 makeLeft and makeRight

```
class Either<TLeft, TRight> {
    private readonly value: TLeft | TRight;
    private readonly left: boolean;          left tells us whether we
                                             are storing a TLeft.

    private constructor(value: TLeft | TRight, left: boolean) {
        this.value = value;
        this.left = left;          left is assigned in the private
    }                              constructor that only makeLeft
                                   and makeRight can call.

    /* ... */

    static makeLeft<TLeft, TRight>(value: TLeft) {
        return new Either<TLeft, TRight>(value, true);
    }                                                      makeLeft and makeRight
                                                           initialize left to the
    static makeRight<TLeft, TRight>(value: TRight) {       appropriate value.
        return new Either<TLeft, TRight>(value, false);
    }
}
```

When we want to take the value out, as a caller, it is our responsibility to first check which of the two types the value is. If we have an Either<Triangle, Square> and want a Triangle, we start by calling isLeft(). If true is returned, we call getLeft() and end up with a Triangle, as the following listing shows.

Listing 4.11 Triangle or Square

```
declare const triangleType: unique symbol;
class Triangle {
    [triangleType]: void;
    /* ... */
}                                     Triangle and
declare const squareType: unique symbol;   Square types
class Square {
    [squareType]: void;
    /* ... */
}

function slot(triangle: Triangle) {
    /* ... */
}                                         From here on, myTriangle.value is of type
                                          Triangle | Square; the compiler no longer
let myTriangle: Either<Triangle,Square>   knows that we placed a Triangle there.
    = Either.makeLeft(new Triangle());
```

```
if (myTriangle.isLeft())
    slot(myTriangle.getLeft());
```

getLeft() casts the value
back to a Triangle.

Internally, our `getLeft()` implementation performs whatever checks it needs (in this case by checking that `this.isLeft()` is true) and handles an invalid call however we want (in this case by throwing `Error`). When all that is out of the way, it casts the value to the type. The type checker forgot which type the value was when we assigned it, so now we remind it, as shown in the following code, as we were keeping track of the type in `left`.

Listing 4.12 `isLeft()` and `getLeft()`

```
class Either<TLeft, TRight> {
    private readonly value: TLeft | TRight;
    private readonly left: boolean;

    /* ... */
    isLeft(): boolean {
        return this.left;
    }

    getLeft(): TLeft {
        if (!this.isLeft()) throw new Error();

        return <TLeft>this.value;
    }

    /* ... */
}
```

Clients can check whether
the value stored is of type
TLeft by calling isLeft().

In case the value is of the wrong type,
we can handle the error. In this case,
we throw an Error. An alternative
would be to return undefined.

The value is cast
to the type TLeft.

In this case, we don't need the `<unknown>` cast: a value of the type `TLeft | TRight` could be a valid value of type `TLeft`, so the compiler won't complain and will trust us with the cast.

When used correctly, casting is powerful because it allows us to refine the type of a value. If we have a `Triangle | Square`, and we know that it is a `Triangle`, we can cast it to a `Triangle`, which the compiler will allow us to fit through a triangular slot.

In fact, most type checkers do several such casts automatically without requiring us to write any code.

> **IMPLICIT AND EXPLICIT TYPE CASTS** An *implicit type cast*, also known as *coercion*, is a type cast that is performed automatically by the compiler. It doesn't require any code to be written. Such casts are usually safe. By contrast, an explicit type cast is a type cast that we need to specify with code. This type cast effectively bypasses the rules of the type system, and we should use it with care.

4.3.3 *Common type casts*

Let's look at a few common types of casts, both implicit and explicit, and see how they can be useful.

UPCASTS AND DOWNCASTS

One example of a common type cast is interpreting an object of a type that inherits from another type as its parent type. If our base class is `Shape`, and we have a `Triangle`, we can always use a `Triangle` whenever a `Shape` is required, as shown in the following code.

Listing 4.13 Upcast

```
class Shape {
    /* ... */
}

declare const triangleType: unique symbol;

class Triangle extends Shape {           The Triangle type
    [triangleType]: void;      ⟵        extends Shape.
    /* ... */
}
                                          useShape() expects an
function useShape(shape: Shape) {  ⟵     argument of type Shape.
    /* ... */
}

let myTriangle: Triangle = new Triangle();
                                          We can pass a Triangle to it, and
useShape(myTriangle);       ⟵            it is automatically cast to Shape.
```

Inside the body of `useShape()`, the compiler treats the argument as a `Shape`, even if we passed in a `Triangle`. Interpreting a derived class (`Triangle`) as a base class (`Shape`) is called an *upcast*. If we know for sure that our Shape is actually a Triangle, we can cast it back to `Triangle`, but this cast needs to be explicit. Casting from a parent class to a derived class is called a *downcast*, shown in the next listing, and most strongly typed languages don't do this automatically.

Listing 4.14 Downcast

```
class Shape {
    /* ... */
}

declare const triangleType: unique symbol;

class Triangle extends Shape {
    [triangleType]: void;                   This version of the function has an
    /* ... */                               additional argument that tracks
}                                           whether a triangle was passed in.

function useShape(shape: Shape, isTriangle: boolean) {   ⟵
    if (isTriangle) {      #B
        let triangle: Triangle = <Triangle>shape;   ⟵    If the argument is in fact
        /* ... */                                         a triangle, we can get the
    }                                                     type back with a cast.
```

```
    /* ... */
}
```

```
let myTriangle: Triangle = new Triangle();

useShape(myTriangle, true);
```
⊲――― **The caller needs to set this flag correctly; otherwise, a run-time error occurs.**

Unlike an upcast, a downcast is not safe. Although it's easy to tell from a derived class what its parent is, the compiler can't automatically determine, given a parent class, which of the possible derived classes a value might be.

Some programming languages store additional type information at run time and include an `is` operator, which can be used to query the type of an object. When we are creating a new object, its associated type is stored alongside, so even if we upcast away some of the type information from the compiler, at run time we can check whether we have an instance of a certain type with `if (shape is Triangle)` ....

Languages and run times that implement this kind of run-time type information provide a safer way to store and query for types, as there is no risk that this information will get out of sync with the objects. This comes at the cost of storing additional data in memory for each object instance.

In chapter 7, when we discuss subtyping, we will look at more complex upcasts and talk about variance. For now, we'll move on to talk about widening and narrowing casts.

WIDENING CASTS AND NARROWING CASTS

Another common implicit cast is from an integer type with a fixed number of bits—say, an 8-bit unsigned integer—to another integer type that represents values with more bits—say, a 16-bit unsigned integer. You can do this implicitly because a 16-bit unsigned integer can represent any 8-bit unsigned integer value and more. This type of cast is called a *widening cast*.

On the other hand, casting a signed integer to an unsigned integer is dangerous, as a negative number can't be represented by an unsigned integer. Similarly, casting an integer with more bits to an integer with fewer bits, such as a 16-bit unsigned integer to an 8-bit unsigned integer, would work only for values that the smaller type can represent.

This type of cast is called a *narrowing cast*. Some compilers force you to be explicit when performing a narrowing cast because it's dangerous. Being explicit helps, in that it makes it clear you didn't do it unintentionally. Other compilers allow narrowing casts but issue a warning. Run-time behavior when the value doesn't fit the new type is similar to the integer overflow that we discussed in chapter 2: depending on the language, we get an error or the value gets chopped so that it fits in the new type (figure 4.5).

Casts are not to be used lightly, as they bypass the type checker, effectively eliminating all the goodness that type checking brings us. They are useful tools, though, especially when we have more information than the compiler does and want to push that

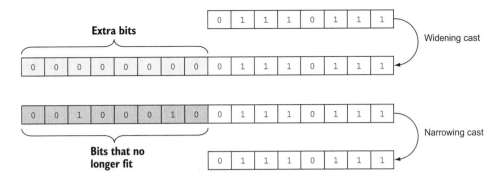

Figure 4.5   Example of widening and narrowing casts. The widening cast is safe: the gray squares represent the extra bits we get, so no information can be lost. On the other hand, the narrowing cast is dangerous: the black squares represent bits that no longer fit in the new type.

information back to the compiler. After we tell the compiler what we know, it can use that information in further analysis. Going back to the `Triangle | Square` example, after we tell the compiler our value is a `Triangle`, there can be no `Square` value farther on. This technique is similar to the one discussed in section 4.2, in which we looked at enforcing constraints, but here, instead of performing a run-time check, we simply tell the compiler to trust us.

In the next section, we'll look at a few other situations in which it's useful to make the compiler "forget" typing information.

4.3.4   *Exercises*

   1   Which of the following casts are considered to be safe?
      a   Upcasts
      b   Downcasts
      c   Upcasts and downcasts
      d   Neither

   2   Which of the following casts are considered to be unsafe?
      a   Widening casts
      b   Narrowing casts
      c   Widening and narrowing casts
      d   Neither

4.4   *Hiding and restoring type information*

One example of hiding type information is wanting to have a collection that can contain a combination of values of different types. If the collection contains values of just one type, such as a bag of cats, it's easy, because we know that whenever we pull some

Homogenous
collection

Heterogeneous
collection

Figure 4.6   If we have a bag that contains only cats, we can bet that whichever item we pull out of it will be a cat. If the bag can also contain groceries, we are no longer able to guarantee what we will pull out.

thing out from the bag, it's going to be a cat. If we want to put groceries in the bag too, when we pull something out, we might end up with either a cat or a grocery item (figure 4.6).

A collection with items of the same type, like our bag of cats, is also called a *homogenous collection*. Because all items have the same type, we don't need to hide their type information. A collection of items of different types is also known as a *heterogenous collection*. In this case, we need to hide some of the typing information to declare such a collection.

4.4.1 *Heterogenous collections*

A document can contain text, pictures, or tables. When we work with the document, we want to keep all its constituent parts together, so we will store them in some collection. But what is the type of the elements of that collection? There are several ways to implement this, all of which involve hiding some type information.

BASE TYPE OR INTERFACE

We can create a class hierarchy and say that all items in the documents must be part of some hierarchy. If everything is a DocumentItem, we can store a collection of DocumentItem values even if, when we add items to the collection, we add types such as Paragraph, Picture, and Table. Similarly, we can declare an IDocumentItem interface and say that the array contains only types that implement this interface, as shown in the following listing.

Listing 4.15   A collection of types implementing IDocumentItem

```
interface IDocumentItem {                          ◁─┐  IDocumentItem is the common
    /* ... */                                           interface for document elements.
}

class Paragraph implements IDocumentItem {         ◁─┐
    /* ... */
}

class Picture implements IDocumentItem {           ◁──  Paragraph, Picture, and
    /* ... */                                           Table all implement
}                                                       IDocumentItem.

class Table implements IDocumentItem {             ◁─┘
    /* ... */
}
```

```
class MyDocument {
    items: IDocumentItem[];                    We store document items as an
                                               array of IDocumentItem objects.
    /* ... */
}
```

We've hidden some of the typing information, so we no longer know whether a particular item in the collection is a `Paragraph`, a `Picture`, or a `Table`, but we know that it implements the `DocumentItem` or `IDocumentItem` contract. If we need only behavior specified by that contract, we can work with the elements of the collection as is. If we need an exact type, such as a picture that we want to pass to an image-enhancing add-on, we have to downcast the `DocumentItem` or `IDocumentItem` back to a `Picture`.

SUM TYPE OR VARIANT

If we know up front all the types we are dealing with, we can use a sum type, as shown in listing 4.16. We can define our document as an array of `Paragraph | Picture | Table` (in which case we must track what each item in the collection is by some other means) or as a type such as `Variant<Paragraph, Picture, Table>` (which keeps track internally of the type it stores).

Listing 4.16　A collection of types as a sum type

```
class Paragraph {
    /* ... */
}
                                    Paragraph, Picture, and
                                    Table no longer
class Picture {                     implement an interface.
    /* ... */
}

class Table {
    /* ... */
}

class MyDocument {
    items: (Paragraph | Picture | Table)[];        The document item collection
                                                   is now an array of objects that
    /* ... */                                      can be either of the types.
}
```

Both `Paragraph | Picture | Table` and `Variant<Paragraph, Picture, Table>` options allow us to store a set of items that don't need to have anything in common (no common base type or implemented interface). The advantage is that we don't impose anything on the types in the collection. The disadvantage is that there is not much we can do with the items in the list without casting them back down to their actual types or, in the `Variant` case, calling `visit()` and having to provide functions for each of the possible types in the collection.

As a reminder, because a type like `Variant` keeps track internally of which type it actually stores, just as `Either` does, it knows which function to pick from a set of functions passed to `visit()`.

UNKNOWN TYPE

At an extreme, we can say we have a collection that can contain anything. As shown in listing 4.17, TypeScript provides the type `unknown` to represent that type of collection. Most object-oriented programming languages have a common base type that is the parent of all other types, usually called `Object`. We'll cover this topic in depth in chapter 7 when we discuss subtyping.

> **Listing 4.17   A collection of unknown type**

```
class MyDocument {
    items: unknown[];           ◁———  The elements of the
    /* ... */                          array can be anything.
}
```

This technique allows us to have a document containing anything. Types don't need to have a shared contract, and we don't even need to know beforehand what the types do. On the other hand, there's even less we can do with the elements of this collection. We'll almost always have to cast them to other types, so we have to keep track of their original types in another way.

Table 4.1 summarizes the different approaches and trade-offs.

Table 4.1   Pros and cons of heterogenous list implementations

	Pros	Cons
Hierarchy	Can easily use any property or method of the base type without casting	Types in the collection must be related by base type or implemented interface
Sum type	No requirement that types be related	Need to cast back to actual type to use items if we don't have `Variant`'s `visit()`
Unknown type	Can store anything	Need to keep track of actual types and cast back to them to use items

All these examples have pros and cons, depending on how flexible we want our collection to be in terms of what can be stored there and how often we expect to have to restore the items to their original types. That being said, all the examples hide some amount of type information when we put items in the collection. Another example of hiding and restoring type information is serialization.

4.4.2   *Serialization*

When we write information to a file and want to load it back and use it in our program, or when we connect to an internet service and send and retrieve some data, that data travels as a sequence of bits. *Serialization* is the process of taking a value of a

Figure 4.7 A compact car with two doors and front-wheel drive serialized as JSON and then deserialized back into a car

certain type and encoding it as a sequence of bits. The opposite operation, *deserialization*, involves taking a sequence of bits and decoding it into a data structure we can work with (figure 4.7).

The exact encoding depends on the protocol we use. It can be JSON, XML, or any other of the multitude of available protocols. From a type perspective, the important part is that after serialization, we end up with a value that should be equivalent to the typed value we started with, but all typing information becomes unavailable to the type system. Effectively, we end up with a string or an array of bytes. The JSON.stringify() method takes an object and returns a JSON representation of that object as a string. If we stringify a Cat, as the next listing shows, we can write the result to disk, to the network, or even to the screen, but we cannot get it to meow().

Listing 4.18 Serializing a cat

```
class Cat {
    meow() {                  ◁——  A Cat type that has
        /* ... */                   a meow() method.
    }
}

let serializedCat: string = JSON.stringify(new Cat());

// serializeCat.meow();      ◁——  Obviously, we can't use a
                                    method like meow() because
                                    serializedCat is a string.
```

> We serialize a Cat object as a JSON string by using JSON.stringify().

We still know what the value is, but the type checker no longer does. The opposite operation involves taking a serialized object and turning it back into a typed value. In this case, we can use the JSON.parse() method, which takes a string and returns a JavaScript object. Because this technique works for any string, the result of calling it is of type any.

THE ANY TYPE   TypeScript provides an any type. This type is used for interoperability with JavaScript when typing information is unavailable. any is a dangerous type because the compiler does no type checking on instances of this type, which can be freely converted to and from any other type. It's up to the developer to ensure that no misinterpretations happen.

If we know that we have a serialized Cat, we can assign it to a new Cat object by using Object.assign() as shown in the following listing, and then cast it back to its type, as Object.assign() returns a value of type any.

Listing 4.19   Deserializing a Cat

```
class Cat {
    meow() {
        /* ... */
    }
}

let serializedCat: string = JSON.stringify(new Cat());

let deserializedCat: Cat =
    <Cat>Object.assign(new Cat(), JSON.parse(serializedCat));

deserializedCat.meow();
```

> We deserialize the object by using JSON.parse(), assign it to a new Cat instance, and cast it to the Cat type.

> We can call meow() on the object, as it is of type Cat and has a meow() method.

In some cases, we can get and deserialize any number of possible types, in which case it might be a good idea to encode some of the typing information in the serialized object too. We can define a protocol in which each object is prefixed with a character that represents its type. Then we can encode a Cat and prefix the resulting string with "c" for Cat. If we get a serialized object, we check the first character. If it's "c", we can safely restore our Cat. If it's "d", for Dog, we know not to deserialize a Cat, as shown in the following listing.

Listing 4.20   Serializing and tracking type

```
class Cat {
    meow() { /* ... */ }
}

class Dog {
    bark() { /* ... */ }
}

function serializeCat(cat: Cat): string {
    return "c" + JSON.stringify(cat);
}

function serializeDog(dog: Dog): string {
    return "d" + JSON.stringify(dog);
}
```

> We serialize a Cat object by prefixing a "c" to the JSON representation.

> We serialize a Dog object by prefixing a "d" to the JSON representation.

Given a serialized Cat or Dog, we
can attempt to deserialize a Cat.

```
function tryDeserializeCat(from: string): Cat | undefined {
    if (from[0] != "c") return undefined;

    return <Cat>Object.assign(new Cat(), JSON.parse(from.substr(1)));
}
```

**Otherwise, JSON.parse()
the rest of the string and
assign it to a Cat object.**

**If the first character is not "c", return
undefined because we can't deserialize a Cat.**

If we serialize a `Cat` object and call `tryDeserializeCat()` on its serialized representation, we get back a `Cat` object. If, on the other hand, we serialize a `Dog` object and call `tryDeserializeCat()`, we get back undefined. Then we can check to see whether we got an `undefined` and see whether we have a `Cat`, as shown in the next listing.

Listing 4.21 Deserializing with tracked type

```
let catString: string = serializeCat(new Cat());
let dogString: string = serializeDog(new Dog());

let maybeCat: Cat | undefined = tryDeserializeCat(catString);

if (maybeCat != undefined) {
    let cat: Cat = <Cat>maybeCat;
    cat.meow();
}

maybeCat = tryDeserializeCat(dogString);
```

**We serialize a Cat
and a Dog to strings.**

**Calling tryDeserializeCat gives
us either a Cat or undefined.**

**If we did, we can cast to Cat and get
an object we can call meow() on.**

**We can check
whether we got a Cat.**

**Attempting to deserialize a Cat
object from a serialized Dog
object will give us undefined.**

The reason why we can compare `maybeCat` with `undefined`, even though we couldn't compare `Triangle` with `TLeft` previously, is that `undefined` is a special unit type in TypeScript. The `undefined` type has a single possible value, which is undefined. In the absence of this type, we can always use a type like `Optional<Cat>`. We described `Optional<T>` in chapter 3 as a type that contains a value of type `T` or nothing.

As we've seen throughout this chapter, types enable whole new levels of safety for our code. We can capture what would've been implicit assumptions in type declaration and make them explicit by avoiding primitive obsession and letting the type checker make sure that we don't misinterpret values. We can further restrict the allowed values of a certain type and ensure that constraints are met during instance creation, so that we have a guarantee that when we have an instance of a given type, it will always be valid.

On the other hand, we want to be more flexible in some situations and handle multiple types in the same way. In such situations, we can hide some of the type information and expand the possible values that a variable can take. In most cases, we would still like to keep track of the original type of the value so we can restore it later.

We do that outside the type system by storing the type somewhere else, such as in another variable. As soon as we no longer need the extra flexibility and want to rely on the type checker again, we can restore the type by using a type cast.

4.4.3   Exercises

1   Which type should we use if we want to assign any possible value to it?

 a   `any`

 b   `unknown`

 c   `any | unknown`

 d   Either `any` or `unknown`

2   What is the best way to represent an array of numbers and strings?

 a   `(number | string)[]`

 b   `number[] | string[]`

 c   `unknown[]`

 d   `any[]`

Summary

- The primitive obsession antipattern shows up when we declare values as basic types and make implicit assumptions about their meaning.
- The alternative to using primitive obsession is defining types that explicitly capture the meaning of the values and prevent misinterpretations.
- If we have additional constraints that we want to impose but can't at compile time, we can enforce them in constructors or factories, so that when we have an object of the type, we are guaranteed that it is valid.
- Sometimes, we know more than the type checker does, as we can store typing information outside the type system itself as data.
- We can use this information to perform safe type casts, adding more information for the type checker.
- We may want to treat different types the same way, perhaps to store values of different types in a single collection or serialize them.
- We can hide type information by casting to a type that includes our type, a type our type inherits from, a sum type, or a type that can store values of any other type.

So far we've looked at basic types, ways to compose them, and other ways in which we can leverage the type systems to increase the safety of our code. In chapter 5, we'll look at something radically different: What new possibilities will be open to us when we can assign types to functions and treat functions like any other values in our code?

Answers to exercises

AVOIDING PRIMITIVE OBSESSION TO PREVENT MISINTERPRETATION

1   c—Specifying the measurement unit is a safer approach.

ENFORCING CONSTRAINTS

1 Here is a possible solution:

```
declare const percentageType: unique symbol;

class Percentage {
    readonly value: number;
    [percentageType]: void;

    private constructor(value: number) {
        this.value = value;
    }

    static makePercentage(value: number): Percentage {
        if (value < 0) value = 0;
        if (value > 100) value = 100;

        return new Percentage(value);
    }
}
```

ADDING TYPE INFORMATION

1 a—Upcasts are safe (casting child to parent type).

2 b—Narrowing casts are unsafe (might lose information).

HIDING AND RESTORING TYPE INFORMATION

1 b—unknown is a safer option than any.

2 a—unknown and any remove too much type information.

Function types 5

This chapter covers

- Simplifying the strategy pattern with function types
- Implementing a state machine without `switch` statements
- Implementing lazy values as lambdas
- Using the fundamental data processing algorithms `map`, `filter`, and `reduce` to reduce code duplication

We covered basic types and types built up from them. We also looked at how we can declare new types to increase the safety of our programs and enforce various constraints on their values. This is about as far as we can get with algebraic data types or the ability to combine types as sum types and product types.

The next feature of type systems we are going to cover, which unlocks a whole new world of expressiveness, is the ability to type functions. If we can name function types and use functions in the same places we use values of other types—as variables, arguments, and function returns—we can simplify the implementation of several common constructs and abstract common algorithms to library functions.

In this chapter, we'll look at how we can simplify the implementation of the strategy design pattern. (We'll also have a quick refresher on the pattern, in case you forgot it.) Then we'll talk about state machines and how they can be implemented more succinctly with function properties. We'll cover lazy values, or how we can defer expensive computation in the hope that we won't need it. Finally, we'll deep dive into the fundamental map(), reduce(), and filter() algorithms.

All these applications are enabled by function types, the next step in the evolution of type systems after basic types and their combinations. Because most programming languages nowadays support these types, we'll get a fresh look at some old, tried, and tested concepts.

5.1 A simple strategy pattern

One of the most commonly used design patterns is the strategy pattern. The strategy design pattern is a behavioral software design pattern that enables selecting an algorithm at run time from a family of algorithms. It decouples the algorithms from the components using them, which improves the flexibility of the overall system. The pattern is usually presented as in figure 5.1.

Let's look at a concrete example. Suppose that we have a car wash with two types of services: a Standard wash and a Premium wash (which, for an extra $3, provides additional polish).

We can implement this example as a strategy, in which our IWashingStrategy interface provides a wash() method. Then we provide two implementations of this

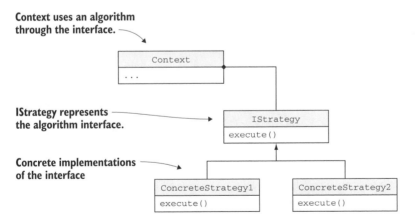

Figure 5.1 Strategy pattern made up of an IStrategy interface, ConcreteStrategy1 and ConcreteStrategy2 implementations, and a Context that uses the algorithms through the IStrategy interface.

interface: a `StandardWash` and a `PremiumWash`. Our `CarWash` is the context that
applies an `IWashingStrategy.wash()` to a car depending on which service the cus-
tomer paid for.

Listing 5.1   Car-wash strategy

```
class Car {
    /* Represents a car */                ◄——┐  The Car class represents
}                                              a car to be washed.

interface IWashingStrategy {           ◄——┐  IWashingStrategy is the
    wash(car: Car): void;                     interface of our strategy pattern
}                                             declaring a wash() method.

class StandardWash implements IWashingStrategy {   ◄——┐
    wash(car: Car): void {
        /* Perform standard wash */                    StandardWash and
    }                                                  PremiumWash are
}                                                      concrete implementations
                                                       of the strategy.
class PremiumWash implements IWashingStrategy {    ◄——┘
    wash(car: Car): void {
        /* Perform premium wash */
    }
}

class CarWash {
    service(car: Car, premium: boolean) {
        let washingStrategy: IWashingStrategy;

        if (premium) {                              ◄——┐
            washingStrategy = new PremiumWash();
        } else {                                       Depending on a flag, we
            washingStrategy = new StandardWash();      select the algorithm to
        }                                              use and then wash() the
                                                       car instance with it.
        washingStrategy.wash(car);                  ◄——┘
    }
}
```

This code works, but it is needlessly verbose. We've introduced an interface and two
implementing types, each providing a single `wash()` method. These types are not
really important; the valuable part of our code is the washing logic. This code is just a
function, so we can simplify our code a lot if we move from interfaces and classes to a
function type and the two concrete implementations.

5.1.1   A functional strategy

We can define `WashingStrategy` to be a type representing a function that receives a
`Car` as an argument and returns `void`. Then we can implement the two types of

washes as two functions—standardWash() and premimumWash()—both taking a Car and returning void. The CarWash can select one of them to apply to a given car.

Listing 5.2 Car-wash strategy revisited

```
class Car {
    /* Represents a car */
}

type WashingStrategy = (car: Car) => void;

function standardWash(car: Car): void {
    /* Perform standard wash */
}

function premiumWash(car: Car): void {
    /* Perform premium wash */
}

class CarWash {
    service(car: Car, premium: boolean) {
        let washingStrategy: WashingStrategy;

        if (premium) {
            washingStrategy = premiumWash;
        } else {
            washingStrategy = standardWash;
        }

        washingStrategy(car);
    }
}
```

> **WashingStrategy is a function that takes a Car and returns void.**

> **standardWash() and premiumWash() implement our car-washing logic.**

> **Now we can assign a function directly to washingStrategy when we select the algorithm.**

> **Because the washingStrategy variable is a function, we can simply call it.**

This implementation has fewer parts than the preceding one, as we can see in figure 5.2.

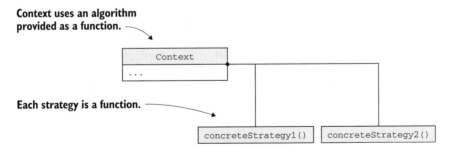

Context uses an algorithm provided as a function.

Each strategy is a function.

Figure 5.2 Strategy pattern made up of a Context that uses a function: either concreteStrategy1() or concreteStrategy2()

Let's zoom in on the function type declaration, because we're using one for the first time.

5.1.2 *Typing functions*

The function `standardWash()` takes an argument of type `Car` and returns `void`, so its type is *function from Car to void* or, in TypeScript syntax, `(car: Car) => void`. The function `premiumWash()`, even though it has a different implementation, has exactly the same argument type and return type, so it has the same type.

> **FUNCTION TYPE OR SIGNATURE**   The type of a function is given by the type of its arguments and its return type. If two functions take the same arguments and return the same type, they have the same type. The set of arguments plus return type is also known as the *signature* of a function.

We want to refer to this type, so we give it a name by declaring `type WashingStrategy = (car: Car) => void`. Whenever we use `WashingStrategy` as a type, we mean the function type `(car: Car) => void`. We refer to it in the `CarWash.service()` method.

   Because we can type functions, we can have variables that represent functions. In our example, the `washingStrategy` variable represents a function with the signature we just named. We can assign any function that takes a `Car` and returns `void` to this variable. We can also call it as we would a function. In the first example that used an `IWashingStrategy` interface, we ran our car-washing logic by calling `washing-Strategy.wash(car)`. In our second example, in which `washingStrategy` is a function, we simply called `washingStrategy(car)`.

> **FIRST-CLASS FUNCTIONS**   The ability to assign functions to variables and treat them like any other values in the type system results in what are called *first-class functions*. That means the language treats functions like first-class citizens, granting them the same rights as other values: they have types; and they can be assigned to variables and passed around as arguments, checked for validity, and converted (if compatible) to other types.

5.1.3 *Strategy implementations*

Earlier, we saw two ways to implement a strategy pattern. Contrasting the two implementations, the by-the-book strategy implementation in the first example requires a lot of extra machinery: we need to declare an interface, and we need to have multiple classes implementing that interface to provide the concrete logic of the strategy. The second implementation is boiled down to the essence of what we are trying to achieve: we have two functions implementing the logic, and we refer to them directly.

   Both implementations achieve the same goals. The reason why the first one, which relies on interfaces, is more widespread is that when design patterns became all the rage in the 1990s, not all mainstream programming languages supported first-order functions. In fact, few of them did. This is no longer the case. Most languages can type functions now, and we can leverage that capability to provide more-succinct implementations of some design patterns.

   It's important to keep in mind that the *pattern* is the same: we are still encapsulating a family of algorithms and selecting at run time the one to use. The difference is in the implementation, which modern capabilities allow us to express more easily. We're replacing an interface and two classes (each class implementing a method) with a type declaration and two functions.

In most cases, the more-succinct implementation is enough. We might need to reconsider the interface and classes implementation when the algorithms are not representable as simple functions. Sometimes, we need multiple functions or need to track some state, in which case the first implementation would be better suited, as it groups the related pieces of a strategy under a common type.

5.1.4 First-class functions

Before we move on, let's quickly review some of the terms introduced in this section:

- The set of arguments plus the return value of a function is called the *signature* of a function. The following two functions have the same signature:

```
function add(x: number, y: number): number {
    return x + y;
}

function subtract(x: number, y: number): number {
    return x - y;
}
```

- The signature of a function is equivalent to its *type* in languages that can type functions. The preceding two functions have the type *function from (number, number) to number*, or (x: number, y: number) => number. Note that the actual name of the arguments doesn't matter; (a: number, b: number) => number has the same type as (x: number, y: number) => number.
- When languages treat functions as they do any other values, we say that they support *first-class functions*. Functions can be assigned to variables, passed as arguments, and used like other values, which makes code more expressive.

5.1.5 Exercises

1 What is the type of a function isEven() that takes a number as an argument and returns true if the number is even and false otherwise?

  a [number, boolean]

  b (x: number) => boolean

  c (x: number, isEven: boolean)

  d {x: number, isEven: boolean}

2 What is the type of a function check() that takes a number and a function of the same type as isEven() as arguments and returns the result of applying the given function to the given value?

  a (x: number, func: number) => boolean

  b (x: number) => (x: number) => boolean

  c (x: number, func: (x: number) => boolean) => boolean

  d (x: number, func: (x: number) => boolean) => void

5.2 *A state machine without switch statements*

One very useful application of first-class functions enables us to define a property of a class as having a function type. Then we can assign different functions to it, changing the behavior at run time. This acts as a plug-in method on the class, and we can swap it as needed.

We can implement a pluggable `Greeter`, for example. Instead of implementing a `greet()` method, we implement a `greet` property with a function type. Then we can assign multiple greeting functions to it, such as `sayGoodMorning()` and `sayGood-Night()`.

Listing 5.3 Pluggable `Greeter`

```
function sayGoodMorning(): void {
    console.log("Good morning!");
}

function sayGoodNight(): void {
    console.log("Good night!");
}

class Greeter {
    greet: () => void = sayGoodMorning;
}

let greeter: Greeter = new Greeter();

greeter.greet();

greeter.greet = sayGoodNight;

greeter.greet();
```

Two greeting functions that output their respective greetings to the console

greet is a function with no arguments that returns void and defaults to sayGoodMorning().

Because greet is a function property, we can call it as a method of the class.

We can assign another function to it.

The second call will invoke sayGoodNight().

This follows from the strategy pattern implementation discussed in the previous section, but it's worth noting that this approach enables us to easily add pluggable behavior to a class. If we want to add a new greeting, we simply need to add another function with the same signature and assign it to the `greet` property.

5.2.1 *Early Programming with Types*

While working on an early draft of this book, I wrote a small script to help me keep the source code in sync with the text. The draft was written in the popular Markdown format. I kept the source code in separate TypeScript files so I could compile them and ensure that even if I update the code samples, they'll still work.

I needed a way to ensure that the Markdown text always contains the latest code samples. The code samples always appear between a line containing ```ts and a line containing ```. When HTML is generated from the Markdown source, ```ts is interpreted as the beginning of a TypeScript code block, which gets rendered with

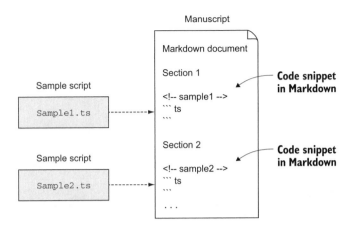

Figure 5.3   Two TypeScript (.ts) files containing code samples that should be inlined in the Markdown document between ```ts and ``` markers. The `<!-- ... -->` comments annotate the code samples for my script.

TypeScript syntax highlighting, whereas ``` marks the end of that code block. The contents of these code blocks had to be inlined from actual TypeScript source files that I could compile and validate outside the text (figure 5.3).

To determine which code sample went where, I relied on a small trick. Markdown allows raw HTML in the document text, so I annotated each code sample with an HTML comment, such as `<!-- sample1 -->`. HTML comments do not get rendered, so when Markdown is converted to HTML, they became invisible. On the other hand, my script could use these comments to determine which code sample to inline where.

When all code samples were loaded from disk, I had to process each Markdown document of the draft and produce an updated version as follows:

- In text processing mode, simply copy each line of the input text to the output document as is. When a marker is encountered (`<!-- sample -->`), grab the corresponding code sample, and switch to marker processing mode.
- In marker processing mode, again copy each line of the input text to the output document until we encounter a code block marker (```ts). When the code marker is encountered, output the latest version of the code sample as loaded from the TypeScript file, and switch to code processing mode.
- In code processing mode, we already ensured that the latest version of the code is in the output document, so we can skip the potentially outdated version in the code block. We skip each line until we encounter the end of code block marker (```). Then we switch back to text processing mode.

With each run, the existing code samples in the document preceded by a `<!-- ... -->` marker get updated to the latest version of the TypeScript files on disk. Other code blocks that aren't preceded by `<!-- ... -->` don't get updated, as they are processed in text processing mode.

As an example, here is a helloWorld.ts code sample.

Listing 5.4 helloWorld.ts

```
console.log("Hello world!");
```

We want to embed this code in Chapter1.md and make sure that it's kept up to date, as shown in the next listing.

Listing 5.5 Chapter1.md

```
# Chapter 1

Printing "Hello world!".
<!-- helloWorld -->
```ts
console.log("Hello");
```
```

> This is not quite up to date. The string here is "Hello", which does not match helloWorld.ts.

This document gets processed line by line as follows:

1. In text processing mode, "`# Chapter 1`" is copied to the output as is.
2. "" (blank line) is copied to the output as is.
3. "`Printing "Hello world!".`" is copied to the output as is.
4. "`<!-- helloWorld -->`" is copied to the output as is. This is a marker, though, so we keep track of the code sample to be inlined (helloWorld.ts) and switch to marker processing mode.
5. "` ```ts `" is copied to the output as is. This marker is a code block marker, so immediately after copying it to the output, we also output the contents of helloWorld.ts. We also switch to code processing mode.
6. "`console.log("Hello");`" is skipped. We don't copy lines in code processing mode, as we are replacing them with the latest in the code sample file.
7. "` ``` `" is an end-of-code-block marker. We insert it and then switch back to text processing mode.

5.2.2 *State machines*

The behavior of our text processing script is best modeled as a state machine. A state machine has a set of states and a set of transitions between pairs of states. The machine starts in a given state, also known as the *start state*; if certain conditions are met, it can transition to another state.

This is exactly what our text processor does with its three processing modes. Input lines are processed in a certain way in *text processing mode*. When some condition is met (a `<!-- sample -->` marker is encountered), our processor transitions to *marker processing mode*. Again, when some other condition is met (a ` ```ts ` code-block marker is encountered), it transitions to *code pro-cessing mode*. When the end of the code-block marker is encountered (```), it transitions back to *text processing mode* (figure 5.4).

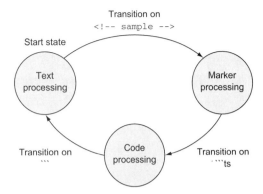

Now that we've modeled the solution, let's look at how we would implement it. One way to implement a state machine is to define the set of states as an enumeration, keeping track of the current state, and get the desired behavior with a `switch` statement that covers all possible states. In our case, we can define a `TextProcessingMode` enum.

Figure 5.4 Text processing state machine with the three states (text processing, marker processing, code processing) and transitions between the states based on input. Text processing is the initial state or start state.

Our `TextProcessor` class will keep track of the current state in a mode property and implement the `switch` statement in a `processLine()` method. Depending on the state, this method will in turn invoke one of the three processing methods: `processTextLine()`, `processMarkerLine()`, or `processCodeLine()`. These functions will implement the text processing and then, when appropriate, transition to another state by updating the current state.

Processing a Markdown document consisting of multiple lines of text means processing each line in turn, using our state machine, and then returning the final result to the caller, as shown in the next listing.

Listing 5.6 State machine implementation

```
enum TextProcessingMode {          ◁─┐  States are represented
    Text,                            │  as an enum.
    Marker,
    Code,
}

class TextProcessor {
    private mode: TextProcessingMode = TextProcessingMode.Text;
    private result: string[] = [];
    private codeSample: string[] = [];

    processText(lines: string[]): string[] {
        this.result = [];
        this.mode = TextProcessingMode.Text;

        for (let line of lines) {          ◁─┐  Processing a text document means
            this.processLine(line);          │  processing each line and returning
        }                                    │  the resulting string array.

        return this.result;
    }
```

```
    private processLine(line: string): void {
        switch (this.mode) {
            case TextProcessingMode.Text:
                this.processTextLine(line);
                break;
            case TextProcessingMode.Marker:
                this.processMarkerLine(line);
                break;
            case TextProcessingMode.Code:
                this.processCodeLine(line);
                break;
        }
    }
```

> The state machine switch statement calls the appropriate processor based on the current state.

```
    private processTextLine(line: string): void {
        this.result.push(line);

        if (line.startsWith("<!--")) {
            this.loadCodeSample(line);

            this.mode = TextProcessingMode.Marker;
        }
    }
```

> Processes a line of text. If the line starts with "<!--", load code sample and transition to next state.

```
    private processMarkerLine(line: string): void {
        this.result.push(line);

        if (line.startsWith("```ts")) {
            this.result = this.result.concat(this.codeSample);

            this.mode = TextProcessingMode.Code;
        }
    }
```

> Processes marker. If the line starts with "```ts", inline code sample and transition to next state.

```
    private processCodeLine(line: string): void {
        if (line.startsWith("```")) {
            this.result.push(line);

            this.mode = TextProcessingMode.Text;
        }
    }
```

> Process code by skipping lines. If the line starts with "```", transition to text processing state.

```
    private loadCodeSample(line: string) {
        /* Load sample based on marker, store in this.codeSample */
    }
}
```

> The body of this function is omitted, as it's not important for this example.

We omitted the code to load a sample from an external file, as it isn't particularly relevant to our state machine discussion. This implementation works but can be simplified if we use a pluggable function.

Note that all our text processing functions have the same signature: they take a line of text as a `string` argument and return `void`. What if, instead of having `processLine()` implement a big switch statement and forward to the appropriate function, we make `processLine()` one of those functions?

Instead of implementing `processLine()` as a method, we can define it as a property of the class with type `(line: string) => void` and initialize it with `processTextLine()`, as shown in the following code. Then, in each of the three text processing methods, instead of setting `mode` to a different enum value, we set `processLine` to a different method. In fact, we no longer need to keep track of our state externally. We don't even need an enum!

Listing 5.7   Alternative state machine implementation

```
class TextProcessor {
    private result: string[] = [];
    private processLine: (line: string) => void = this.processTextLine;
    private codeSample: string[] = [];

    processText(lines: string[]): string[] {
        this.result = [];
        this.processLine = this.processTextLine;

        for (let line of lines) {
            this.processLine(line);
        }

        return this.result;
    }

    private processTextLine(line: string): void {
        this.result.push(line);

        if (line.startsWith("<!--")) {
            this.loadCodeSample(line);

            this.processLine = this.processMarkerLine;
        }
    }

    private processMarkerLine(line: string): void {
        this.result.push(line);

        if (line.startsWith("```ts")) {
            this.result = this.result.concat(this.codeSample);

            this.processLine = this.processCodeLine;
        }
    }

    private processCodeLine(line: string): void {
        if (line.startsWith("```")) {
            this.result.push(line);

            this.processLine = this.processTextLine;
        }
    }

    private loadCodeSample(line: string) {
```

State transitions are now done by updating this.processLine to the appropriate method.

```
    /* Load sample based on marker, store in this.codeSample  */
  }
}
```

The second implementation gets rid of the `TextProcessingMode` enum, the `mode` property, and the `switch` statement that forwarded processing to the appropriate method. Instead of handling forwarding, `processLine` now *is* the appropriate processing method.

This implementation removes the need to keep track of states separately and keep that in sync with the processing logic. If we ever wanted to introduce a new state, the old implementation would've forced us to update the code in several places. Besides implementing the new processing logic and state transitions, we would've had to update the enum and add another case to the `switch` statement. Our alternative implementation removes the need for that task: a state is represented purely by a function.

State machines with sum types

One caveat is that for state machines with many states, capturing states and even transitions explicitly might make the code easier to understand. Even so, instead of using enums and `switch` statements, another possible implementation represents each state as a separate type and the whole state machine as a sum type of the possible states, allowing us to break it apart into type-safe components. Following is an example of how we would implement the state machine by using a sum type. The code is a bit more verbose, so if possible, we should try the implementation we've discussed so far, which is another alternative to a `switch`-based state machine.

When a sum type is used, each state is represented by a different type, so we have a `TextLineProcessor`, a `MarkerLineProcessor`, and a `CodeLine-Processor`. Each keeps track of the processed lines so far in a `result` member and provides a `process()` method to handle a line of text.

State machine with sum type

```
class TextLineProcessor {
    result: string[];

    constructor(result: string[]) {            TextLineProcessor returns
        this.result = result;                  either a TextLineProcessor
    }                                           or a MarkerLineProcessor
                                                to process the next line.
    process(line: string): TextLineProcessor | MarkerLineProcessor {  ◁─
        this.result.push(line);

        if (line.startsWith("<!--")) {                 ◁─┐ If the line starts with
            return new MarkerLineProcessor(              │ "<!--", return a new
                this.result, this.loadCodeSample(line)); │ MarkerLineProcessor;
        } else {                                         │ otherwise, return
            return this;                                 │ this processor.
        }
    }
}
```

```
        private loadCodeSample(line: string): string[] {
            /* Load sample based on marker, store in this.codeSample */
        }
    }

class MarkerLineProcessor {
    result: string[];
    codeSample: string[]

    constructor(result: string[], codeSample: string[]) {
        this.result = result;
        this.codeSample = codeSample;
    }

    process(line: string): MarkerLineProcessor | CodeLineProcessor {
        this.result.push(line);

        if (line.startsWith("```ts")) {
            this.result = this.result.concat(this.codeSample);

            return new CodeLineProcessor(this.result);
        } else {
            return this;
        }
    }
}

class CodeLineProcessor {
    result: string[];

    constructor(result: string[]) {
        this.result = result;
    }

    process(line: string): CodeLineProcessor | TextLineProcessor {
        if (line.startsWith("```")) {
            this.result.push(line);

            return new TextLineProcessor(this.result);
        } else {
            return this;
        }
    }
}

function processText(lines: string): string[] {
    let processor: TextLineProcessor | MarkerLineProcessor
        | CodeLineProcessor = new TextLineProcessor([]);

    for (let line of lines) {
        processor = processor.process(line);
    }

    return processor.result;
}
```

MarkerLineProcessor returns either a MarkerLineProcessor or a CodeLineProcessor.

If we encounter "```ts", load the code sample and return a new CodeLineProcessor; otherwise, return this processor.

CodeLineProcessor returns a CodeLineProcessor or a TextLineProcessor.

If the line starts with "```", append it to the result and return a new TextLineProcessor; otherwise, return this processor.

The states are represented by the processor, which is a sum type of TextLineProcessor, MarkerLineProcessor, and CodeLineProcessor.

processor gets updated after each line processed, in case there is a state change.

(continued)

All our processors return a processor instance: `this`, if there is no state change, or a new processor as state changes. The `processText()` runs the state machine by calling `process()` on each line of text and updating `processor` as state changes by reassigning it to the result of the method call.

Now the set of states is spelled out explicitly in the signature of the `processor` variable, which can be a `TextLineProcessor`, a `MarkerLineProcessor`, or a `CodeLineProcessor`.

The possible transitions are captured in the signatures of the `process()` methods. `TextLineProcessor.process` returns `TextLineProcessor | MarkerLine-Processor`, for example, so it can stay in the same state (`TextLineProcessor`) or transition to the `MarkerLineProcessor` state. These state classes can have more properties and members if needed. This implementation is slightly longer than the one that relies on functions, so if we don't need the extra features, we are better off using the simpler solution.

5.2.3 *State machine implementation recap*

Let's quickly review the alternative implementations discussed in this section and then look at other applications of function types:

- The "classical" implementation of a state machine uses an enum to define all the possible states, a variable of that enum type to keep track of the current state, and a big `switch` statement to determine which processing should be performed based on the current state. State transitions are implemented by updating the current state variable. The drawback of this implementation is that states are removed from the processing that we want to run during each state, so the compiler can't prevent mistakes when we run the wrong processing while in a given state. Nothing stops us, for example, from calling `process-CodeLine()` even when we're in `TextProcessingMode.Text`. We also have to maintain state and transitions as a separate enum, with the risk of running out of sync. (We might add a new value to the enum but forget to add a case for it in the `switch` statement, for example.)
- The functional implementation represents each processing state as a function and relies on a function property to track the current state. State transitions are implemented by assigning the function property to another state. This implementation is lightweight and should work for many cases. There are two drawbacks: sometimes, we need to associate more information with each state; and we might want to be explicit when declaring the possible states and transitions.
- The sum type implementation represents each processing state as a class and relies on a variable representing the sum type of all the possible states to keep track of the current state. State transitions are implemented by reassigning the variable to another state, which allows us to add properties and members to

each state and keep them grouped together. The drawback is that the code is more verbose than the functional alternative.

This concludes our discussion of state machines. In the next section, we look at another use of function types: implementing lazy evaluation.

5.2.4 Exercises

1 Model a simple connection that can be `open` or `closed` as a state machine. A connection is opened with `connect` and closed with `disconnect`.

2 Implement the preceding connection as a functional state machine with a `process()` function. In a closed connection, `process()` opens a connection. In an open connection, `process()` calls a `read()` function that returns a string. If the string is empty, the connection is closed; otherwise, the read string is logged to the console. `read()` is given as `declare function read(): string;`.

5.3 Avoiding expensive computation with lazy values

Another advantage of being able to use functions as any other value is that we can store them and invoke them only when needed. Sometimes, a value we may want is expensive to compute. Let's say that my program can build a `Bike` and a `Car`. I may want a `Car`. But a `Car` is expensive to build, so I might decide to ride my bike instead. A `Bike` is extremely cheap to build, so I'm not worried about the cost. Instead of always building a `Car` with each run of the program, just so I can use it if I want it, wouldn't it be better to give me the ability to ask for a `Car`? In that case, I would ask for it when I really needed it and execute the expensive building logic then. If I never asked for it, no resources would be wasted.

The idea is to postpone expensive computation as much as possible, in the hope that it may not be needed at all. Because computation is expressed as functions, we can pass around functions instead of actual values and call them when and whether we need the values. This process is called *lazy evaluation*. The opposite is *eager evaluation*, in which we produce the values immediately and pass them around even if we decide later to discard them.

Listing 5.8 Eager `Car` production

```
class Bike { }          Car and Bike. Let's assume
class Car { }           that Car is expensive to create.

function chooseMyRide(bike: Bike, car: Car): Bike | Car {
    if (isItRaining()) {                    The chooseMyRide() function
        return car;                         will pick Bike or Car,
    } else {                                depending on some condition.
        return bike;
    }
}
                                            To call chooseMyRide(),
chooseMyRide(new Bike(), new Car());        we need to create a Car.
```

In our eager `Car` production example, to call `chooseMyRide()`, we need to supply a `Car` object, so we're already paying the cost of building a `Car`. If the weather is nice and I decide to ride my bike, the `Car` instance was created for nothing.

Let's switch to a lazy approach. Instead of providing a `Car`, let's provide a function that returns a `Car` when called.

Listing 5.9   Lazy `Car` production

```
class Bike { }                                      Instead of a Car argument,
class Car { }                                       chooseMyRide() now takes a
                                                    function that returns a Car.
function chooseMyRide(bike: Bike, car: () => Car): Bike | Car {
    if (isItRaining()) {
        return car();            We call this function only
    } else {                     when we know for sure
        return bike;             that we need a Car.
    }
}

function makeCar(): Car {
    return new Car();
}                                     We wrap car-making in a function
                                      and pass that to chooseMyRide().
chooseMyRide(new Bike(), makeCar);
```

The lazy version will not create an expensive `Car` unless it's really needed. If I decide to ride my bike instead, the function never gets called, and no `Car` gets created.

This is something we could achieve with pure object-oriented constructs, albeit with a lot more code. We could declare a `CarFactory` class that wraps a `makeCar()` method and use that as the argument to `chooseMyRide()`. We would then create a new instance of `CarFactory` when calling `chooseMyRide()`, which would invoke the method when needed. But why write more code when we can write less? In fact, we can make our code even shorter.

5.3.1   *Lambdas*

Most modern programming languages support *anonymous functions*, or *lambdas*. Lambdas are similar to normal functions but don't have names. We would use lambdas whenever we have a one-off function: a function we usually refer to only once, so going through the trouble of naming it becomes extra work. Instead, we can provide an inline implementation.

In our lazy car example, a good candidate is `makeCar()`. Because `chooseMyRide()` needs a function with no arguments that returns a `Car`, we had to declare this new function that we refer to only once: when we pass it as an argument to `chooseMyRide()`. Instead of this function, we can use an anonymous function, as shown in the following listing.

Listing 5.10 Anonymous `Car` production

```
class Bike { }
class Car { }

function chooseMyRide(bike: Bike, car: () => Car): Bike | Car {
    if (isItRaining()) {
        return car();
    } else {
        return bike;
    }
}

chooseMyRide(new Bike(), () => new Car());        ◁── A lambda that doesn't take any
                                                     arguments and returns a Car
```

The TypeScript lambda syntax is very similar to the function type declaration: we have the list of arguments (none in this particular case) in parentheses, then =>, and then the body of the function. If the function had multiple lines, we would've put them between { and }, but because we have only a single call to new Car(), this is implicitly considered to be the return statement for the lambda, so we get rid of makeCar() and put the construction logic in a one-liner.

> **LAMBDA OR ANONYMOUS FUNCTION** A lambda, or anonymous function, is a function definition that doesn't have a name. Lambdas are usually used for one-off, short-lived processing and are passed around like data.

Lambdas wouldn't be very useful if we were unable to type functions. What would we do with an expression such as () => new Car()? If we couldn't store it in a variable or pass it as an argument to another function, there really wouldn't be much use for it. On the other hand, having the ability to pass functions around like values enables scenarios like the preceding one, in which producing a Car instance lazily is just a few characters longer than the eager version.

Lazy evaluation

A common feature of many functional programming languages is *lazy evaluation*. In such languages, everything is evaluated as late as possible, and we don't have to be explicit about it. In such languages, chooseMyRide() would by default construct neither a Bike nor a Car. Only when we actually try to use the object returned by chooseMyRide()—by calling ride() on it, for example—would the Bike or Car be created.

Imperative programming languages such as TypeScript, Java, C#, and C++ are *eagerly evaluated*. That being said, as we saw previously, we can simulate lazy evaluation fairly easily when necessary. We'll see more examples of this when we discuss generators later.

5.3.2   *Exercise*

1   Which of the following implements a lambda that adds two numbers?

    a `function add(x: number, y: number) => number { return x + y; }`

    b `add(x: number, y: number) => number { return x + y; }`

    c `add(x: number, y: number) { return x + y; }`

    d `(x: number, y: number) => x + y;`

5.4   *Using map, filter, and reduce*

Let's look at another capability unlocked by typed functions: functions that take as arguments or return other functions. A "normal" function that accepts one or more nonfunction arguments and returns a nonfunction type is also known as a *first-order function*, or a regular, run-of-the-mill function. A function that takes a first-order function as an argument or returns a first-order function is called a *second-order function*.

We could climb up the ladder and say that a function that takes a second-order function as an argument or returns a second-order function is called a *third-order function*, but in practice, we simply refer to all functions that take or return other functions as *higher-order functions*.

An example of a higher-order function is the second iteration of `choose-MyRide()` from the preceding section. That function requires an argument of type `() => Car`, which would be a function itself.

In fact, it turns out that several very useful algorithms can be implemented as higher-order functions, the most fundamental ones being `map()`, `filter()`, and `reduce()`. Most programming languages ship with libraries that provide versions of these functions, but in DIY fashion, we'll look at possible implementations and go over the details.

5.4.1   *map()*

The premise behind `map()` is very straightforward: given a collection of values of some type, call a function on each of those values, and return the collection of results. This type of processing shows up over and over in practice, so it makes sense to reduce code duplication.

Let's take two scenarios as examples. First, we have an array of numbers, and we want to square each number in the array. Second, we have an array of strings, and we want to compute the length of each string in the array.

We could implement these examples with a couple of `for` loops, but looking at them side by side, as shown in the next listing, should give us a feeling that some of the commonality could be abstracted away into shared code.

Listing 5.11   Ad hoc mapping

```
let numbers: number[] = [1, 2, 3, 4, 5];          ◁───┐ Array of numbers
let squares: number[] = [];

for (const n of numbers) {                  ┐ For each number in the array, we square
    squares.push(n * n);              ◁────┘ it and add it to the squares array.
}
```

```
let strings: string[] = ["apple", "orange", "peach"];        ⊲⎯⎤ Array of strings
let lengths: number[] = [];

for (const s of strings) {                    ⎡ For each string in the array, we
    lengths.push(s.length);           ⊲⎯⎦ add its length to the lengths array.
}
```

Although the arrays and transformations are different, the structure is obviously very similar (figure 5.5).

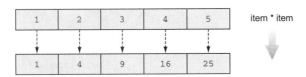

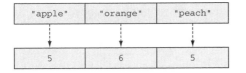

Figure 5.5 Squaring numbers and getting string lengths are very different scenarios, but the overall structure of the transformation is the same: take an input array, apply a function, and produce an output array.

DIY MAP

Let's look at an implementation of map() for arrays and see how we can avoid writing this kind of loop over and over. We'll use generic types T and U, as the implementation works regardless of what T and U are. This way, we can use this function with different types, as opposed to restricting it to, say, arrays of numbers.

Our function takes an array of Ts and a function that takes an item T as argument and returns a value of type U. It collects the result in an array of Us. The implementation in the next listing simply goes over each item in the array of Ts, applies the given function to it, and then stores the result in the array of Us.

Listing 5.12   map()

map() takes an array of items of type T and a function from T to U, and returns an array of Us.

```
function map<T, U>(items: T[], func: (item: T) => U): U[] {        ⊲⎯⎤
    let result: U[] = [];                          ⊲⎯⎡ Start with an empty
                                                        ⎦ array of Us.
    for (const item of items) {
        result.push(func(item));          ⊲⎯⎡ For each item, push the result
    }                                           ⎦ of func(item) to the array of Us.

    return result;        ⊲⎯⎡ Return the
}                              ⎦ array of Us.
```

This simple function encapsulates the common processing of the preceding example. With `map()`, we can produce the array of squares and the array of string lengths with a couple of one-liners, as the following listing shows.

Listing 5.13   Using `map()`

> **Call map() with the lambda (item) => item * item. (In this case, item is a number.)**

```
let numbers: number[] = [1, 2, 3, 4, 5];
let squares: number[] = map(numbers, (item) => item * item);      ◁────────

let strings: string[] = ["apple", "orange", "peach"];
let lengths: number[] = map(strings, (item) => item.length);      ◁────────
```

> **Call map() with the lambda (item) => item.length. (In this case, item is a string.)**

`map()` encapsulates the application of the function that we give it as argument. We just hand it an array of items and a function, and we get back the array resulting from the application of the function. Later, when we discuss generics, we'll see how we can generalize this even further to make it work with any data structure, not only arrays. Even with the current implementation, though, we get a very good abstraction for applying functions to sets of items, which we can reuse in many situations.

5.4.2   *filter()*

The next very common scenario, the cousin of `map()`, is `filter()`. Given a collection of items and a condition, filter out the items that don't meet the condition and return the collection of items that do.

Going back to our numbers and strings examples, let's filter the list so that we keep only the even numbers and the strings of length 5. `map()` can't help us here, as it processes all elements in the collection, but in this case, we want to discard some. The ad-hoc implementation would again consist of looping over the collections and checking whether the condition is met, as shown in the next listing.

Listing 5.14   Ad hoc filtering

```
let numbers: number[] = [1, 2, 3, 4, 5];
let evens: number[] = []

for (const n of numbers) {
    if (n % 2 == 0) {              ◁──┐  Push item only
        evens.push(n);                │  if it is even
    }
}

let strings: string[] = ["apple", "orange", "peach"];
let length5Strings: string[] = [];
```

```
for (const s of strings) {
    if (s.length == 5) {
        length5Strings.push(s);
    }
}
```

Push item only
if it has length 5

Again, we immediately see a common underlying structure (figure 5.6).

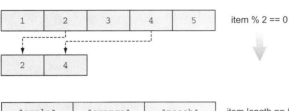

item % 2 == 0

item.length == 5

Figure 5.6 **Even numbers and
strings with length 5 share a
structure. We traverse the input,
apply the filter, and output the items
for which the filter returns `true`.**

DIY FILTER

Just as we did with `map()`, we can implement a generic `filter()` higher-order function that takes as arguments an input array and a filter function, and returns the filtered output, as shown in the following code. In this case, if the input array is of type `T`, the filter function is a function that takes a `T` as argument and returns a `boolean`. A function that takes a single argument and returns a `boolean` is also called a *predicate*.

Listing 5.15   `filter()`

```
function filter<T>(items: T[], pred: (item: T) => boolean): T[] {
    let result: T[] = [];

    for (const item of items) {
        if (pred(item)) {
            result.push(item);
        }
    }

    return result;
}
```

filter() takes an array of Ts
and a predicate (a function
from T to boolean).

If the predicate returns true, the
item is added to the result array;
otherwise, it's skipped.

Let's see what the filtering code looks like when we use the common structure that we implemented in our `filter()` function. Both the even numbers and strings of length 5 become one-liners in the next listing.

Listing 5.16   Using `filter()`

```
let numbers: number[] = [1, 2, 3, 4, 5];
let evens: number[] = filter(numbers, (item) => item % 2 == 0);

let strings: string[] = ["apple", "orange", "peach"];
let length5Strings: string[] = filter(strings, (item) => item.length == 5);
```

The arrays are filtered by using a predicate—in the first case, a lambda that returns `true` if the number is divisible by 2, and in the second case, a lambda that returns `true` if the string has length 5.

With the second common operation implemented as a generic function, let's move on to the third and last operation covered in this chapter.

5.4.3   *reduce()*

So far, we can apply a function to a collection of items by using `map()`, and we can remove items that don't meet certain criteria from a collection by using `filter()`. The third common operation involves merging all the collection items into a single value.

We might want to calculate the product of all numbers in a number array, for example, and concatenate all the strings in a string array to form one big string. These scenarios are different but have a common underlying structure. First, let's look at the ad hoc implementation.

Listing 5.17   Ad hoc reducing

```
let numbers: number[] = [1, 2, 3, 4, 5];      In the product case, we start
let product: number = 1;                  ◁── with an initial value of 1.

for (const n of numbers) {                 We proceed to multiply product by every number
    product = product * n;           ◁──  in our collection, accumulating the result.
}

let strings: string[] = ["apple", "orange", "peach"];   In the string case, we start
let longString: string = "";                      ◁──  with an empty string.

for (const s of strings) {                 We append each string to the empty
    longString = longString + s;     ◁──  string, accumulating the result.
}
```

In both scenarios, we start with an initial value; then we accumulate the result by going over the collections and combining each item with the accumulator. When we're done going over the collections, `product` contains the product of all the numbers in the numbers array, and `longString` is the concatenation of all strings in the strings array (figure 5.7).

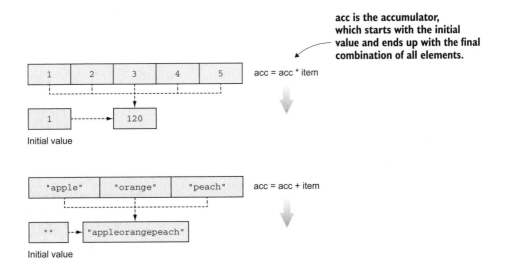

Figure 5.7   Common structure of combining the numbers in a number array and strings in a string array. In the first case, the initial value is 1, and the combination we apply is multiplication with each item. In the second case, the initial value is " ", and the combination we apply is concatenation with each item.

DIY REDUCE

In listing 5.18, we'll implement a generic function that takes an array of Ts, an initial value of type T, and a function that takes two arguments of type T and returns a T. We'll store the running total in a local variable and update it by applying the function to it and each element of the input array in turn.

Listing 5.18   reduce()

```
function reduce<T>(items: T[], init: T, op: (x: T, y: T) => T): T {
    let result: T = init;

    for (const item of items) {
        result = op(result, item);
    }

    return result;
}
```

reduce() takes an array of Ts, an initial value, and an operation combining two Ts into one.

Each item in the array is combined with the running total by using the given operation.

This function has three arguments, and the others have two. The reason why we need an initial value instead of starting with, say, the first element of the array is that we need to handle the case when the input array is empty. What would `result` be if there was no item in the collection? Having an initial value covers that case, as we would simply return that.

Let's see how we can update our ad-hoc implementations to use reduce().

Listing 5.19 Using reduce()

> **For numbers, we start with an
> initial value of 1 and the operation
> (x, y) => x * y (multiplication).**

```
let numbers: number[] = [1, 2, 3, 4, 5];
let product: number = reduce(numbers, 1, (x, y) => x * y);

let strings: string[] = ["apple", "orange", "peach"];
let longString: string = reduce(strings, "", (x, y) => x + y);
```

> **For strings, we start with an initial
> value of " " and the operation
> (x, y) => x + y (concatenation).**

reduce() has a few subtleties that the other two functions don't. Besides requiring an initial value, the order in which the items are combined may affect the final result. For the operations and initial values in our example, that's not the case. But what if our initial string was "banana"? Then, concatenating from left to right, we would get "bananaappleorangepeach". But if we traversed the array from right to left, always adding the item to the beginning of the string, we would get "appleorangepeach-banana".

Or if our combining operation appended the first letters of each string together, applying that to "apple" and "orange" first would give us "ao". Applying it again to "ao" and "peach" would give us "ap". On the other hand, if we started with "orange" and "peach", we would have "op". Then "apple" and "op" would give us "ao" (figure 5.8).

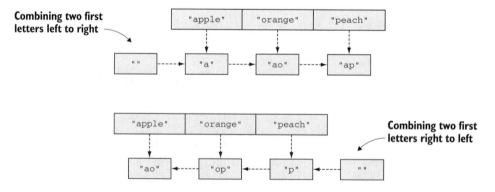

Figure 5.8 Combining an array of strings with the operation "first letter of both strings" gives us different results when applied from left to right and when applied from right to left. In the first case, we start with an empty string and "apple", then "a" and "orange", then "ao" and "peach", giving us "ap". In the second case, we start with "peach" and an empty string, followed by "orange" and "p", giving us "op"; and then "apple" and "op", giving us "ao".

Conventionally, `reduce()` is applied left to right, so whenever you encounter it as a library function, it should be safe to assume that's how it works. Some libraries also provide a right-to-left version. The JavaScript `Array` type, for example, has both `reduce()` and `reduceRight()` methods. See the sidebar "Monoids" if you want to learn more about the math behind this.

Monoids

In abstract algebra, we deal with sets and operations on those sets. As we saw previously, we can think of a type as a set of possible values. An operation on type `T` that takes two `T`s and returns another `T`, `(T, T) => T`, can be interpreted as an operation on the set of values `T`. The set of `number` and `+`, which is `(x, y) => x + y`, for example, forms an algebraic structure.

These structures are defined by the properties of their operations. An *identity* is an element `id` of `T` for which the operation `op(x, id) == op(id, x) == x`. In other words, combining `id` with any other element leaves the other element unchanged. Identity is `0` when the set is `number` and the operation is addition, `1` when the set is `number` and the operation is multiplication, and `""` (the empty string) when the set is `string` and the operation is string concatenation.

Associativity is a property of the operation that says the order in which we apply it to a sequence of elements doesn't matter, as we'll get the same result in the end. For any `x, y, z` of `T`, `op(x, op(y, z)) == op(op(x, y), z)`. This is true, for example, for number addition and multiplication but not true for subtraction or our "first letter of both strings" operation.

If a set `T` with an operation `op` has an identity element and the operation is associative, the resulting algebraic structure is called a *monoid*. For a monoid, starting with the identity as the initial value, reducing from left to right or right to left yields the same result. We can even remove the requirement for an initial value and default to the identity if the collection is empty. We can also parallelize reduction. We could reduce the first half and the second half of the collection in parallel and combine the results, for example, because the associativity property guarantees that we'll get the same result. For `[1, 2, 3, 4, 5, 6]`, we can combine `1 + 2 + 3` and, in parallel, `4 + 5 + 6`, and then add the results together.

As soon as we drop one of the properties, we lose these guarantees. If we don't have associativity, but just a set, an operation, and an identity element, although we still don't require an initial value (we use the identity element), the direction in which we apply the operations becomes important. If we drop the identity element but keep associativity, we have a *semigroup*. Without an identity, it matters whether we put the initial value on the left of the first element or the right of the last element.

The key takeaway is that `reduce()` works seamlessly on a monoid, but if we don't have a monoid, we should be careful what we use for our initial value and the direction we're reducing on.

5.4.4 *Library support*

As mentioned at the start of this section, most programming languages have library support for these common algorithms. They may show up under different names, though, as there is no golden standard for naming them.

In C#, `map()`, `filter()`, and `reduce()` show up in the `System.Linq` namespace as `Select()`, `Where()`, and `Aggregate()` respectively. In Java, they show up as `map()`, `filter()`, and `reduce()` in `java.util.stream`.

`map()` is also known as `Select()` or `transform()`. `filter()` is also known as `Where()`. `reduce()` is also known as `accumulate()`, `Aggregate()`, or `fold()`, depending on the language and library.

Even though they have many names, these algorithms are fundamental and useful across a broad range of applications. We'll discuss many similar algorithms later in the book, but these three form the foundation of data processing using higher-order functions.

Google's famous MapReduce large-scale data processing framework uses the same underlying principles of the `map()` and `reduce()` algorithms by running a massively parallel `map()` operation on multiple nodes and combining the results via a `reduce()`-like operation.

5.4.5 *Exercises*

1 Implement a `first()` function that takes an array of Ts and a function `pred` (for predicate) that takes a T as an argument and returns a `boolean`. `first()` will return the first element of the array for which `pred()` returns `true` or `undefined` if `pred()` returns `false` for all elements.

2 Implement an `all()` function that takes an array of Ts and a function `pred` (for predicate) that takes a T as an argument and returns a `boolean`. `all()` will return true if `pred()` is `true` for all the elements of the array; otherwise, it will return `false`.

5.5 *Functional programming*

Although the material covered in this chapter was a bit more complex, the good news is that we went over most of the key ingredients of functional programming. The syntax of some functional languages may be off-putting if you're used to imperative, object-oriented languages. Their type systems usually offer some combinations of sum types, product types, and first-order function support, as well as a set of library functions such as `map()`, `filter()`, and `reduce()` to process data. Many functional languages employ lazy evaluation, which we also discussed in this chapter.

With the ability to type functions, many of the concepts originating from functional programming languages can be implemented in languages that aren't functional (or purely functional). We saw this throughout this chapter; we touched on all these topics and provided imperative implementations for all these key components.

Summary

- If we can type functions, we can implement the strategy pattern in a much simpler way by focusing on the functions that implement the logic and discarding the surrounding scaffolding.
- The ability to plug a function into a class as a property and call it as a method allows us to implement state machines that don't rely on big `switch` statements. This way, the compiler can prevent mistakes like accidentally applying the wrong processing in some given state.
- Another alternative to `switch` statements for a state machine implementation is a sum type in which each state is captured by a different type.
- We can defer expensive computation by relying on lazy values, which are functions we pass around that wrap the expensive computation. We call them when needed to produce a value, but if we never need them, we can skip the expensive computation.
- Lambdas are nameless functions we can use for one-off logic in which naming a function wouldn't be very useful.
- A higher order function is a function that takes another function as an argument or returns a function.
- `map()`, `filter()`, and `reduce()` are three fundamental higher-order functions, with many applications in data processing.

In chapter 6, we'll look at a few more applications of typed functions. We'll learn about closures and how we can use them to simplify another common design pattern: the decorator pattern. We'll also talk about promises, as well as tasking and event-driven systems. All these applications are made possible by the ability to represent computation (functions) as first-class citizens of the type system.

Answers to exercises

A SIMPLE STRATEGY PATTERN

1 b—That is the only function type; the other declarations do not represent functions.

2 c—The function takes a `number` and an `(x: number) => boolean` and returns `boolean`.

A STATE MACHINE WITHOUT SWITCH STATEMENTS

1 We can model the connection as a state machine with two states—open and closed—and two transitions—connect transitions from `closed` to `open` and disconnect transitions from `open` to `closed`.

2 A possible implementation:

```
declare function read(): string;

class Connection {
    private doProcess: () => void = this.processClosedConnection;
```

```
public process(): void {
    this.doProcess();
}

private processClosedConnection() {
    this.doProcess = this.processOpenConnection;
}

private processOpenConnection() {
    const value: string = read();

    if (value.length == 0) {
        this.doProcess = this.processClosedConnection;
    } else {
        console.log(value);
    }
}
}
```

AVOIDING EXPENSIVE COMPUTATION WITH LAZY VALUES

1 d—The other implement named functions; this is the only anonymous implementation.

USING MAP, FILTER, AND REDUCE

1 A possible implementation for `first()`:

```
function first<T>(items: T[], pred: (item: T) => boolean):
    T | undefined {
    for (const item of items) {
        if (pred(item)) {
            return item;
        }
    }

    return undefined;
}
```

2 A possible implementation for `all()`:

```
function all<T>(items: T[], pred: (item: T) => boolean): boolean {
    for (const item of items) {
        if (!pred(item)) {
            return false;
        }
    }

    return true;
}
```

Advanced applications
of function types

This chapter covers

- Using a simplified decorator pattern
- Implementing a resumable counter
- Handling long-running operations
- Writing clean asynchronous code by using promises and `async/await`

In chapter 5, we covered the basics of function types and scenarios enabled by the ability to treat functions like other values by passing them as arguments and returning them as results. We also looked at some powerful abstractions that implement common data processing patterns: `map()`, `filter()`, and `reduce()`.

In this chapter, we'll continue our discussion of function types with some more advanced applications. We'll start by looking at the decorator pattern, its by-the-book implementation, and an alternative implementation. (Again, don't worry if you forgot it; we'll have a quick refresher.) We'll introduce the concept of a *closure* and see how we can use it to implement a simple counter. Then we'll look at another way to implement a counter, this time with a generator: a function that yields multiple results.

Next, we'll talk about asynchronous operations. We'll go over the two main asynchronous execution models—threads and event loops—and look at how we can sequence several long-running operations. We'll start with callbacks; then we'll look at promises, and finally, we'll cover the `async/await` syntax provided nowadays by most mainstream programming languages.

All the topics discussed in this chapter are made possible because we can use functions as values, as we'll see in the following pages.

6.1 *A simple decorator pattern*

The decorator pattern is a behavioral software design pattern that extends the behavior of an object without modifying the class of the object. A decorated object can perform work beyond what its original implementation provides. The pattern looks like figure 6.1.

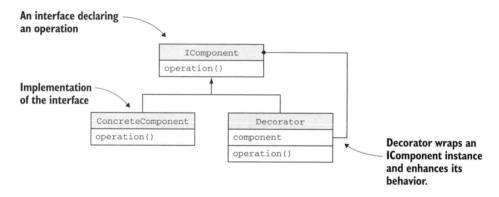

Figure 6.1   Decorator pattern: an `IComponent` interface, a concrete implementation via `ConcreteComponent`, and a `Decorator` that enhances an `IComponent` with additional behavior

As an example, suppose that we have an `IWidgetFactory` that declares a `makeWidget()` method returning a `Widget`. The concrete implementation, `WidgetFactory`, implements the method to instantiate new `Widget` objects.

Suppose that we want to reuse a `Widget`, so instead of always creating a new one, we want to create just one and keep returning it (that is, have a singleton). Without

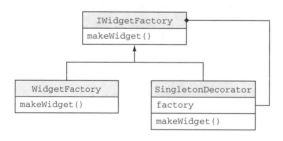

Figure 6.2   Decorator pattern for the widget factory. `IWidgetFactory` is the interface, `WidgetFactory` is a concrete implementation, and `SingletonDecorator` adds singleton behavior to an `IWidgetFactory`.

modifying our `WidgetFactory`, we can create a decorator called `Singleton-Decorator`, which wraps an `IWidgetFactory`, as shown in the next listing, and extends its behavior to ensure that only a single `Widget` gets created (figure 6.2).

> **Listing 6.1** `WidgetFactory` decorator

```
class Widget { }

interface IWidgetFactory {
    makeWidget(): Widget;
}

class WidgetFactory implements IWidgetFactory {
    public makeWidget(): Widget {              WidgetFactory simply
        return new Widget();                   creates a new Widget.
    }
}

class SingletonDecorator implements IWidgetFactory {   SingletonDecorator
    private factory: IWidgetFactory;                   wraps an IWidgetFactory.
    private instance: Widget | undefined = undefined;

    constructor(factory: IWidgetFactory) {
        this.factory = factory;
    }

    public makeWidget(): Widget {
        if (this.instance == undefined) {              makeWidget() implements
            this.instance = this.factory.makeWidget(); the singleton logic and
        }                                              ensures that only a single
                                                       Widget is created.
        return this.instance;
    }
}
```

The advantage of using this pattern is that it supports the *single-responsibility principle*, which says that a class should have just one responsibility. In this case, the `Widget-Factory` is responsible for creating widgets, whereas the `SingletonDecorator` is responsible for the singleton behavior. If we want multiple instances, we use the `WidgetFactory` directly. If we want a single instance, we use `SingletonDecorator`.

6.1.1 *A functional decorator*

Let's see how we can simplify this implementation, again by using typed functions. First, let's get rid of the `IWidgetFactory` interface and replace it with a function type. That would be the type of a function that takes no arguments and returns a `Widget`: `() => Widget`.

Now we can replace our `WidgetFactory` class with a simple function, `make-Widget()`. Whenever we would've used an `IWidgetFactory` before, passing in an instance of `WidgetFactory`, we now require a function of type `() => Widget` and pass in `makeWidget()`, as the following listing shows.

Listing 6.2   Functional widget factory

```
class Widget { }

type WidgetFactory = () => Widget;          Function type for
                                            a widget factory

function makeWidget(): Widget {             makeWidget() is of
    return new Widget();                    type WidgetFactory.
}

function use10Widgets(factory: WidgetFactory) {     use10Widgets() requires a
    for (let i = 0; i < 10; i++) {                  WidgetFactory, which it uses
        let widget = factory();                     to create 10 Widget instances.
        /* ... */
    }
}
                                            Example call: we pass the makeWidget
use10Widgets(makeWidget);                   function as an argument.
```

With the functional widget factory, we use a technique very similar to the strategy pattern in chapter 5: we get a function as an argument and call it when needed. Now let's see how we can add the singleton behavior.

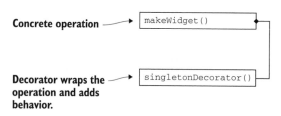

Concrete operation → makeWidget()

Decorator wraps the → singletonDecorator()
operation and adds
behavior.

Figure 6.3   Functional decorator: we now have only a makeWidget() function and a singletonDecorator() function.

We provide a new function, singletonDecorator(), that takes a WidgetFactory-type function and returns another WidgetFactory-type function. Remember from chapter 5 that a lambda is a function without a name, which we can return from another function. In the next listing, our decorator will take a factory and use it to build a new function that handles the singleton behavior (figure 6.3).

Listing 6.3   Functional widget factory decorator

```
class Widget { }

type WidgetFactory = () => Widget;

function makeWidget(): Widget {
    return new Widget();
}

function singletonDecorator(factory: WidgetFactory): WidgetFactory {
    let instance: Widget | undefined = undefined;

    return (): Widget => {                          singletonDecorator() returns a lambda that
        if (instance == undefined) {                implements the singleton behavior and uses
            instance = factory();                   the given factory to create a Widget.
        }
```

```
        return instance;
    };
}

function use10Widgets(factory: WidgetFactory) {
    for (let i = 0; i < 10; i++) {
        let widget = factory();
        /* ... */
    }
}

use10Widgets(singletonDecorator(makeWidget));
```

> Because singletonDecorator() returns a WidgetFactory, we can pass it as an argument to use10Widgets().

Now, instead of constructing 10 `Widget` objects, `use10Widgets()` will call the lambda, which will reuse the same `Widget` instance for all calls.

This code reduces the number of components from an interface and two classes, each with a method (the concrete operation and the decorator) to two functions.

6.1.2 Decorator implementations

As with our strategy pattern, the object-oriented and functional approaches implement the same decorator pattern. The object-oriented version requires an interface declaration (`IWidgetFactory`), at least one implementation of that interface (`WidgetFactory`), and a decorator class that handles the added behavior (`SingletonDecorator`). By contrast, the functional implementation simply declares the type of the factory function (`() => Widget`) and uses two functions: a factory function (`makeWidget()`) and a decorator function (`singletonDecorator()`).

One thing to note is that in the functional case, the decorator does not have the same type as `makeWidget()`. Whereas the factory doesn't expect any arguments and returns a `Widget`, the decorator takes a widget factory and returns another widget factory. In other words, `singletonDecorator()` takes a function as an argument and returns a function as its result. This wouldn't be possible without first-class functions: the ability to treat functions as any other variables and use them as arguments and return values.

The more-succinct implementation, enabled by modern type systems, is good for many situations. We can use the more-verbose object-oriented solution when we are dealing with more than a single function. If our interface declares several methods, we can't replace it with a single function type.

6.1.3 Closures

Let's zoom in on the `singletonDecorator()` implementation in listing 6.4. You may have noticed something interesting: even though the function returns a lambda, the lambda references both the `factory` argument and the variable `instance`, which should be local to the `singletonDecorator()` function.

```
function singletonDecorator(factory: WidgetFactory): WidgetFactory {
    let instance: Widget | undefined = undefined;

    return (): Widget => {
        if (instance == undefined) {
            instance = factory();
        }

        return instance;
    };
}
```

Even after we return from `singletonDecorator()`, the `instance` variable is still alive, as it was "captured" by the lambda, which is known as a *lambda capture*.

CLOSURES AND LAMBDA CAPTURES   A lambda capture is an external variable captured within a lambda. Programming languages implement lambda captures through closures. A *closure* is something more than a simple function: it also records the environment in which the function was created, so it can maintain state between calls.

In our case, the `instance` variable in `singletonDecorator()` is part of that environment. The lambda we return will still be able to reference `instance` (figure 6.4).

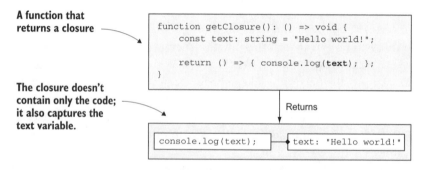

A function that returns a closure

The closure doesn't contain only the code; it also captures the text variable.

```
function getClosure(): () => void {
    const text: string = "Hello world!";

    return () => { console.log(text); };
}
```

Returns

```
console.log(text);          text: "Hello world!"
```

Figure 6.4   A simple function that returns a closure: a lambda that references a variable local to the function. Even after `getClosure()` returns, the variable is still referenced by the closure, so it outlives the function in which it appeared.

Closures make sense only if we have higher-order functions. If we can't return a function from another function, there is no environment to capture. In that case, all functions are in the global scope, which is their environment. They can reference global variables.

Another way to think about closures is to contrast them with objects. An object represents some state with a set of methods; a *closure* represents a function with some captured state. Let's look at another example in which closures can be used: implementing a counter.

6.1.4 Exercises

1 Implement a function, `loggingDecorator()`, that takes as argument another function, `factory()`, that takes no arguments and returns a `Widget` object. Decorate the given function so that whenever it is called, it logs `"Widget created"` before returning a `Widget` object.

6.2 Implementing a counter

Let's look at a very simple scenario: we want to create a counter that gives us consecutive numbers starting from 1. Although this example may seem trivial, it covers several possible implementations that generalize to any scenario in which we need to generate values. One way is to use a global variable and a function that returns that variable and then increments, as shown in the following code.

Listing 6.5 Global counter

```
let n: number = 1;                    The counter is stored
                                      in a global variable.
function next() {
    return n++;                       next() returns n
}                                     and increments.

console.log(next());
console.log(next());                  This will log 1 2 3.
console.log(next());
```

This implementation works, but it's not ideal. First, n is a global variable, so anyone has access to it. Other code might change it from underneath us. Second, this implementation gives us a single counter. What if we want two counters, both starting from 1?

6.2.1 An object-oriented counter

The first implementation we will look at is an object-oriented one, which should be familiar. We create a `Counter` class, which stores the state of the counter as a private member. We provide a `next()` method, which returns and increments that counter. In this way, we encapsulate the counter so that external code can't change it and we can create as many counters as we want as instances of this class.

Listing 6.6 Object-oriented counter

```
class Counter {
    private n: number = 1;            The counter value is
                                      now private to the class.
    next(): number {
        return this.n++;
    }
}

let counter1: Counter = new Counter();    We can create
let counter2: Counter = new Counter();    multiple counters.
```

```
console.log(counter1.next());
console.log(counter2.next());
console.log(counter1.next());
console.log(counter2.next());
```

This will log 1 1 2 2.

This approach works better. In fact, most modern programming languages provide an interface for types such as our counter, which provides a value on each call and has special syntax to iterate over it. In TypeScript, this is done with the `Iterable` interface and `for ... of` loop. We cover this topic later in the book, when we discuss generic programming. For now, we'll just note that this pattern is common. C# implements it with the `IEnumerable` interface and the `foreach` loop, whereas Java does it with the `Iterable` interface and the `for : loop`.

Next, let's look at a functional alternative that leverages closures to implement the counter.

6.2.2 A functional counter

In the next listing, we'll implement the functional counter through a `makeCounter()` function that returns a counter function when called. We will initialize the counter as a variable local to `makeCounter()` and then capture it in the return function.

Listing 6.7 Functional counter

```
type Counter = () => number;
```

We define a Counter type as a function that takes no arguments and returns a number.

```
function makeCounter(): Counter {
    let n: number = 1;

    return () => n++;
}
```

The counter value is declared as a variable and captured by the lambda.

```
let counter1: Counter = makeCounter();
let counter2: Counter = makeCounter();

console.log(counter1());
console.log(counter2());
console.log(counter1());
console.log(counter2());
```

This will log 1 1 2 2.

Each counter is a function now, so instead of calling `counter1.next()`, we simply call `counter1()`. We also see that each counter captures a separate value: calling `counter1()` does not affect `counter2()` because whenever we call `make-Counter()`, a new n gets created. Each function returned keeps its own n. The counters are closures. Also, these values persist between calls. This behavior is different from that of variables that are local to a function, which are created when the function is called and disposed of when the function returns (figure 6.5).

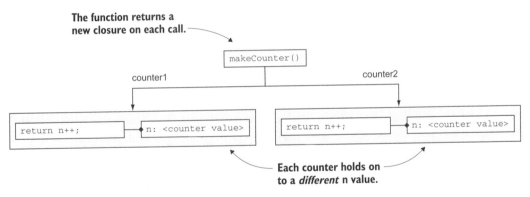

The function returns a
new closure on each call.

Each counter holds on
to a *different* n value.

Figure 6.5 It's important to understand that each closure (in our case, `counter1` and `counter2`) ends up with a different n. Whenever we call `makeCounter()`, a new n is initialized to 1 and captured by the returned closure. Because the values are separate, they don't interfere with each other.

6.2.3 A resumable counter

Another way to define a counter is to use a resumable function. An object-oriented counter keeps track of state via a private member. A functional counter keeps track of state in its captured context.

> **RESUMABLE FUNCTIONS** A *resumable function* is a function that keeps track of its own state and, whenever it gets called, doesn't run from the beginning; rather, it resumes executing from where it left off the last time it returned.

In TypeScript, instead of using the keyword `return` to exit the function, we use the keyword `yield`, as shown in listing 6.8. This keyword suspends the function, giving control back to the caller. When called again, execution is resumed from the `yield` statement.

There are a couple more constraints for using `yield`: the function must be declared as a generator, and its return type must be an iterable iterator. A generator is declared by prefixing the function name with an asterisk.

Listing 6.8 Resumable counter

```
function* counter(): IterableIterator<number> {      The function is declared
    let n: number = 1;                                as a generator.

    while (true) {
        yield n++;          We call yield
    }                       instead of return.
}

let counter1: IterableIterator<number> = counter();   Our counters are objects implementing
let counter2: IterableIterator<number> = counter();   the IterableIterator interface.

console.log(counter1.next());
console.log(counter2.next());
console.log(counter1.next());       This logs 1 1 2 2.
console.log(counter2.next());
```

This implementation is in a way a mix between our object-oriented and functional counters. The implementation of the counter reads like a function: we start with n being 1 and then loop forever, yielding the counter value and incrementing it. On the other hand, the code generated by the compiler is object-oriented: our counter is actually an `IterableIterator<number>`, and we call `next()` on it to get the next value.

Even though we implement this with a `while (true)` statement, we don't get stuck in an infinite loop; the function keeps yielding values and gets suspended after each `yield`. Behind the scenes, the compiler translates the code we wrote into something that looks more like our previous implementations.

The type of this function is `() => IterableIterator<number>`. Notice that the fact that it is a generator doesn't affect its type. A function with no arguments that would return an `IterableIterator<number>` would have exactly the same type. The `*` declaration is used by the compiler to allow `yield` statements but is transparent to the type system.

We will come back to iterators and generators in a later chapter and discuss them at length.

6.2.4 *Counter implementations recap*

Before moving on, let's quickly recap the four ways to implement a counter and the various language features we learned about:

- A global counter is implemented as a simple function that references a global variable. This counter has multiple drawbacks: the counter value is not properly encapsulated, and we cannot have two separate instances of the counter.
- The object-oriented counter implementation is straightforward: the counter value is private state, and we expose a `next()` method to read and increment it. Most languages declare an interface like `Iterable` to support such scenarios and provide syntactic sugar to consume them.
- A functional counter is a function that returns a function. The returned function is a counter. This implementation leverages lambda captures to hold the state of the counter. The code is more succinct than the object-oriented version.
- A generator employs special syntax to create a resumable function. Instead of returning, a generator yields; it provides a value to the caller but also keeps track of where it was and picks up from there on subsequent calls. A generator function must return an iterable iterator.

Next, we'll look at another common application of function types: asynchronous functions.

6.2.5 *Exercises*

1. Implement a function that returns the next number in the Fibonacci sequence whenever it is called by using a closure.
2. Implement a function that returns the next number in the Fibonacci sequence whenever it is called by using a generator.

6.3   *Executing long-running operations asynchronously*

We want our applications to be as fast and responsive as possible, even when certain operations take longer to complete. Running all our code sequentially might introduce unacceptable delays. If we can't respond to our users clicking a button because we're waiting for a download to complete, the users get frustrated.

In general, we don't want to wait for a long-running operation to execute a faster operation. It's best to execute such long-running tasks asynchronously so we can keep the UI interactive while our download completes. Asynchronous execution means that the operations don't run one after another, in the order in which they show up in the code. They could be running in parallel, but that's not mandatory. JavaScript is single-threaded, so asynchronous execution is achieved by the run time with an event loop. We'll go over a high-level description of both parallel execution using multiple threads and event loop–based execution with a single thread, but first, let's look at an example in which running code asynchronously comes in handy.

Suppose that we want to perform two operations: greet our users and take them to www.weather.com so that they can see today's weather. We'll do this with two functions: a greet() function that asks for the user's name and greets them, and a weather() function, which launches a browser for today's weather. Let's look at a synchronous implementation and then contrast it with an asynchronous one.

6.3.1   *Synchronous execution*

We will implement greet() by using the readline-sync node package, as shown in listing 6.9. This package provides a way to read input from stdin with the question() function. The function returns the string typed by the user. Execution blocks until the user types their answer and presses return. We can install the package with npm install –save readline-sync.

To implement weather(), we will use the open Node package, which allows us to launch a URL in the browser. We can install the package with npm install --save open.

Listing 6.9   Synchronous execution

```
function greet(): void {
    const readlineSync = require('readline-sync');

    let name: string = readlineSync.question("What is your name? ");      ◁─┐
    console.log(`Hi ${name}!`);
}                                                     Calling question() blocks
                                                       execution until the user
function weather(): void {                               enters their answer.
    const open = require('open');
    open('https://www.weather.com/');
}

greet();           │ We first call greet();
weather();         │ then we call weather().
```

Let's step through what happens when we run this code. First, `greet()` is called, and we ask the user to give us their name. Execution stops here until we receive a reply from the user, after which it proceeds by outputting a greeting. After `greet()` returns, `weather()` is called, launching www.weather.com.

This implementation works, but it's not optimal. The two functions—greeting the user and taking them to a website—are independent in this case, so one of them shouldn't be blocked until the other one finishes. We could call the functions in a different order, because in this case, it's obvious that requesting user input takes longer than launching an application. But in practice, we can't always tell which one of two functions will take longer to complete. A better approach is to run the functions asynchronously.

6.3.2 *Asynchronous execution: callbacks*

An asynchronous version of `greet()` prompts the user for their name but does not block and wait for the reply. Execution will continue by calling `weather()`. We still want to print the user's name after they enter it, so we need a way to be notified of their answer. This is done with a callback.

A *callback* is a function that we provide to an asynchronous function as an argument. The asynchronous function does not block execution; the next line of code gets executed. When the long-running operation completes (in this case, waiting for the user to answer with their name), the callback function is executed, so we can handle the result.

Let's see the asynchronous `greet()` implementation in the next listing. We will use the `readline` module provided by Node. In this case, the `question()` function does not block execution; rather, it takes a callback as an argument.

Listing 6.10 Asynchronous execution with callback

```
function greet(): void {
    const readline = require('readline');          // Using readline instead
                                                   // of readline-sync

    const rl = readline.createInterface({          // createInterface() is extra setup
        input: process.stdin,                      // required by readline and not
        output: process.stdout                     // important for our example.
    });

    rl.question("What is your name? ", (name: string) => {
        console.log(`Hi ${name}!`);                // The callback is a lambda
        rl.close();                                // that will receive the
    });                                            // name and print it.
}

function weather(): void {
    const open = require('open');
    open('https://www.weather.com/');
}

greet();
weather();
```

Stepping through this program, as soon as `question()` is called and the user is prompted, execution continues without waiting for the user's answer, returning from `greet()` and calling `weather()`. Running this program prints "What is your name?" on the terminal, but www.weather.com will be open before the user provides their answer.

When an answer comes in, the lambda gets called. The lambda prints the greeting to the screen with `console.log()` and closes the interactive session (so that no more user input is requested) with `rl.close()`.

6.3.3 *Asynchronous execution models*

As briefly mentioned at the start of this section, asynchronous execution can be achieved with threads or with an event loop. The choice depends on how your run time and the library you are using implement asynchronous operations. In JavaScript, asynchronous execution is implemented with an event loop.

THREADS

Each application runs as a process. A process starts with a main thread, but we can create multiple other threads on which to run code. On POSIX-compliant systems such as Linux and macOS, new threads are created with `pthread_create()`, whereas Windows provides `CreateThread()`. These APIs are provided by the operating systems. Programming languages provide libraries with different interfaces, but those libraries end up using the OS APIs internally.

Separate threads can run at the same time. Multiple CPU cores can execute instructions in parallel, each handling a different thread. If the number of threads is larger than the hardware can run in parallel, the operating system ensures that each thread gets a fair amount of run time. Threads get paused and resumed by the thread scheduler to achieve this result. The thread scheduler is a core component of the OS kernel.

We won't look at a code sample for threads, as JavaScript (and, thus, TypeScript) has been historically single-threaded. Node recently enabled experimental support for worker threads, but this development is fairly recent at the time of this writing. That being said, if you program in any other mainstream language, you are probably familiar with how to create new threads and execute code on them in parallel (figure 6.6).

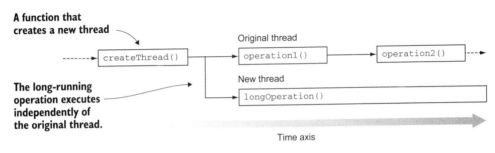

Figure 6.6 `createThread()` creates a new thread. The original thread continues to execute `operation1()` and then `operation2()`, and the new thread executes `longRunningOperation()` in parallel.

EVENT LOOPS

An alternative to multiple threads is an event loop. An *event loop* uses a queue: asynchronous functions get enqueued, and they themselves can enqueue other functions. As long as the queue is not empty, the first function in line gets dequeued and executed.

As an example, let's look at a function that counts down from a given number, shown in the following listing. Instead of blocking execution until the countdown is complete, this function will use an event queue and enqueue another call to itself until it reaches 0 (figure 6.7).

Listing 6.11   Counting down in an event loop

```
type AsyncFunction = () => void;          We'll restrict our asynchronous
                                          functions to functions without
                                          arguments that return void.

let queue: AsyncFunction[] = [];          Our queue will be
                                          an array of functions.

function countDown(counterId: string, from: number): void {
    console.log(`${counterId}: ${from}`);    The counter prints its
                                             id and current value.
    if (from > 0)
        queue.push(() => countDown(counterId, from - 1));    If greater than 0, the counter enqueues
}                                                            another call to countDown(),
                                                             decrementing the value.
queue.push(() => countDown('counter1', 4));

while (queue.length > 0) {
    let func: AsyncFunction = <AsyncFunction>queue.shift();
    func();                                   While there is a function in the
}                                             queue, dequeue it and call it.
```

We kick off the process by queueing
a call to countDown() from 4.

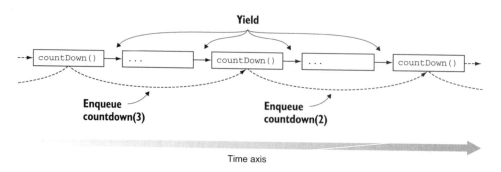

Figure 6.7   `countDown()` counts one step; then it yields and allows other code to run. It also enqueus another call to `countDown()` with the decremented counter value. If the counter reaches 0, `countDown()` doesn't enqueue another call to itself.

This code will output

```
counter1: 4
counter1: 3
counter1: 2
counter1: 1
counter1: 0
```

When the counter reaches 0, it will not enqueue another call, so the program will stop. So far, this isn't much more interesting than simply counting in a loop. But what happens if we start by enqueuing two counters?

Listing 6.12 Two counters in an event loop

```
type AsyncFunction = () => void;

let queue: AsyncFunction[] = [];

function countDown(counterId: string, from: number): void {
    console.log(`${counterId}: ${from}`);

    if (from > 0)
        queue.push(() => countDown(counterId, from - 1));
}

queue.push(() => countDown('counter1', 4));
queue.push(() => countDown('counter2', 2));

while (queue.length > 0) {
    let func: AsyncFunction = <AsyncFunction>queue.shift();
    func();
}
```

> **The only difference from the preceding sample is that now we enqueue a second counter.**

This time around, the output is

```
counter1: 4
counter2: 2
counter1: 3
counter2: 1
counter1: 2
counter2: 0
counter1: 1
counter1: 0
```

As we can see, this time the counters are interleaved. Each counter counts down one step; then the other one gets a chance to count. We couldn't achieve this result if we just counted down in a loop. Using the queue, the two functions yield after each step of the countdown and allow other code to run before they count down again.

The two counters do not run at the same time; either `counter1` or `counter2` gets some time to run. But they do run asynchronously, or independently, of each other.

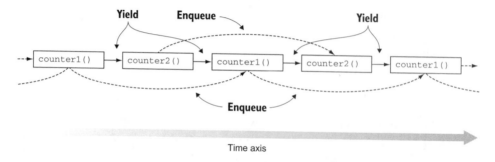

Figure 6.8   **Each counter runs and then enqueues another operation. Execution proceeds in the order in which operations are enqueued. Everything runs on a single thread.**

Either of them can finish execution first, regardless of how much longer the other one takes (figure 6.8).

For operations that wait for input, such as from the keyboard, the run time can ensure that an operation to handle that input is queued only after input is received, in which case other code can run while the input is being provided. This way, a long-running operation that requires input can be split into two shorter-running ones; the first requests input and returns, and the second processes input when it arrives. The run time handles scheduling the second operation after input is available.

Event loops don't work as well for long-running operations that cannot be split into multiple chunks. If we enqueue an operation that doesn't yield and runs for a long time, the event loop will be stuck until it finishes.

6.3.4   *Asynchronous functions recap*

If we execute long-running operations synchronously, no other code runs until the long-running operation completes. Input/output operations are good examples of long-running operations, as reading from disk or from the network has higher latency than reading from memory.

Instead of executing such operations synchronously, we can execute them asynchronously and provide a callback function to be called when the long-running operation completes. There are two main models of executing asynchronous code: one that uses multiple threads and one that uses an event loop.

Threads can run in parallel on separate CPU cores, which is their main advantage, as different pieces of code can run at the same time, and the overall program finishes faster. A drawback is the synchronization overhead: passing data between threads requires careful synchronization. We won't cover the topic in this book, but you've probably heard of problems such as *deadlock* and *livelock*, in which two threads never complete because they wait on each other.

An event loop runs on a single thread but enables a mechanism to put long-running code at the back of the queue while it awaits input. The advantage of using an event loop is that it doesn't require synchronization, as everything runs on a single thread. The disadvantage is that although queuing up I/O operations as they wait for data works fine, CPU-intensive operations still block. A CPU-intensive operation, like a complex computation, can't just be queued; as it's not waiting for data, it requires CPU cycles. Threads are much better suited to this task.

Most mainstream programming languages use threads, JavaScript being a notable exception. That being said, even JavaScript is being extended with support for web worker threads (background threads running in the browser), and Node has experimental support for similar worker threads outside the browser.

In the next section, we look at how we can make our asynchronous code cleaner and easier to read.

6.3.5 Exercises

1 Which of the following can be used to implement an asynchronous execution model?

   a Threads
   b An event loop
   c Neither a nor b
   d Both a and b

2 Can two functions execute at the same time in an event-loop-based asynchronous system?

   a Yes
   b No

3 Can two functions execute at the same time in a thread-based asynchronous system?

   a Yes
   b No

6.4 Simplifying asynchronous code

Callbacks work in the same way as our counter in the preceding example. Whereas the counter enqueues another call to itself after each run, an asynchronous function can take another function as an argument and enqueue a call to that function when it completes execution.

As an example, let's enhance our counter in the next listing with a callback that gets queued after the counter reaches 0.

Listing 6.13 Counter with callback

```
function countDown(counterId: string, from: number,
    callback: () => void): void {
    console.log(`${counterId}: ${from}`);

    if (from > 0)
        queue.push(() => countDown(counterId, from - 1, callback));
```

We add the callback argument, which is a function with no arguments that returns void.

```
    else
        queue.push(callback);
}
```
| When we're done counting down, we queue the callback to be executed.

```
queue.push(() => countDown('counter1', 4,
    () => console.log('Done')));
```
| We provide a callback that prints "Done" when the counter completes.

Callbacks are a common pattern for dealing with asynchronous code. In our example, we used a callback without arguments, but callbacks can also receive arguments from the asynchronous function. That was the case with our asynchronous `question()` call from the `readline` module, which passed the string provided by the user to the callback.

Chaining multiple asynchronous functions with callbacks leads to a lot of nested functions, as we can see in listing 6.14, in which we want to ask the user's name with a `getUserName()` function, ask their birthday with a `getUserBirthday()` function, ask their email address, and so on. The functions depend on one another because each of them requires some information from the preceding one. (`getUser-Birthday()` requires the user's name, for example.) Each function is also asynchronous, as it is potentially long-running, so it takes a callback to provide its result. We use these callbacks to call the next function in the chain.

Listing 6.14   Chaining callbacks

```
declare function getUserName(
    callback: (name: string) => void): void;
declare function getUserBirthday(name: string,
    callback: (birthday: Date) => void): void;
declare function getUserEmail(birthday: Date,
    callback: (email: string) => void): void;

getUserName((name: string) => {
    console.log(`Hi ${name}!`);
    getUserBirthday(name, (birthday: Date) => {
        const today: Date = new Date();
        if (birthday.getMonth() == today.getMonth() &&
            birthday.getDay() == today.getDay())
            console.log('Happy birthday!');

        getUserEmail(birthday, (email: string) => {
            /* ... */
        });
    })
});
```
| We won't provide implementations for these functions—just declarations.

| The callback to getUserName() calls getUserBirthday().

| The callback to getUserBirthday() calls getUserEmail() and so on.

In the callback invoked when `getUserName()` obtains the name, we call `getUser-Birthday()`, passing it the name. In the callback invoked when `getUserBirthday()` obtains the birthday, we call `getUserEmail()` passing in the birthday and so on.

We won't go over the actual implementation of all the `getUser...` functions in this example, as they would be similar to the `greet()` implementation in the preceding section. We're more concerned here with the overall structure of the calling code.

Structuring code this way makes it hard to read, as the more callbacks we chain together, the more nested lambdas inside lambdas we end up with. It turns out that there is a better abstraction for this pattern of asynchronous function calls: promises.

6.4.1 Chaining promises

We start by observing that a function such as `getUserName(callback: (name: string) => void)` is an asynchronous function that will, at some point in time, determine the user's name and then hand it over to a callback we provide. In other words, `getUserName()` "promises" to give back a name string eventually. We also observe that whenever the function has the promised value, we want it to call another function, passing that value as an argument.

> **PROMISES AND CONTINUATIONS** A *promise* is a proxy for a value that will be available at a future point in time. Until the code that produces the value runs, other code can use the promise to set up how the value will be processed when it arrives, what to do in case of error, and even to cancel the future execution. A function set up to be called when the result of a promise is available is called a *continuation*.

The two main ingredients of a promise are a value of some type `T` that our function "promises" to give us and the ability to specify a function from `T` to some other type `U` (`(value: T) => U`), to be called when the promise is fulfilled and we have our value (a continuation). This is an alternative to supplying the callback directly to a function.

First, let's update the declarations of our functions in listing 6.15 so that instead of taking a callback argument, they return a `Promise`. `getUserName()` will return a `Promise<string>`, `getUserBirthday()` will return a `Promise<Date>`, and `getUserEmail()` will return another `Promise<string>`.

Listing 6.15 Functions returning promises

```
declare function getUserName(): Promise<string>;
declare function getUserBirthday(name: string): Promise<Date>;
declare function getUserEmail(birthday: Date): Promise<string>;
```

JavaScript (and, thus, TypeScript) provides a built-in `Promise<T>` type that implements this abstraction. In C#, `Task<T>` implements this, and in Java, `Completable-Future<T>` provides similar functionality.

A promise provides a `then()` method that allows us to pass in our continuation. Each `then()` function returns another promise, so we can chain `then()` calls together. This process eliminates the nesting we saw in the callback-based implementation.

Listing 6.16 Chaining promises

```
getUserName()
    .then((name: string) => {           ◁─── We call then() on the promise
        console.log(`Hi ${name}!`);           returned by getUserName().
```

```
        return getUserBirthday(name);
})
.then((birthday: Date) => {
    const today: Date = new Date();
    if (birthday.getMonth() == today.getMonth() &&
        birthday.getDay() == today.getDay())
        console.log('Happy birthday!');
    return getUserEmail(birthday);
})
.then((email: string) => {
    /* ... */
});
```

In this continuation, we use the value provided by getUserName().

Because then() returns another promise, we can call then() on the returned value again . . .

. . . and again.

As we can see, instead of having a callback within a callback within a callback, continuations are chained together in a pattern that's easier to follow: we run a function, then() we run another function, and so on.

6.4.2 *Creating promises*

If we want to use this pattern, we should also look at how we can create a promise. The principle is straightforward, though it relies on higher-order functions—a promise takes as argument a function that takes as argument another function—so it may seem mind-bending at first.

A promise for a value of a certain type, such as `Promise<string>`, doesn't really know how to compute that value. It provides a `then()` method for the continuation chaining we saw before, but it cannot determine what the string is. In the case of `getUserName()`, the promised string is the name of the user, and in the case of `getUserEmail()`, the promised string is an email address. How, then, could a generic `Promise<string>` be able to determine that value? The answer is that it can't without help. The constructor of a promise takes as an argument a function that actually handles computing the value. For `getUserName()`, that function would prompt the user for their name and get their reply. The promise can then use this function by calling it directly, queuing it for the event loop, or scheduling its execution on a thread, depending on the implementation, which differs from language to language and library to library.

So far, so good. The `Promise<string>` gets some code that will provide the value. But because that code might run at a later time, we also need a mechanism for that code to tell the promise that the value has arrived. For that task, the promise will pass a function called `resolve()` to that code. When the value is determined, the code can call `resolve()` and hand the value back to the promise (figure 6.9).

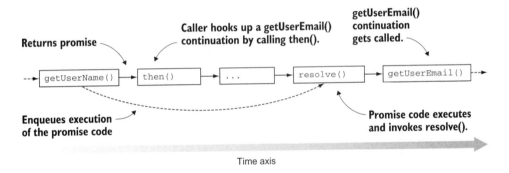

Figure 6.9 `getUserName()` enqueues the code to get the username and returns a `Promise<string>`. The caller of `getUserName()` can call `then()` on the promise to hook up the `getUserEmail()` continuation—code to be run when we have a username. At some later time, the code to get the user name runs and calls `resolve()` with the username. At this point, the continuation `getUserEmail()` gets called with the now-available user name.

Let's look at how we can implement `getUserName()` in the next listing to return a promise.

Listing 6.17 `getUserName()` returning a promise

```
function getUserName(): Promise<string> {
    return new Promise<string>(
        (resolve: (value: string) => void) => {
        const readline = require('readline');

        const rl = readline.createInterface({
            input: process.stdin,
            output: process.stdout
        });

        rl.question("What is your name? ", (name: string) => {
            rl.close();
            resolve(name);
        });
    });
}
```

We pass a lambda to the Promise constructor, which expects as argument a resolve() function.

We use the same code as in greet() to read a string from stdin.

Finally, when we have a name, we call the provided resolve() function and pass it the name.

`getUserName()` simply creates and returns a promise. The promise is initialized with a function that takes a `resolve` argument of type `(value: string) => void`. This function contains the code to ask the user to provide their name, and when the name is provided, the function calls `resolve()` to pass the value to the promise.

If we implement long-running functions to return promises, we can chain these asynchronous calls together by using `Promise.then()` to make our code more readable.

6.4.3   *More about promises*

There's more to promises than providing continuations. Let's see how promises handle errors and a couple more ways to sequence their execution beyond using `then()`.

HANDLING ERRORS

A promise can be in one of three states: pending, settled, and rejected. *Pending* means that the promise has been created but not yet resolved (that is, the provided function responsible for providing a value hasn't called `resolve()` yet). *Settled* means that `resolve()` was called and a value is provided, at which point continuations are called. But what happens if there is an error? When the function responsible for providing a value throws an exception, the promise enters the *rejected* state.

In fact, the function responsible for providing a value to the promise can take an additional function as an argument, so it can set the promise in the rejected state and provide a reason for that. Instead of providing

```
(resolve: (value: T) => void) => void
```

to the constructor, callers can provide a

```
(resolve: (value: T) => void, reject: (reason: any) => void) => void
```

The second argument is a function `(reason: any) => void`, which can provide a reason of any type to the promise and mark it as rejected.

Even without calling `reject()`, if the function throws an exception, the promise will automatically consider itself to be rejected. Besides the `then()` function, a promise exposes a `catch()` function in which we can provide a continuation to be called when the promise is rejected for whatever reason (figure 6.10).

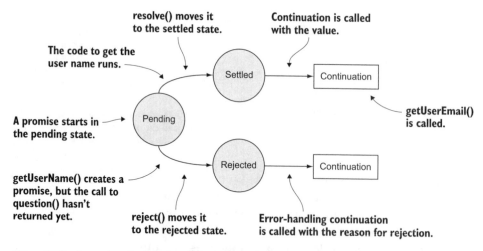

Figure 6.10   A promise starts in the *pending* state. (`getUserName()` scheduled the code to prompt the user, but `question()` hasn't returned yet.) `resolve()` transitions it to the *settled* state and invokes a continuation if one is provided (after the user provided their name). A value is available so the continuation can be called (`getUserEmail()`, in our case). `reject()` transitions the promise to the rejected state and invokes an error-handling continuation, if one is provided. A value is not available; a reason for the error is available instead.

Let's extend our `getUserName()` function to reject an empty string in the next listing.

Listing 6.18   Rejecting a promise

```
function getUserName(): Promise<string> {
    const readline = require('readline');

    const rl = readline.createInterface({
        input: process.stdin,
        output: process.stdout
    });

    return new Promise<string>(
        (resolve: (value: string) => void,
         reject: (reason: string) => void) => {        ◁──  We provide the
            rl.question("What is your name? ", (name: string) => {   additional reject
                rl.close();                                          argument.

                if (name.length != 0) {
                    resolve(name);
                } else {
                    reject("Name can't be empty");    ◁──  If name.length is 0,
                }                                           we reject the promise.
            });
        });
}

getUserName()                                              The new continuation hooked up
    .then((name: string) => { console.log(`Hi ${name}!`); })   with catch() gets called on reject
    .catch((reason: string) => { console.log(`Error: ${reason}`); });   (or if an exception is thrown). ◁──
```

Not only does a promise get rejected, either via a call to `reject()` or due to an error being thrown, but also all other promises chained to it via `then()` get rejected. A `catch()` continuation added at the end of a chain of `then()` calls will get called if any of the promises in the chain is rejected.

CHAINING SYNCHRONOUS FUNCTIONS

There are more ways to chain continuations together than what we've covered so far. First, a continuation doesn't have to return a promise. We don't always chain asynchronous functions; maybe the continuation is short-running and can be executed synchronously. Let's take another look at our original example in the following listing, in which all our continuations returned promises.

Listing 6.19   Chaining functions returning promises

```
getUserName()                          ◁──  getUserName() returns
    .then((name: string) => {               a Promise<string>.
        console.log(`Hi ${name}!`);
        return getUserBirthday(name);  ◁──  getUserBirthday() returns
    })                                      a Promise<Date>.
    .then((birthday: Date) => {
        const today: Date = new Date();
        if (birthday.getMonth() == today.getMonth() &&
            birthday.getDay() == today.getDay())
```

```
            console.log('Happy birthday!');
        return getUserEmail(birthday);
    })
    .then((email: string) => {
        /* ... */
    });
```

getUserEmail() returns a
Promise<string>.

In this case, all our functions need to run asynchronously, as they expect user input. But what if after we get the user's name, we simply want to splice it inside a string and return that? If our continuation is just return `Hi ${name}!`, it returns a string, not a promise. But that's OK; the then() function automatically converts it in a Promise<string> so that it can be further processed by another continuation, as shown in the following code.

Listing 6.20 Chaining functions that don't return promises

```
getUserName()
    .then((name: string) => {
        return `Hi ${name}!`;
    })
    .then((greeting: string) => {
        console.log(greeting);
    });
```

In this case, we don't return a
promise, but then() converts
this to a Promise<string>.

This should make sense intuitively: even if our continuation just returns a string, because it is chained to a promise, it can't execute right away. That fact automatically makes it a promise to be settled when the original promise is settled.

OTHER WAYS TO COMPOSE PROMISES

So far, we've looked at then() (and catch()), which chain promises together so that they settle one after the other. There are a couple more ways to schedule the execution of asynchronous functions: via Promise.all() and Promise.race(). These are static methods provided on the Promise class. Promise.all() takes as arguments a set of promises and returns a promise that is settled when *all* the provided promises are settled. Promise.race() takes a set of promises and returns a promise that is settled when *any one* of the promises is settled.

We can use Promise.all() when we want to schedule a set of independent asynchronous functions, such as fetching user inbox messages from a database and their profile picture from a CDN, and then passing both values to the UI, as shown in listing 6.21. We don't want to sequence these fetching functions one after another, because they don't depend on one another. On the other hand, we do want to gather their results and pass them to another function.

Listing 6.21 Using Promise.all() to sequence execution

```
class InboxMessage { /* ... */ }
class ProfilePicture { /* ... */ }

declare function getInboxMessages(): Promise<InboxMessage[]>;
declare function getProfilePicture(): Promise<ProfilePicture>;
```

getInboxMessages() and getProfilePicture() are
independent asynchronous functions.

```
declare function renderUI(
    messages: InboxMessage[], picture: ProfilePicture): void;

Promise.all([getInboxMessages(), getProfilePicture()])
    .then((values: [InboxMessage[], ProfilePicture]) => {
        renderUI(values[0], values[1]);
    });
```

renderUI() needs the result from both functions.

values is a tuple containing both results.

We pass the values retrieved to renderUI().

Promise.all() creates a promise settled when both functions resolve their promises.

A pattern like this would be significantly harder to achieve with callbacks, as there is no mechanism to join them.

Let's look at an example of using `Promise.race()` in the next listing. Suppose that the user profile is replicated across two nodes. We try to fetch it from both, and whichever is the fastest wins. In this case, as soon as we get a result from any one of the nodes, we can proceed.

Listing 6.22   Using `Promise.race()` to sequence execution

```
class UserProfile { /* ... */ }

declare function getProfile(node: string): Promise<UserProfile>;

declare function renderUI(profile: UserProfile): void;

Promise.race([getProfile("node1"), getProfile("node2")])
    .then((profile: UserProfile) => {
        renderUI(profile);
    });
```

We call getProfile() once for each of the nodes.

The argument to the continuation is a single UserProfile in this case—the one that won the race.

This scenario would be more difficult to achieve by using callbacks without promises (figure 6.11).

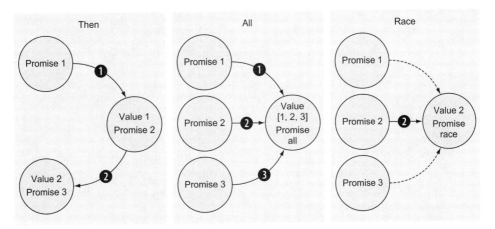

Figure 6.11   Different ways to combine a promise. *Then:* Promise 1 settles and hands out Value 1 to Promise 2; Promise 2 settles and hands out Value 2 to Promise 3. *All:* Promise 1, 2, and 3 settle. When all of them are settled, Promise.all gets all their values and can proceed, settling its own value. *Race:* One of the promises settles first (in this case, Promise 2). Promise.race gets Value 2 and can proceed, settling its own value.

Promises provide a clean abstraction for running asynchronous functions. They not only make code more readable than using callbacks through the `then()` and `catch()` methods, which enable sequencing, but also handle error propagation and joining or racing multiple promises via `Promise.all()` and `Promise.race()`. Promise libraries are available in most mainstream programming languages, and they all provide similar functionality, even if the name of the methods is slightly different. (`race()` is sometimes called `any()`, for example.)

This is about as far as libraries can go in helping us write clean asynchronous code. Making asynchronous code more readable requires updates to the syntax of the language itself. Much as a `yield` statement allows us to more easily express a generator function, many languages extended their syntax with `async` and `await` to enable us to write asynchronous functions more easily.

6.4.4   *async/await*

Using promises, we prompted our user for various pieces of information, using continuations to sequence the questions. Let's take another look at that implementation in the next listing. We're going to wrap it into a `getUserData()` function.

Listing 6.23   Chaining promises review

```
function getUserData(): void {
    getUserName()
        .then((name: string) => {
            console.log(`Hi ${name}!`);
            return getUserBirthday(name);
        })
        .then((birthday: Date) => {
            const today: Date = new Date();
            if (birthday.getMonth() == today.getMonth() &&
                birthday.getDay() == today.getDay())
                console.log('Happy birthday!');
            return getUserEmail(birthday);
        })
        .then((email: string) => {
            /* ... */
        });
}
```

Notice again that each continuation takes as argument a value of the same type as the type of the promise from the preceding function. `async/await` allows us to express this better in code. We can draw a parallel with generators and the `*`/`yield` syntax we discussed in a previous section.

`async` is a keyword that comes before the keyword `function`, much as the `*` appears after the keyword `function` in generators. In the same way that `*` can be used only if the function returns an `Iterator`, `async` can appear only in a function that returns a `Promise`, just as `*`, `async` does not change the type of the function.

`function getUserData(): Promise<string>` and `async function getUser-Data(): Promise<string>` have the same type: `() => Promise<string>`. The same way that `*` marks a function as a generator and allows us to call `yield` inside it, `async` marks a function as asynchronous and allows us to call `await` inside it.

We can use `await` before a function that returns a promise to get the value returned when that promise settles. Instead of writing `getUserName().then ((name: string) => { /* … */ })`, we write `let name: string = await getUserName()`. Before walking through how this works, let's look at how we would write `getUserData()` with `async` and `await`.

Listing 6.24 Using `async`/`await`

```
async function getUserData(): Promise<void> {
    let name: string = await getUserName();
    console.log(`Hi ${name}!`);

    let birthday: Date = await getUserBirthday(name);
    const today: Date = new Date();
    if (birthday.getMonth() == today.getMonth() &&
        birthday.getDay() == today.getDay())
        console.log('Happy birthday!');

    let email: string = await getUserEmail(birthday);
    /* ... */
}
```

getUserData() must return a Promise because it is marked as async.

We can use this name string in this same function.

We await getUserName() to settle and give us a name string.

We await getUserBirthday() to settle and give us a birthday.

The same is true for getUserEmail(); we await the settled promise and get the string value.

We immediately see that writing our `getUserData()` this way makes it even more readable than chaining promises with `then()`. The compiler generates the same code; there is nothing special under the hood. This technique is simply a nicer way to express a chain of continuations. Instead of putting each continuation in a separate function and connecting them via `then()`, we can write all the code in a single function, and whenever we call another function that returns a promise, we `await` its result.

Each `await` is the equivalent of taking the code after it and placing it in a `then()` continuation: this reduces the number of lambdas we need to write and makes asynchronous code read just like synchronous code. As for `catch()`, if there is no value to return, perhaps because we encountered an exception, the exception is thrown from the `await` call and can be caught with a regular `try/catch` statement. Simply wrap the `await` call in a `try` block to catch the expected errors.

6.4.5 *Clean asynchronous code recap*

Let's quickly review the approaches to writing asynchronous code that we covered in this section. We started with callbacks, passing a callback function to an asynchronous function that calls it when its work is done. This approach works, but we'll usually end up with a lot of nested callbacks within callbacks, which makes code harder to follow. It's also very difficult to join several independent asynchronous functions if we need the results from all of them to proceed.

Next, we looked at promises. Promises provide an abstraction for writing asynchronous code. They handle scheduling the execution of the code (in languages that rely on threads, they get scheduled on threads) and provide a way for us to provide functions called continuations, which get called when the promise is settled (has a value) or rejected (encountered an error). Promises also provide ways to join and race a set of promises via `Promise.all()` and `Promise.race()`.

Finally, `async/await` syntax, now common in most mainstream programming languages, provides an even-cleaner way to write asynchronous code that reads just like regular code. Instead of providing a continuation with `then()`, we `await` the result of a promise and continue from there. The underlying code executed by the computer is the same, but the syntax is much nicer to read.

6.4.6   *Exercises*

1 Which state does a promise start in?

   a Settled

   b Rejected

   c Pending

   d Any

2 Which of the following chains a continuation to be called when the promise is rejected?

   a `then()`

   b `catch()`

   c `all()`

   d `race()`

3 Which of the following chains a continuation to be called when a whole set of promises is settled?

   a `then()`

   b `catch()`

   c `all()`

   d `race()`

Summary

- A closure is a lambda that also holds on to a piece of state from its surrounding function.
- We can implement a simpler decorator pattern by using a closure and capturing the decorated function instead of implementing a whole new type.
- We can implement a counter by using a closure that tracks the counter state.

- A generator, written using */yield syntax, is a resumable function.
- Long-running operations should run asynchronously so that they don't block the rest of the program.
- The two main models for asynchronous execution are threads and event loops.
- A callback is a function passed to an asynchronous function that is invoked when the asynchronous function completes.
- Promises provide a common abstraction for running asynchronous functions and provide continuations as an alternative to callbacks. A promise can be pending, settled (value obtained), or rejected (error encountered).
- `Promise.all()` and `Promise.race()` are mechanisms for joining and racing a set of promises.
- `async/await` is modern syntax for writing promise-based code as though it were synchronous code.

Now that we've covered applications of function types in depth, from the basics of passing functions as arguments all the way to generators and asynchronous functions, we'll move on to the next major topic: subtypes. As we'll see in chapter 7, there is a lot more to subtypes than inheritance.

Answers to exercises

A SIMPLE DECORATOR PATTERN

1 A possible implementation returning a function that adds logging to the wrapped factory:

```
function loggingDecorator(factory: () => Widget): () => Widget {
    return () => {
        console.log("Widget created");
        return factory();
    }
}
```

IMPLEMENTING A COUNTER

2 A possible implementation using a closure that captures a and b from the wrapping function:

```
function fib(): () => number {
    let a: number = 0;
    let b: number = 1;

    return () => {
        let next: number = a;
        a = b;
        b = b + next;
        return next;
    }
}
```

3 A possible implementation using a generator that yields the next number in the sequence:

```
function *fib2(): IterableIterator<number> {
    let a: number = 0;
    let b: number = 1;

    while (true) {
        let next: number = a;
        a = b;
        b = a + next;
        yield next;
    }
}
```

EXECUTING LONG-RUNNING OPERATIONS ASYNCHRONOUSLY

1 d—Both threads and an event loop can be used to implement asynchronous execution.

2 b—An event loop does not execute code in parallel. It can queue and execute functions asynchronously, but not at the same time.

3 a—Threads allow parallel execution; multiple threads can run multiple functions at the same time.

SIMPLIFYING ASYNCHRONOUS CODE

1 c—A promise starts in the pending state.

2 c—We use catch() to chain a continuation that gets called when a promise is rejected.

3 c—We use all() to chain a continuation that gets called when all promises are settled.

Subtyping 7

This chapter covers

- Disambiguating types in TypeScript
- Safe deserialization
- Values for error cases
- Type compatibility for sum types, collections, and functions

Now that we've covered primitive types, composition, and function types, it's time to look at another aspect of type systems: relationships between types. In this chapter, we'll introduce the subtyping relationship. Although you may be familiar with it from object-oriented programming, we will not cover inheritance in this chapter. Instead, we will focus on a different set of applications of subtyping.

First, we'll talk about what subtyping is and the two ways in which programming languages implement it: structural and nominal. Then we will revisit our Mars Climate Orbiter example and explain the `unique symbol` trick we used in chapter 4 when discussing type safety.

Because a type can be a subtype of another type, and it can also have other subtypes, we will look at this type hierarchy: we usually have a type that sits at the top of this hierarchy and, sometimes, a type that sits at the bottom. We'll see how we can use this top type in a scenario such as deserialization, in which we don't have a lot of typing information readily available. We'll also see how to use a bottom type as a value for error cases.

In the second half of the chapter, we will look at how more-complex subtyping relationships are established. This helps us understand what values we can substitute for what other values. Do we need to implement wrappers, or can we simply pass a value of another type as is? If a type is a subtype of another type, what is the subtyping relationship between collections of those two types? What about functions that take or return arguments of these types? We'll take a simple example involving shapes and see how we can pass them around as sum types, collections, and functions, a process also known as *variance*. We'll also learn about the different types of variance. But first, let's see what subtyping means in TypeScript.

7.1 *Distinguishing between similar types in TypeScript*

Most of the examples in this book, even though presented in TypeScript, are language-agnostic and can be translated for most other mainstream programming languages. This section is an exception; we'll discuss a technique specific to TypeScript. We'll do this because it's a great segue into a discussion of subtyping.

Let's revisit the pound-force second/Newton-second example from chapter 4. Remember that we were modeling two different units of measurements as two different classes. We wanted to make sure that the type checker wouldn't allow us to misinterpret a value of one type as the other, so we used `unique symbol` to disambiguate them. We didn't go into the details of why we had to do this then, but let's do it now in the following listing.

Listing 7.1   Pound-force second and Newton-second types

```
declare const NsType: unique symbol;

class Ns {
    value: number;
    [NsType]: void;

    constructor(value: number) {
        this.value = value;
    }
}

declare const LbfsType: unique symbol;

class Lbfs {
    value: number;
    [LbfsType]: void;

    constructor(value: number) {
        this.value = value;
    }
}
```

We declare NsType as a unique symbol and add a property named [NsType] of type void to Ns.

We also declare a LbfsType as a unique symbol and add a [LbfsType] property of type void to Lbfs.

If we omit these two declarations, an interesting thing happens: we can pass a Ns object as a Lbfs object, and vice versa, without getting any errors from the compiler. Let's implement a function to demonstrate this process: a function named acceptNs() that expects a Ns argument. Then we'll try to pass a Lbfs object to acceptNs() in the next listing.

Listing 7.2   Pound-force second and Newton-second without unique symbols

```
class Ns {                              ◁─────┐
    value: number;                            │
                                              │   Ns and Lbfs no longer have
    constructor(value: number) {              │   a unique symbol property.
        this.value = value;                   │
    }                                         │
}                                             │
                                              │
class Lbfs {                            ◁─────┘
    value: number;

    constructor(value: number) {
        this.value = value;
    }
}
                                                        acceptNs() takes a Ns object as
function acceptNs(momentum: Ns): void {      ◁──────┐   an argument and logs its value.
    console.log(`Momentum: ${momentum.value} Ns`);
}                                                    We pass a Lbfs
                                                     instance to acceptNs().
acceptNs(new Lbfs(10));                      ◁──────┘
```

Surprisingly, this code works and logs Momentum: 10 Ns., which is definitely not what we want. The reason why we defined these two separate types was to avoid confusing the two units of measure and crashing the Mars Climate Orbiter. What's going on? To understand what is happening, we need to understand subtyping.

> **SUBTYPING**   A type S is a subtype of a type T if an instance of S can be safely used anywhere an instance of T is expected.

This is an informal definition of the famous *Liskov substitution principle*. Two types are in a subtype-supertype relationship if we can use an instance of the subtype whenever an instance of the supertype is expected without having to change the code.

There are two ways in which subtyping relationships are established. The first one, which most mainstream programming languages (such as Java and C#) use, is called *nominal subtyping*. In nominal subtyping, a type is the subtype of another type if we explicitly declare it as such, using syntax like class Triangle extends Shape. Now we can use an instance of Triangle whenever an instance of Shape is expected (such as as argument to a function). If we don't declare Triangle as extending Shape, the compiler won't allow us to use it as a Shape.

On the other hand, *structural subtyping* doesn't require us to state the subtyping relationship explicitly in code. An instance of a type, such as Lbfs, can be used instead of another type, such as Ns, as long as it has all the members that the other type declares. In other words, if a type has a similar structure to another type (the same members and optionally additional members), it is automatically considered to be a subtype of that other type.

> **NOMINAL AND STRUCTURAL SUBTYPING**   In nominal subtyping, a type is a subtype of another type if we explicitly declare it as such. In structural subtyping, a type is a subtype of another type if it has all the members of the supertype and, optionally, additional members.

Unlike C# and Java, TypeScript uses structural subtyping. That's the reason why, if we declare Ns and Lbfs as classes with only a value member of type number, they can still be used interchangeably.

7.1.1   *Structural and nominal subtyping pros and cons*

In many cases, structural subtyping is useful, as it allows us to establish relationships between types even if they are not under our control. Suppose that a library we use defines a User type as having a name and age. In our code, we have a Named interface that requires a name property on implementing types. We can use an instance of User whenever a Named is expected, even though User does not explicitly implement Named, as shown in the next listing. (We don't have the declaration class User implements Named.)

Listing 7.3   User is structurally a subtype of Named

```
/* Library code */
class User {                        User is a type from
    name: string;                   an external library that
    age: number;                    we can't modify.

    constructor(name: string, age: number) {
        this.name = name;
        this.age = age;
    }
}

/* Our code */
interface Named {
    name: string;
}
                                    greet() expects an instance
function greet(named: Named): void {   conforming to the Named interface.
    console.log(`Hi ${named.name}!`);
}
                                    We can pass a User
greet(new User("Alice", 25));       instance as a Named.
```

If we had to explicitly declare that User implements Named, we would be in trouble, because User is a type that comes from an external library. We can't change library code, so we would have to work around this situation by declaring a new type that extends `User` and implements `Named` (`class NamedUser extends User implements Named {}`) just to connect the two types. We don't need to do this if our type system uses structural subtyping.

On the other hand, in some situations we absolutely don't want a type to be considered a subtype of another type based simply on its structure. A `Lbfs` instance should never be used instead of a `Ns` instance, for example. In nominal subtyping, this is the default, which makes it very easy to avoid mistakes. On the other hand, structural subtyping requires us to do more work to ensure that a value is of the type we expect it to be rather than a value of a type with a similar shape. In such scenarios, structural subtyping is much better.

If we want to use nominal subtyping, we can use several techniques to enforce it in TypeScript. One of them is the `unique symbol` trick we've used throughout the book. Let's zoom in on it.

7.1.2 *Simulating nominal subtyping in TypeScript*

In our `Ns`/`Lbfs` case, we are effectively trying to simulate nominal subtyping. We want to make sure that the compiler considers a type to be a subtype of `Ns` only if we explicitly declare it as such, not just because it has a `value` member.

To achieve this, we need to add a member to `Ns` that no other type can declare accidentally. In TypeScript, `unique symbol` generates a "name" that's guaranteed to be unique across all the code. Different `unique symbol` declarations will generate different names, and no user-declared name can ever match a generated name.

We declare a unique symbol to represent our `Ns` type as `NsType`. The unique symbol declaration looks like this: `declare const NsType: unique symbol` (as in listing 7.1). Now that we have a unique name, we can create a property with that name by putting the name in square brackets. We need to define a type for this property, but we aren't really going to assign anything to it because we're just using it to disambiguate types. Because we don't care about its actual value, a unit type is best suited for this purpose, so we use `void`.

We do the same for `Lbfs`, and now the types have different structures: one of them has a `[NsType]` property, and the other has a `[LbfsType]` property, as shown in listing 7.4. Because we used `unique symbol`, it's impossible to accidentally define a property with the same name on another type. The only way to come up with a subtype for `Ns` and `Lbfs` now is to explicitly inherit from them.

Listing 7.4 Simulating nominal subtyping

```
declare const NsType: unique symbol;

class Ns {
    value: number;
    [NsType]: void;

    constructor(value: number) {
        this.value = value;
```

```
    }
}

declare const LbfsType: unique symbol;

class Lbfs {
    value: number;
    [LbfsType]: void;

    constructor(value: number) {
        this.value = value;
    }
}

function acceptNs(momentum: Ns): void {
    console.log(`Momentum: ${momentum.value} Ns`);
}

acceptNs(new Lbfs(10));
```

This no longer compiles.

When we try to pass a Lbfs instance as a Ns, we get the following error:

```
Argument of type 'Lbfs' is not assignable to parameter of
type 'Ns'. Property '[NsType]' is missing in type 'Lbfs'
but required in type 'Ns'.
```

In this section, we saw a definition of subtyping and learned about the two ways in which the subtyping relationship between two types can be established: nominally (because we say so) and structurally (because the types have the same structure). We also saw how, even though TypeScript uses structural subtyping, we can simulate nominal subtyping by using unique symbols for the situations in which structural subtyping is not appropriate.

7.1.3 *Exercises*

1 In TypeScript, is Painting a subtype of Wine for the types defined as

```
class Wine {
    name: string;
    year: number;
}

class Painting {
    name: string;
    year: number;
    painter: Painter;
}
```

2 In TypeScript, is Car a subtype of Wine for the types defined as
```
class Wine {
    name: string;
    year: number;
}
```

```
class Car {
    make: string;
    model: string;
    year: number;
}
```

7.2   Assigning anything to, assigning to anything

Now that we've learned about subtyping, let's look at a couple of extremes: a type to which we can assign anything and a type that we can assign to anything. The first one is a type we can use to store absolutely anything. The second is a type we can use instead of any other type if we don't have an instance of that other type handy.

7.2.1   Safe deserialization

We covered the unknown and any types in chapter 4. unknown is a type that can store a value of any other type. We mentioned that other object-oriented languages usually provide a type named Object with similar behavior. In fact, TypeScript has an Object type too; it provides a few common methods such as toString(). But the story doesn't end there, as we'll see in this section.

The any type is more dangerous. We can not only assign any value to it, but also assign an any value to any other type, bypassing type checking. This type is used for interoperability with JavaScript code but may have unintended consequences. Suppose that we have a function that deserializes an object using the standard JSON.parse(), as shown in the next listing. Because JSON.parse() is a JavaScript function with which TypeScript interoperates, it is not strongly typed; its return type is any. Assume that we are expecting to deserialize a User instance that has a name property.

Listing 7.5   Deserializing any

```
class User {
    name: string;                          ◁─── The User type has
                                                a name property.
    constructor(name: string) {
        this.name = name;
    }
}

function deserialize(input: string): any {    deserialize() simply wraps
    return JSON.parse(input);              ◁─── JSON.parse() and returns
}                                               a value of type any.

function greet(user: User): void {            greet() uses the name property
    console.log(`Hi ${user.name}!`);       ◁─── of the given User object.
}
                                              We deserialize a
greet(deserialize('{ "name": "Alice" }'));  ◁─── valid User JSON.
greet(deserialize('{}'));        ◁─── We can also deserialize an
                                     object that is not a User object.
```

The last call to greet() will log "Hi undefined!" because any bypasses type check-ing, and the compiler allows us to treat the returned value as a value of type User, even when we didn't get a value of that type. This result is clearly not ideal. We need to check that we have the right type before we call greet().

In this case, we'd want to ensure that the object we have has a name property of type string, which in our case is enough to cast it into a User. We should also check that our object is not null or undefined, which are special types in TypeScript. One way of doing this is to update our code with such a check and call it before calling greet(). Note that this type check is done at run time, because it depends on the input value and is not something that can be enforced statically.

Listing 7.6   Run-time type checking for `User`

```
class User {
    name: string;

    constructor(name: string) {
        this.name = name;
    }
}

function deserialize(input: string): any {
    return JSON.parse(input);
}

function greet(user: User): void {
    console.log(`Hi ${user.name}!`);
}

function isUser(user: any): user is User {          ⟵  This function checks whether
    if (user === null || user === undefined)             the given argument is of type
        return false;                                    User. We consider a variable
                                                         with a name property of type
    return typeof user.name === 'string';                string to be of User type.
}

let user: any = deserialize('{ "name": "Alice" }');
if (isUser(user))                                   ⟵⎤
    greet(user);                                         Checks that user has a
                                                         property name of type
user = undefined;                                        string before each use.
if (isUser(user))                                   ⟵⎦
    greet(user);
```

The `user is User` return type of isUser() is a bit of TypeScript-specific syntax, but I hope that it's not too confusing. This type is very much like a boolean return type, but it carries extra meaning for the compiler. If the function returns true, the vari-able user has type User, and the compiler can use that information in the caller. Effectively, within each if block in which isUser() returned true, user has type User instead of any.

This approach works. Running the code executes only the first call when our user-name is Alice. The second call to greet() will not be executed because in this case, there is no name property on user. There's still a problem with this approach, though: we are not forced to implement this check. Because no enforcement is going on, we could make a mistake and forget to call it, which would allow an arbitrary result from deserialize() to make its way to greet(), and there's nothing to stop it from doing so.

Wouldn't it be great if we had another way of saying, "This object can be of absolutely any type" but without the additional "Trust me, I know what I'm doing" that any implies? We need another type—a type that is a supertype of any other type in the system, which means that regardless of what JSON.parse() returns, it will be a subtype of this type. From there on, the type system will ensure that we add the proper type checking before we cast it to User.

TOP TYPE   A type to which we can assign any value is also called a *top type* because any other type is a subtype of this type. In other words, this type sits at the top of the subtyping hierarchy (figure 7.1).

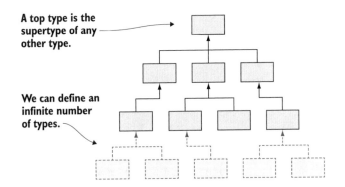

A top type is the supertype of any other type.

We can define an infinite number of types.

Figure 7.1   A top type is the supertype of any other type. We can define any number of types, but any of them would be a subtype of the top type. We can use a value of any type wherever the top type is expected.

Let's update our implementation. We can start with the Object type, which is the supertype of *most* types in the type systems, with two exceptions: null and undefined. The TypeScript type system has some great safety features, one of them being the ability to keep null and undefined values outside the domain of other types. Remember the billion-dollar-mistake sidebar in chapter 3—the fact that in most languages, we can assign null to any type. This is not allowed in TypeScript if we use the --strictNullChecks compiler flag (which is strongly recommended). TypeScript considers null to be of type null and undefined to be of type undefined. So our top type, the supertype of absolutely anything, is the sum of these three types: Object | null | undefined. This type is actually defined out of the box as unknown. Let's rewrite our code to use unknown, as shown in the next listing, and then we can discuss the differences between using any and unknown.

Listing 7.7 Stronger typing using `unknown`

```
class User {
    name: string;

    constructor(name: string) {
        this.name = name;
    }
}

function deserialize(input: string): unknown {      ◁─┐ We make deserialize()
    return JSON.parse(input);                            return unknown.
}

function greet(user: User): void {
    console.log(`Hi ${user.name}!`);
}

function isUser(user: any): user is User {      ◁─┐ We keep the isUser()
    if (user === null || user === undefined)        argument as any.
        return false;

    return typeof user.name === 'string';
}
                                                      ┌ We declare our variable
let user: unknown = deserialize('{ "name": "Alice" }');  ◁─┘ as having type unknown.
if (isUser(user))
    greet(user);

user = deserialize("null");
if (isUser(user))
    greet(user);
```

The change is subtle but powerful: as soon as we get a value from `JSON.parse()`, we convert it from `any` to `unknown`. This process is safe, because anything can be converted to `unknown`. We keep the argument of `isUser()` as `any`, because it makes our implementation easier. (We wouldn't be allowed to perform a check such as `typeof user.name` on an `unknown` without extra casting.)

The code works as before, the distinction being that if we remove any of the `isUser()` calls, the code no longer compiles. The compiler issues the following error:

```
Argument of type 'unknown' is not assignable to parameter
of type 'User'.
```

We can't simply pass a variable of type `unknown` to `greet()`, which expects a `User`. The function `isUser()` helps, as whenever it returns `true`, the compiler automatically considers the variable to have type `User`.

With this implementation, we simply cannot forget to check; the compiler will not allow us. It allows us to use our object as a `User` only after we confirm that `user is User`.

DIFFERENCE BETWEEN UNKNOWN AND ANY　Although we can assign anything to both unknown and any, there is a difference in how we use a variable of one of these types. In the unknown case, we can use the value as some type (such as User) only after we confirm that the value actually has that type (as we did with the function that returns the user as User). In the any case, we can use the value as a value of any other type right away. any bypasses type checking.

Other languages provide different mechanisms to determine whether a value is of a given type. C# has the is keyword, for example, and Java has instanceof. In general, when we deal with a value that could be *anything*, we start by considering it to be a top type. Then we use the appropriate checks to ensure that it is of the type we need before we downcast it to the required type.

7.2.2　Values for error cases

Now let's look at an opposite problem: a type that can be used instead of any other type. Let's take a simple example in listing 7.8. In our game, we can turn our spaceship Left or Right. We'll represent these possible directions as an enumeration. We want to implement a function that takes a direction and converts it to an angle by which we rotate our spaceship. Because we want to make sure that we cover all cases, we'll throw an error if the enumeration has a value different from the two expected Left and Right values.

Listing 7.8　TurnDirection to angle conversion

```
enum TurnDirection {
    Left,
    Right
}

function turnAngle(turn: TurnDirection): number {     A Left turn becomes –90
    switch (turn) {                                   degrees; a Right turn
        case TurnDirection.Left: return -90;          becomes 90 degrees.
        case TurnDirection.Right: return 90;
        default: throw new Error("Unknown TurnDirection");
    }
}
```

We throw an error in case we encounter an unexpected value.

So far, so good. But what if we have a function that handles error scenarios? Suppose that we want to log the error before throwing it. This function would always throw, so we'll declare it as returning the type never, as we saw in chapter 2. As a reminder, never is the empty type that cannot be assigned any value. We use it to explicitly show that a function never returns, either because it loops forever or because it throws, as shown in the next listing.

Listing 7.9   Error reporting

```
function fail(message: string): never {
    console.error(message);
    throw new Error(message);
}
```

Print error to console and then throw.

fail() never returns (always throws), so we declare it as returning never.

If we want to replace the throw statement in turnAngle() with fail(), we end up with something like the following.

Listing 7.10   turnAngle() using fail()

```
function turnAngle(turn: TurnDirection): number {
    switch (turn) {
        case TurnDirection.Left: return -90;
        case TurnDirection.Right: return 90;
        default: fail("Unknown TurnDirection");
    }
}
```

We replace throw with a call to fail().

This code almost works, but not quite. Compilation fails in strict mode (with --strict flag) with the following error:

```
Function lacks ending return statement and return type
does not include "undefined".
```

The compiler doesn't see a return statement on the default branch and flags that as an error. One fix would be to return a dummy value as shown in the next listing, knowing that we throw before reaching it anyway.

Listing 7.11   turnAgain() using fail() and returning a dummy value

```
enum TurnDirection {
    Left,
    Right
}

function turnAngle(turn: TurnDirection): number {
    switch (turn) {
        case TurnDirection.Left: return -90;
        case TurnDirection.Right: return 90;
        default: {
            fail("Unknown TurnDirection");
            return -1;
        }
    }
}
```

Dummy value that will never actually be returned because fail() throws

But what if, at some point in the future, we update fail() in such a way that it doesn't always throw? Then our code would end up returning a dummy value, even though it should never do so. There's a better solution: return the result of fail(), as the following listing shows.

Listing 7.12   `turnAngle()` using `fail()` and returning its result

```
function turnAngle(turn: TurnDirection): number {
    switch (turn) {
        case TurnDirection.Left: return -90;
        case TurnDirection.Right: return 90;
        default: return fail("Unknown TurnDirection");
    }
}
```

Just return whatever
fail() returns.

The reason why this code works is that besides being the type without values, `never` is the type that is the subtype of all other types in the system.

> **BOTTOM TYPE**   A type that is the subtype of any other type is called a *bottom type* because it sits at the bottom of the subtyping hierarchy. To be a subtype of any other possible type, it must have the members of any other possible type. Because we can have an infinite number of types and members, the bottom type would also have to have an infinite number of members. Because that is impossible, the bottom type is always an empty type: a type for which we can't create an actual value (figure 7.2).

Because we can assign `never` to any other type, due to it being a bottom type, we can return it from the function. The compiler will not complain, as this is an upcast (converting a value from a subtype to a supertype), which can be done implicitly. We're saying, "Take this value that is impossible to create and turn it into a string," which is fine. Because the `fail()` function never returns, we never end up in a situation in which we actually have something to turn into a string.

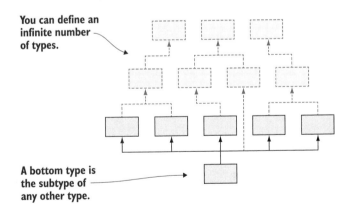

You can define an
infinite number
of types.

A bottom type is
the subtype of
any other type.

Figure 7.2   A bottom type is the subtype of any other type. We can define any number of types, but any of these would be a supertype of the bottom type. We can pass a value of the bottom type wherever a value of any type is required (although we can never produce such a value).

This approach is better than the preceding one because, if we update `fail()` so that it doesn't `throw` in some cases, the compiler will force us to fix all our code. First, it will force us to change the return type of `fail()` from `never` to something else, such as `void`. Then it will see that we are trying to pass that as a `string`, which does not type-check. We will have to update our implementation of `turnAngle()`, perhaps by bringing back the explicit `throw`.

A bottom type allows us to pretend that we have a value of any type even if we can't come up with one.

7.2.3   *Top and bottom types recap*

Let's quickly recap what we covered in this section. Two types can be in a subtyping relationship, in which one of them is the supertype and the other is the subtype. At the extreme, we have a type that is the supertype of any other type and a type that is the subtype of any other type.

The supertype of any other type, called the top type, can be used to hold a value of any other type. That type is `unknown` in TypeScript. One situation in which this comes in handy is when we are dealing with data that can be anything, such as as a JSON document read from a NoSQL database. We initially type such data as the top type and then perform the required checks to cast it down to a type we can work with.

The subtype of any other type, called the bottom type, can be used to produce a value of any other type. This type is `never` in TypeScript. One example application is producing a return value when none can be produced via a function that always throws.

Note that although most mainstream languages provide a top type, few of them provide a bottom type. The DIY implementation we saw in chapter 2 makes a type empty but not bottom. Unless worked into the compiler, there is no way to define our custom bottom type.

Next, let's look at subtyping for more complex types and see how that works.

7.2.4   *Exercises*

1   If we have a function `makeNothing()` that returns `never`, can we initialize a variable x of type `number` with its result (without casting)?

```
declare function makeNothing(): never;

let x: number = makeNothing();
```

2   If we have a function `makeSomething()` that returns `unknown`, can we initialize a variable x of type `number` with its result (without casting)?

```
declare function makeSomething(): unknown;

let x: number = makeSomething();
```

7.3   *Allowed substitutions*

So far, we've looked at a few simple examples of subtyping. We observed, for example, that if `Triangle extends Shape`, `Triangle` is a subtype of `Shape`. Now let's try to answer a few trickier questions:

- What is the subtyping relationship between the sum types `Triangle | Square` and `Triangle | Square | Circle`?
- What is the subtyping relationship between an array of triangles (`Triangle[]`) and an array of shapes (`Shape[]`)?
- What is the subtyping relationship between a generic data structure such as `List<T>`, for `List<Triangle>` and `List<Shape>`?
- What about the function types `() => Shape` and `() => Triangle`?
- Conversely, what about the function type `(argument: Shape) => void` and the function type `(argument: Triangle) => void`?

These questions are important, as they tell us which of these types can be substituted for their subtypes. Whenever we see a function that expects an argument of one of these types, we should understand whether we can provide a subtype instead.

The challenge in the preceding examples is that things aren't as straightforward as `Triangle extends Shape`. We are looking at types that are defined *based* on `Triangle` and `Shape`. `Triangle` and `Shape` are part of the sum types, the types of elements of a collection, or a function's argument types or return types.

7.3.1 Subtyping and sum types

Let's take the simplest example first: the sum type. Suppose that we have a `draw()` function that can draw a `Triangle`, a `Square`, or a `Circle`. Can we pass a `Triangle` or `Square` to it? As you might have guessed, the answer is yes. We can check that such code compiles in the following listing.

Listing 7.13 `Triangle | Square` as `Triangle | Square | Circle`

```
declare const TriangleType: unique symbol;
class Triangle {
    [TriangleType]: void;
    /* Triangle members */
}

declare const SquareType: unique symbol;
class Square {
    [SquareType]: void;
    /* Square members */
}

declare const CircleType: unique symbol;
class Circle {
    [CircleType]: void;
    /* Circle members */
}
declare function makeShape(): Triangle | Square;          ◁── makeShape() returns a Triangle or a Square (implementation omitted).
declare function draw(shape: Triangle | Square | Circle): void;   ◁──┐

draw(makeShape());                                                   draw() accepts a Triangle,
                                                                     a Square, or a Circle
                                                                     (implementation omitted).
```

We enforce nominal subtyping throughout these examples because we're not providing full implementations for these types. In practice, they would have various different properties and methods to distinguish them. We simulate these different properties with unique symbols for our examples, as leaving the classes empty would make all of them equivalent due to TypeScript's structural subtyping.

As expected, this code compiles. The opposite doesn't: if we can draw a `Triangle` or a `Square` and attempt to draw a `Triangle`, `Square`, or `Circle`, the compiler will complain, because we might end up passing a `Circle` to the `draw()` function, which wouldn't know what to do with it. We can confirm that the following code doesn't compile.

Listing 7.14 `Triangle | Square | Circle as Triangle | Square`

```
declare function makeShape(): Triangle | Square | Circle;
declare function draw(shape: Triangle | Square): void;

draw(makeShape());
```

This no longer compiles.

We flipped the types so that makeShape() could also return a Circle, whereas draw() no longer accepts a Circle.

`Triangle | Square` is a subtype of `Triangle | Square | Circle`: we can always substitute a `Triangle` or `Square` for a `Triangle`, `Square`, or `Circle` but not the other way around.

This situation may seem to be counterintuitive, because `Triangle | Square` is "less" than `Triangle | Square | Circle`. Whenever we use inheritance, we end up with a subtype that has more properties than its supertype. For sum types, it works the opposite way: the supertype has more types than the subtype (figure 7.3).

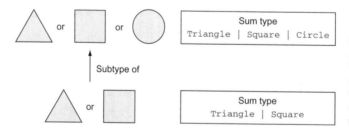

Figure 7.3 `Triangle | Square` **is a subtype of** `Triangle | Square | Circle` **because whenever a** `Triangle`, `Square`, **or** `Circle` **is expected, we can use a** `Triangle` **or a** `Square`.

Say we have an `EquilateralTriangle` which inherits from `Triangle`, as shown in the next listing.

Listing 7.15 `EquilateralTriangle` **declaration**

```
declare const EquilateralTriangleType: unique symbol;
class EquilateralTriangle extends Triangle {
    [EquilateralTriangleType]: void;
    /* EquilateralTriangle members */
}
```

As an exercise, check what happens when we mix sum types with inheritance. Does `makeShape()` returning `EquilateralTriangle | Square` and `draw()` accepting `Triangle | Square | Circle` work? What about `makeShape()` returning `Triangle | Square` and `draw()` accepting `EquilateralTriangle | Square | Circle`?

This form of subtyping is something that has to be supported by the compiler. With a DIY sum type like the `Variant` we looked at in chapter 3, we would not get the same subtyping behavior. Remember the `Variant` can wrap a value of one of several types, but it is not itself any of those types.

7.3.2 Subtyping and collections

Now let's look at types that contain a set of values of some other type. Let's start with arrays in the next listing. Can we pass an array of `Triangle` objects to a `draw()` function that accepts an array of `Shape` objects if `Triangle` is a subtype of `Shape`?

Listing 7.16 `Triangle[]` as `Shape[]`

```
class Shape {
    /* Shape members */
}
declare const TriangleType: unique symbol;       Triangle is a
class Triangle extends Shape {               <--  subtype of Shape.
    [TriangleType]: void;
    /* Triangle members */
}
                                                  makeTriangles() returns an
declare function makeTriangles(): Triangle[];  <-- array of Triangle objects.
declare function draw(shapes: Shape[]): void;  <-- draw() accepts an
                                                   array of Shape objects.
draw(makeTriangles());    <--  We can use an array of
                               Triangle objects as an
                               array of Shape objects.
```

This observation may not be surprising, but it is important: *arrays preserve the subtyping relationship of the underlying types that they are storing.* As expected, the opposite doesn't work: if we try to pass an array of `Shape` objects when an array of `Triangle` objects is expected, the code won't compile (figure 7.4).

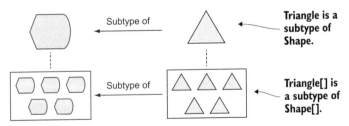

Figure 7.4 If `Triangle` is a subtype of `Shape`, an array of triangles is a subtype of an array of shapes. If we can use a `Triangle` as a `Shape`, we can use an array of `Triangle` objects as an array of `Shape` objects.

As we saw in chapter 2, arrays are basic types that come out of the box in many programming languages. What if we define a custom collection, such as a `LinkedList<T>`?

> **Listing 7.17** `LinkedList<Triangle>` as `LinkedList<Shape>`

```
class LinkedList<T> {
    value: T;                                              ◁── A generic linked
    next: LinkedList<T> | undefined = undefined;              list collection

    constructor(value: T) {
        this.value = value;
    }

    append(value: T): LinkedList<T> {
        this.next = new LinkedList(value);
        return this.next;
    }
}                                                          ◁── makeTriangle() now
                                                               returns a linked list
declare function makeTriangles(): LinkedList<Triangle>;    ◁── of triangles.
declare function draw(shapes: LinkedList<Shape>): void;    ◁── draw() accepts a
                                                               linked list of shapes.
draw(makeTriangles());    ◁── The code
                              compiles.
```

Even without a primitive type, TypeScript correctly establishes that `LinkedList-<Triangle>` is a subtype of `LinkedList<Shape>`. As before, the opposite doesn't compile; we can't pass a `LinkedList<Shape>` as a `LinkedList<Triangle>`.

COVARIANCE   A type that preserves the subtyping relationship of its underlying type is called *covariant*. An array is covariant because it preserves the subtyping relationship: `Triangle` is a subtype of `Shape`, so `Triangle[]` is a subtype of `Shape[]`.

Various languages behave differently when dealing with arrays and collections such as `LinkedList<T>`. In C#, for example, we would have to explicitly state covariance for a type such as `LinkedList<T>` by declaring an interface and using the `out` keyword (`ILinkedList<out T>`). Otherwise, the compiler will not deduce the subtyping relationship.

An alternative to covariance is to simply ignore the subtyping relationship between two given types and consider a `LinkedList<Shape>` and `LinkedList<Triangle>` to be types with no subtyping relationship between them. (Neither is a subtype of the other.) This is not the case in TypeScript, but it is in C#, in which a `List<Shape>` and a `List<Triangle>` have no subtyping relationship.

INVARIANCE   A type that ignores the subtyping relationship of its underlying type is called *invariant*. A C# `List<T>` is invariant because it ignores the subtyping relationship "Triangle is a subtype of Shape", so `List<Shape>` and `List<Triangle>` have no subtype–supertype relationship.

Now that we've looked at how collections relate to one another in terms of subtyping and have seen two common types of variance, let's see how function types are related.

7.3.3 *Subtyping and function return types*

We'll start with the simpler case first: let's see what substitutions we can make between a function that returns a `Triangle` and a function that returns a `Shape`, as shown in listing 7.18. We'll declare two factory functions: a `makeShape()` that returns a `Shape` and a `makeTriangle()` that returns a `Triangle`.

Then we'll implement a `useFactory()` function that takes a function of type `() => Shape` as argument and returns a `Shape`. We'll try passing `makeTriangle()` to it.

Listing 7.18 () => Triangle as () => Shape

```
declare function makeTriangle(): Triangle;
declare function makeShape(): Shape;

function useFactory(factory: () => Shape): Shape {
    return factory();
}

let shape1: Shape = useFactory(makeShape);
let shape2: Shape = useFactory(makeTriangle);
```

> useFactory() takes a function with no arguments that returns a Shape and calls it.

> Both makeTriangle() and makeShape() can be used as arguments to useFactory().

Nothing is out of the ordinary here: we can pass a function that returns a `Triangle` as a function that returns a `Shape` because the return value (a `Triangle`) is a subtype of `Shape`, so we can assign it to a `Shape` (figure 7.5).

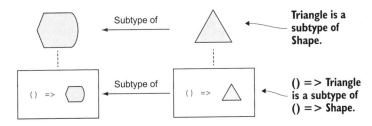

Figure 7.5 If `Triangle` is a subtype of `Shape`, we can use a function that returns a `Triangle` instead of a function that returns a `Shape` because we can always assign a `Triangle` to a caller that expects a `Shape`.

The opposite doesn't work: if we change our `useFactory()` to expect a `() => Triangle` argument and try to pass it `makeShape()`, the following code won't compile.

Listing 7.19 () => Shape as () => Triangle

```
declare function makeTriangle(): Triangle;
declare function makeShape(): Shape;
```

```
function useFactory(factory: () => Triangle): Triangle {
    return factory();
}
```
We replace Shape with Triangle here.

```
let shape1: Shape = useFactory(makeShape);
let shape2: Shape = useFactory(makeTriangle);
```
Code fails to compile; we can't use makeShape() as a () => Triangle.

Again, this code is pretty straightforward: we can't use `makeShape()` as a function of type `() => Triangle` because `makeShape()` returns a `Shape` object. That object could be a `Triangle`, but it also might be a `Square`. `useFactory()` promises to return a `Triangle`, so it can't return a supertype of `Triangle`. It could, of course, return a subtype such as `EquilateralTriangle`, given a `makeEquilateralTriangle()`.

Functions are covariant in their return types. In other words, if `Triangle` is a subtype of `Shape`, a function type such as `() => Triangle` is a subtype of a `function () => Shape`. Note that the function types don't have to describe functions that don't take any arguments. If both `makeTriangle()` and `makeShape()` took a couple of number arguments, they would still be covariant, as we just saw.

This behavior is followed by most mainstream programming languages. The same rules are followed for overriding methods in inherited types, changing their return type. If we implement a `ShapeMaker` class that provides a `make()` method that returns a `Shape`, we can override it in a derived class `MakeTriangle` to return `Triangle` instead, as shown in the following listing. The compiler allows this, as calling either of the `make()` methods will give us a `Shape` object.

Listing 7.20 Overriding a method with a subtype as return type

```
class ShapeMaker {
    make(): Shape {
        return new Shape();
    }
}
```
ShapeMaker defines a method make(), which returns a Shape object.

```
class TriangleMaker extends ShapeMaker {
    make(): Triangle {
        return new Triangle();
    }
}
```
TriangleMaker inherits from ShapeMaker.

TriangleMaker overrides make() and changes its return type to Triangle.

Again, this behavior is allowed in most mainstream programming languages, as most consider functions to be covariant in their return type. Let's see what happens to function types whose argument types are subtypes of one another.

7.3.4 *Subtyping and function argument types*

We'll turn things inside out here, so instead of using a function that returns a `Shape` and a function that returns a `Triangle`, we'll take a function that takes a `Shape` as argument and a function that takes a `Triangle` as argument. We'll call these functions `drawShape()` and `drawTriangle()`. How do `(argument: Shape) => void` and `(argument: Triangle) => void` relate to each other?

Let's introduce another function, render(), that takes as arguments a Triangle and an (argument: Triangle) => void function, as the next listing shows. It simply calls the given function with the given Triangle.

Listing 7.21 Draw and render functions

```
declare function drawShape(shape: Shape): void;
declare function drawTriangle(triangle: Triangle): void;

function render(
    triangle: Triangle,
    drawFunc: (argument: Triangle) => void): void {
    drawFunc(triangle);
}
```

drawShape() takes a Shape argument; drawTriangle() takes a Triangle argument.

render() expects a Triangle and a function that takes a Triangle as argument.

render() simply calls the provided function, passing it the triangle it received.

Here comes the interesting bit: in this case, we can safely pass drawShape() to the render() function! We can use a (argument: Shape) => void where an (argument: Triangle) => void is expected.

Logically, it makes sense: we have a Triangle, and we pass it to a drawing function that can use it as an argument. If the function itself expects a Triangle, like our drawTriangle() function, it of course works. But it should also work for a function that expects a *supertype* of Triangle. drawShape() wants a shape—any shape—to draw. Because it doesn't use anything that's triangle-specific, it is more general than drawTriangle(); it can accept any shape as argument, be it Triangle or Square. So in this particular case, the subtyping relationship is reversed.

CONTRAVARIANCE A type that reverses the subtyping relationship of its underlying type is called *contravariant*. In most programming languages, functions are contravariant with regard to their arguments. A function that expects a Triangle as argument can be substituted for a function that expects a Shape as argument. The relationship of the functions is the reverse of the relationship of the argument types. If Triangle is a subtype of Shape, the type of function that takes a Triangle as an argument is a supertype of the type of function that takes a Shape as an argument (figure 7.6).

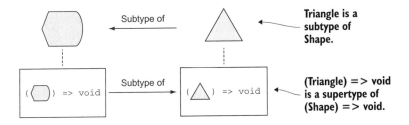

Figure 7.6 If Triangle is a subtype of Shape, we can use a function that expects a Shape as argument instead of a function that expects a Triangle as argument because we can always pass a Triangle to a function that takes a Shape.

We said "most programming languages" earlier. A notable exception is TypeScript. In TypeScript, we can also do the opposite: pass a function that expects a subtype instead of a function that expects a supertype. This choice was an explicit design choice made to facilitate common JavaScript programming patterns. It can lead to run-time issues, though.

Let's look at an example in the next listing. First, we'll define a method `isRight-Angled()` on our `Triangle` type, which would determine whether a given instance describes a right-angled triangle. The implementation of the method is not important.

Listing 7.22   `Shape` and `Triangle` with `isRightAngled()` method

```
class Shape {
    /* Shape members */
}

declare const TriangleType: unique symbol;
class Triangle extends Shape {
    [TriangleType]: void;

    isRightAngled(): boolean {
        let result: boolean = false;

        /* Determine whether it is a right-angled triangle */

        return result;
    }

    /* More Triangle members */
}
```

> The isRightAngled() method tells us whether an instance describes a right-angled triangle.

Now let's reverse the drawing example, as shown in listing 7.23. Suppose that our `render()` function expects a `Shape` instead of a `Triangle` and a function that can draw shapes `(argument: Shape) => void` instead of a function that can draw only triangles `(argument: Triangle) => void`.

Listing 7.23   Updated draw and render functions

```
declare function drawShape(shape: Shape): void;
declare function drawTriangle(triangle: Triangle): void;

function render(
    shape: Shape,
    drawFunc: (argument: Shape) => void): void {
    drawFunc(shape);
}
```

> drawShape() and drawTriangle() are just like before.

> render() simply calls the provided function passing it the shape it received.

> render() expects a Shape and a function that takes a Shape as argument.

Here's how we can cause a run-time error: we can define `drawTriangle()` to use something that is triangle-specific, such as the `isRightAngled()` method we just added. Then we call render with a `Shape` object (not a `Triangle`) and `drawTriangle()`.

Now `drawTriangle()` will receive a `Shape` object and attempt to call `isRight-Angled()` on it in the next listing, but because the `Shape` is not a `Triangle`, this will cause an error.

```
function drawTriangle(triangle: Triangle): void {
    console.log(triangle.isRightAngled());          ◁——  drawTriangle() calls a
    /* ... */                                             Triangle-specific method
}                                                         on the given argument.

function render(
    shape: Shape,
    drawFunc: (argument: Shape) => void): void {
    drawFunc(shape);
}                                                      We can pass a Shape and
                                                       drawTriangle() to render.
render(new Shape(), drawTriangle);          ◁——
```

This code will compile, but it will fail at run time with a JavaScript error, because the run time won't be able to find `isRightAngled()` on the `Shape` object we gave to `drawTriangle()`. This result is not ideal, but as mentioned before, it was a conscious decision made during the implementation of TypeScript.

In TypeScript, if `Triangle` is a subtype of `Shape`, a function of type `(argument: Shape) => void` and a function of type `(argument: Triangle) => void` can be substituted for each other. Effectively, they are subtypes of each other. This property is called *bivariance*.

BIVARIANCE Types are bivariant if, from the subtyping relationship of their underlying types, they become subtypes of each other. In TypeScript, if `Triangle` is a subtype of `Shape`, the function types `(argument: Shape) => void` and `(argument: Triangle) => void` are subtypes of each other (figure 7.7).

Again, the bivariance of functions with respect to their arguments in TypeScript allows incorrect code to compile. A major theme of this book is relying on the type system to

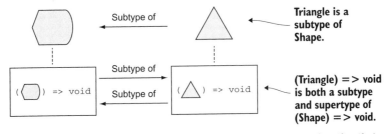

Figure 7.7 If `Triangle` is a subtype of `Shape`, in TypeScript, a function that expects a `Triangle` can be used instead of a function that expects a `Shape`, and a function that expects a `Shape` can be used instead of a function that expects a `Triangle`.

eliminate run-time errors at compile time. In TypeScript, it was a deliberate design decision to enable common JavaScript programming patterns.

7.3.5 *Variance recap*

Throughout this section, we've looked at what types can be substituted for what other types. Although subtyping is straightforward for dealing with simple inheritance, things get more complicated when we add types parameterized on other types. These types could be collections, function types, or other generic types. The way that the subtyping relationships of these parameterized types is removed, preserved, reversed, or made two-way based on the relationship of their underlying types is called variance:

- Invariant types ignore the subtyping relationship of their underlying types.
- Covariant types preserve the subtyping relationship of their underlying types. If `Triangle` is a subtype of `Shape`, an array of type `Triangle[]` is a subtype of an array of type `Shape[]`. In most programming languages, function types are covariant in their return types.
- Contravariant types reverse the subtyping relationship of their underlying types. If `Triangle` is a subtype of `Shape`, the function type `(argument: Shape) => void` is a subtype of the function type `(argument: Triangle) => void` in most languages. This is not true for TypeScript, in which function types are bivariant with regard to their argument types.
- Bivariant types are subtypes of each other when their underlying types are in a subtyping relationship. If `Triangle` is a subtype of `Shape`, the function type `(argument: Shape) => void` and the function type `(argument: Triangle) => void` are subtypes of each other. (Functions of both types can be substituted for each other.)

Although some common rules exist across programming languages, there is no *one way* to support variance. You should understand what the type system of your programming language does and how it establishes subtyping relationships. This is important to know, as these rules tell us what can be substituted for what. Do you need to implement a function to transform a `List<Triangle>` into a `List<Shape>`, or can you just use the `List<Triangle>` as is? The answer depends on the variance of `List<T>` in your programming language of choice.

7.3.6 *Exercises*

In the following exercises, `Triangle` is a subtype of `Shape`. We are going to use the variance rules of TypeScript.

1. Can we pass a `Triangle` variable to a function `drawShape(shape: Shape): void`?
2. Can we pass a `Shape` variable to a function `drawTriangle(triangle: Triangle): void`?
3. Can we pass an array of `Triangle` objects (`Triangle[]`) to a function `drawShapes(shapes: Shape[]): void`?

4   Can we assign the `drawShape()` function to a variable of function type `(triangle: Triangle) => void`?

5   Can we assign the `drawTriangle()` function to a variable of function type `(shape: Shape) => void`?

6   Can we assign a function `getShape(): Shape` to a variable of function type `() => Triangle`?

Summary

- We defined subtyping and the two ways that programming languages determine whether a type is a subtype of another type: structural or nominal.
- We looked at a TypeScript technique to simulate nominal subtyping in a language with structural subtyping.
- We saw an application for the top type, the type that sits at the top of the subtyping hierarchy: safe deserialization.
- We also saw an application for the bottom type, the type that sits at the bottom of the subtyping hierarchy: as a value type for error scenarios.
- We covered subtyping between sum types. The sum type composed of fewer types is the supertype of the sum type composed of more types.
- We learned about covariant types. Arrays and collections are often covariant, and function types are covariant in their return types.
- In some languages, types can be invariant (have no subtyping relationship) even if their underlying types have a subtyping relationship.
- Function types are usually contravariant in their argument types. In other words, their subtyping relationship is the reverse of that of their argument types.
- In TypeScript, functions are bivariant in their argument types. As long as their argument types have a subtyping relationship, each function type is a subtype of the other.
- Variance is implemented differently in different programming languages. It's good to know how your programming language of choice establishes subtyping relationships.

Now that we've covered subtyping at length, we'll move on to the one major application of subtyping we haven't talked about much: object-oriented programming. In chapter 8, we will go over the elements of OOP and their applications.

Answers to exercises

DISTINGUISHING BETWEEN SIMILAR TYPES IN TYPESCRIPT

1   Yes—`Painting` has the same shape as `Wine`, with an additional `painter` property. In TypeScript, due to structural subtyping, `Painting` is a subtype of `Wine`.

2   No—`Car` is missing the `name` property that `Wine` defines, so even with structural subtyping, `Car` cannot be substituted for `Wine`.

ASSIGNING ANYTHING TO, ASSIGNING TO ANYTHING

1 Yes—`never` is a subtype of any other type, including `number`, so we can assign it to a number (even though we would never be able to create an actual value, as `makeNothing()` would never return).

2 No—`unknown` is a supertype of any other type, including `number`. We can assign a `number` to an `unknown`, but not vice versa. First, we have to ensure that the value returned from `makeSomething()` is a number before we can assign it to x.

ALLOWED SUBSTITUTIONS

1 Yes—We can substitute a `Triangle` wherever a `Shape` is expected.

2 No—We cannot use a supertype instead of a subtype.

3 Yes—Arrays are covariant, so we can use an array of `Triangle` objects instead of an array of `Shape` objects.

4 Yes—Functions are bivariant in their arguments in TypeScript, so we can use `(shape: Shape) => void` as `(triangle: Triangle) => void`.

5 Yes—Functions are bivariant in their arguments in TypeScript, so we can use `(triangle: Triangle) => void` as `(shape: Shape) => void`.

6 No—Functions are bivariant in their arguments but not in their return types in TypeScript. We can't use a function of type `() => Shape` as a function of type `() => Triangle`.

Elements of object-oriented programming

This chapter covers

- Defining contracts by using interfaces
- Implementing a hierarchy of expressions
- Implementing the adapter pattern
- Extending behavior with mix-ins
- Considering alternatives to pure OOP

In this chapter, we will cover the elements of object-oriented programming and see how we can employ them effectively. You are probably familiar with these concepts, as they show up in all object-oriented languages, so we'll focus more on their use cases.

We'll start with interfaces and see how we can think of them as contracts. After interfaces, we'll look at inheritance: we can inherit both data and behavior. An alternative to inheritance is *composition*. We'll look at some of the differences between the two approaches and when to use which. We'll talk about extending data and behavior with *mix-ins* or, in TypeScript, *intersection types*. Not all languages support mix-ins. Finally, we'll look at alternatives to OOP and when it might make sense not to use it. This is not because there is something wrong with OOP, but

187

because many developers learn it as the only approach to software engineering, and sometimes it ends up being overused.

Before getting started, let's quickly define OOP.

OBJECT-ORIENTED PROGRAMMING   OOP is a programming paradigm based on the concept of objects, which contain both data and code. The data is the state of the object. The code is one or more methods, also known as *messages*. In an object-oriented system, objects can "talk" to or message one another by invoking each other's methods.

Two key features of OOP are *encapsulation*, which allows us to hide data and methods, and *inheritance*, which extends a type with additional data and/or code.

8.1   *Defining contracts with interfaces*

In this section, we'll try to answer a common OOP question: what is the difference between an abstract class and an interface? Let's take as an example a logging system. We want to provide a `log()` method but still have the ability to use different logging implementations. We can go about this in a couple of ways. First, we can declare an abstract class, `ALogger`, and have the actual implementations, such as `Console-Logger`, inherit from it, as shown in the following listing.

Listing 8.1   Abstract logger

```
abstract class ALogger {          ALogger is an abstract class.
    abstract log(line: string): void;   log() is an abstract method, lacking implementation.
}
class ConsoleLogger extends ALogger {
    log(line: string): void {     ConsoleLogger inherits from
        console.log(line);         ALogger and provides an
    }                              implementation for log().
}
```

A user of the logging system would take an `ALogger` as a parameter. We can pass any subtype of `ALogger`, such as `ConsoleLoger`, anywhere that an `ALogger` is expected.

The alternative is to declare an `ILogger` interface and have `ConsoleLogger` implement that interface, as shown in the next listing.

Listing 8.2   Logger interface

```
interface ILogger {              ILogger interface declares
    log(line: string): void;      a log() method.
}
class ConsoleLogger implements ILogger {   ConsoleLogger implements
    log(line: string): void {              ILogger interface and
        console.log(line);                 provides a log() method.
    }
}
```

A user of the logging system would, in this case, take an `ILogger` as a parameter. We can pass any type implementing the interface, such as `ConsoleLogger`, anywhere that an `ILogger` is expected.

The two approaches are similar, and both work, but in a scenario like this one, we should use an interface because an interface specifies a *contract*.

> **INTERFACES OR CONTRACTS** An *interface*, or a *contract*, is a description of a set of messages that are understood by any object implementing that interface. The messages are methods and include name, arguments, and return type. An interface does not have any state. Just like real-world contracts, which are written agreements, an interface is a written agreement of what implementers will provide.

This is exactly what we need in our case: the logging contract consisting of a `log()` method that clients will call. Declaring the `ILogger` interface makes it clear to whoever reads our code that we are specifying a contract.

An abstract class can do that, but it can do much more: it can contain nonabstract methods or state. The only difference between an abstract and a "normal" or *concrete* class is that we can't directly create an instance of an abstract class. We know that whenever we pass around an instance of the abstract class, such as an `ALogger` argument, we are in fact working with an instance of a type that inherits from `ALogger`, such as `ConsoleLogger`.

This is a subtle but important distinction between abstract classes and interfaces: the relationship between `ConsoleLogger` and `ALogger` is called an *is-a relationship*, as in `ConsoleLogger` is an `ALogger`, because it inherits from it. On the other hand, there is nothing to inherit from `ILogger`, as it just specifies a contract. We have `ConsoleLogger` implement the contract, but it doesn't semantically create an *is-a* relationship. `ConsoleLogger` *satisfies the contract* `ILogger` but *isn't* an `ILogger`. That's the reason why even languages that enforce that a class can inherit from only one other class, such as Java and C#, still allow classes to implement many interfaces.

Note that we can extend an interface, creating a new interface based on it, with additional methods. We can create an `IExtendedLogger` that adds a `warn()` and an `error()` method to the `ILogger` contract, for example, as the following listing shows,

Listing 8.3 Extended logger interface

```
interface ILogger {
    log(line: string): void;
}

interface IExtendedLogger extends ILogger {    ⟵  IExtendedLogger has log(),
    warn(line: string): void;                      warn(), and error() methods.
    error(line: string): void;
}
```

Any object that satisfies the `IExtendedLogger` contract also satisfies the `ILogger` contract automatically. We can also combine multiple interfaces into one. We can take an `ISpeaker` and an `IVolumeControl`, for example, and define an `ISpeakerWith-VolumeControl` contract that combines the two, as shown in listing 8.4. This technique allows us to use as a contract both the speaker capabilities and the volume-control capabilities while still allowing other types to implement only one of them. (We might have volume control for a microphone, for example.)

Listing 8.4   Combining interfaces

```
interface ISpeaker {                              ◁─┐ Speaker
    playSound(/* ... */): void;                        │ interface
}

interface IVolumeControl {                        ◁─┐ Volume-control
    volumeUp(): void;                                  │ interface
    volumeDown(): void;
}                                                              Combined speaker and
                                                               volume-control interface
interface ISpeakerWithVolumeControl extends ISpeaker, IVolumeControl {
}                                                            ◁─┘

class MySpeaker implements ISpeakerWithVolumeControl {   ◁─┐ MySpeaker implementing
    playSound(/* ... */): void {                               │ the combined interface
        // Concrete implementation
    }

    volumeUp(): void {
        // Concrete implementation
    }

    volumeDown(): void {
        // Concrete implementation
    }
}

class MusicPlayer {                               ┌ MusicPlayer requires a speaker
    speaker: ISpeakerWithVolumeControl;       ◁─┘ with volume controls.

    constructor(speaker: ISpeakerWithVolumeControl) {
        this.speaker = speaker;
    }
}
```

We can have `MySpeaker` implement both `ISpeaker` and `IVolumeControl` instead of `ISpeakerWithVolumeControl`, of course, but using a single interface makes it easier for a component such as `MusicPlayer` to request a speaker with volume controls. The ability to combine interfaces like this allows us to create them from smaller, reusable building blocks.

Interfaces ultimately benefit the consumers, not the classes that implement them, so it's generally a good idea to spend some time coming up with the best design. The well-known OOP principle of *coding against interfaces* encourages working with interfaces rather than classes, as we did with `MusicPlayer` in our example. That principle reduces the coupling of the components in the system, as we can modify or even swap out `MySpeaker` for another type without affecting `MusicPlayer`, as long as the `ISpeakerWithVolumeContract` is satisfied.

Dependency injection frameworks take on the responsibility of mapping the concrete implementation we should use for that interface, so the rest of the code simply asks for a certain interface, and the framework provides it. This reduces the "glue" code and allows us to focus on implementing the components themselves. We won't cover dependency injection at length, but it's a good approach to reducing the coupling of the code and especially useful for unit testing, as we usually set up dependencies of components under test to be stubs or mocks.

Next, we'll look at inheritance and some of its applications.

8.1.1 Exercises

1 Instances of types that have a `getName()` function can be used by an `index()` function. What is the best way to model this?

 a Declare a concrete `BaseNamed` base class

 b Declare an `ANamed` abstract base class

 c Declare an `INamed` interface

 d Check whether `getName()` exists at run time

2 In TypeScript, the `Iterable<T>` interface declares a `[Symbol.iterator]` method that returns an `Iterator<T>`, and the `Iterator<T>` interfaces declares a `next()` method returning an `IteratorResult<T>`:

```
interface Iterable<T> {
    [Symbol.iterator](): Iterator<T>;
}

interface Iterator<T> {
    next(): IteratorResult<T>;
}
```

Generators return a combination of these—an `IterableIterator<T>`, which is both iterable and an iterator itself. How would you define the `Iterable-Iterator<T>` interface?

8.2 Inheriting data and behavior

Inheritance is one of the best-known features of object-oriented languages. It allows us to create subclasses of a parent class. The subclasses inherit both the data and the methods of the parent class. A subclass is, obviously, a subtype of the parent class, as an instance of the subclass can always be used whenever the parent class is expected.

8.2.1 The is-a rule of thumb

There seems to be an immediate application: if we already have a class that implements most of the behavior we want, we can inherit from it and add what is missing. The problem with doing this haphazardly is twofold. First, if we abuse inheritance, we end up with deep hierarchies of classes that are very hard to understand and navigate. Second, we end up with an inconsistent data model in which the classes don't make sense.

If we have a `Point` class that tracks x and y coordinates, for example, we could inherit a `Circle` from it and add a `radius` property. We can define a circle by its center and radius, and `Point` can already represent the center. But this definition should feel odd.

Listing 8.5 Bad inheritance

```
class Point {
    x: number;
    y: number;

    constructor(x: number, y: number) {
        this.x = x;
        this.y = y;
    }
}

class Circle extends Point {        ⟵— Circle inherits the x and
    radius: number;                     y coordinates of its
                                        center from Point.
    constructor(x: number, y: number, radius: number) {
        super(x, y);
        this.radius = radius;
    }
}
```

To understand why this feels odd, let's look at the *is-a* relationship we established. Is an instance of the subclass logically an instance of the superclass? In this case, no. A `Circle` is not a `Point`. We can certainly use it as one, the way we defined it, but there doesn't seem to be a reasonable scenario in which we would want to do that.

> **INHERITANCE AND THE IS-A RELATIONSHIP** Inheritance establishes an *is-a* relationship between the child type and its parent type. If our base class is `Shape`, and our derived class is `Circle`, the relationship is "`Circle` is a `Shape`." This is the semantic meaning of inheritance and a good test to apply to two types to determine whether we should use inheritance.

We'll go over the alternative approach of composition in section 8.3. Until then, let's look at a few situations in which it *does* make sense to use inheritance.

8.2.2 Modeling a hierarchy

One instance when we should look at inheritance is when our data model is hierarchical. This fact is fairly obvious, so we won't cover it at length, but this is the best use of inheritance: as we move down the inheritance chain, we refine our types by adding more data and/or more behavior (figure 8.1).

The example in the figure may seem to be simplistic, but it is a perfect use of inheritance. A `Cat` is a `Pet` is an `Animal`, and as we go deeper down the hierarchy, we get more behavior and state.

When we want to deal with a higher abstraction level, we go up the hierarchy. If we just need to `play()` with our animal, we use an argument of type `Pet`. If we need specific meowing behavior, we use an argument of type `Cat`.

This example should be very straightforward, so let's move on to a more interesting application of inheritance, which has a twist: different derived classes implement some behavior differently.

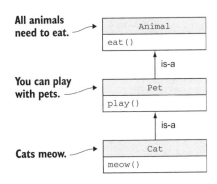

Figure 8.1 **All animals eat. We can play with pets (but they still need to eat). Cats also meow (but they still play and eat).**

8.2.3 *Parameterizing behavior of expressions*

The other situation in which we should use inheritance is when most of the behavior and state we want is common to multiple types, but a small part of it needs to vary across implementations. The multiple types should still pass our *is-a* test.

We have an expression that can be evaluated to a number, we have binary expressions that have two operands, and we have sum and multiply expressions that we evaluate by adding and multiplying the operands.

We can model an expression as an `IExpression` interface with an `eval()` method. We make it an interface because it doesn't hold any state. Next, we implement a `BinaryExpression` abstract class that stores the two operands, as shown in listing 8.6, but we keep `eval()` abstract and let derived classes implement it. `SumExpression` and `MulExpression` each inherit the two operands from `BinaryExpression` and provide their own `eval()` implementation (figure 8.2).

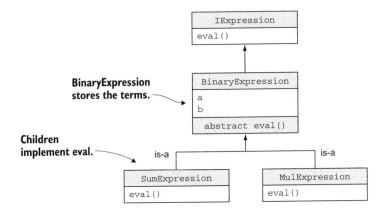

Figure 8.2 **Expression hierarchy with `BinaryExpression` as parent and `SumExpression` and `MulExpression` as children**

```
Listing 8.6   Expression hierarchy
```

```
interface IExpression {          ◄─────┐  IExpression doesn't need to be
    eval(): number;                       a class, as it doesn't hold state.
}

abstract class BinaryExpression implements IExpression {   ◄───  BinaryExpression
    readonly a: number;                                          is a class storing
    readonly b: number;                                          the two operands.

    constructor(a: number, b: number) {
        this.a = a;
        this.b = b;
    }
                                    ┌── eval() is abstract, as we don't
    abstract eval(): number;    ◄───┘   have an implementation for it.
}

class SumExpression extends BinaryExpression {    ◄──┐
    eval(): number {
        return this.a + this.b;                       Both SumExpression and
    }                                                 MulExpression inherit from
}                                                     BinaryExpression and
                                                      implement eval().
class MulExpression extends BinaryExpression {    ◄──┘
    eval(): number {
        return this.a * this.b;
    }
}
```

This should pass our *is-a* test: a SumExpression is a BinaryExpression. As we go down the hierarchy, we inherit the common parts (in our case, the two operands) but parameterize the eval() for each derived class.

One thing to watch out for is coming up with very deep hierarchies of classes, which makes the code harder to navigate, as various parts of the state and methods of an object come from different levels in the hierarchy.

Usually, it's also good to have the children be concrete classes and all parents up the hierarchy be abstract. This technique makes it easier to keep track of things and avoid unexpected behavior. Unexpected behavior can happen when a child class overrides a parent method, but then we upcast it and pass it around as the parent type. Such an object would behave differently from an instance of the parent class, which might not be intuitive for maintainers of the code.

Some languages provide a way to explicitly mark a child class as noninheritable to enforce stopping the hierarchy there. Usually, this is done with keywords such as final or sealed. We should use these as often as we can. If we want to override or extend behavior, we have a better alternative to inheritance: composition.

8.2.4 *Exercises*

1 Which of the following looks like a good use of inheritance?

   a File extends Folder.

   b Triangle extends Point.

    c Parser extends Compiler.

    d None of the above.

  2 Extend the example in this section with a UnaryExpression that has a single operand and a UnaryMinusExpression that toggles the sign of its operand. (Example 1 becomes –1, for example, and –2 becomes 2.)

8.3 *Composing data and behavior*

A well-known principle of object-oriented programming is to prefer composition over inheritance whenever possible. Let's see what composition is about.

Going back to our Point and Circle example, we can make a Circle a child of Point, but that wouldn't be quite right. Let's expand our example and introduce a Shape in listing 8.7. We'll say that all shapes in our system need to have an identifier, so Shape has an id property of type string. A Circle is a Shape, so we can inherit the id. On the other hand, the Circle *has a* center, so it will contain a center property of type Point.

Listing 8.7 Inheritance and composition

```
class Shape {
    id: string;

    constructor(id: string) {
        this.id = id;
    }
}

class Point {
    x: number;
    y: number;

    constructor(x: number, y: number) {
        this.x = x;
        this.y = y;
    }
}

class Circle extends Shape {
    center: Point;
    radius: number;

    constructor(id: string, center: Point, radius: number) {
        super(id);
        this.center = center;
        this.radius = radius;
    }
}
```

Circle inherits the id property from Shape.

Circle contains a Point, which defines the x and y coordinates of its center.

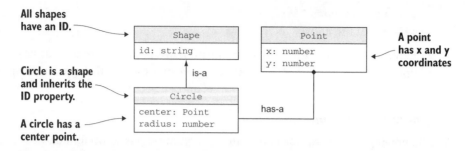

Figure 8.3 All shapes have an id. A circle *Is a* shape, so it inherits the id. A circle *has a* point that defines its center.

8.3.1 *The has-a rule of thumb*

Just like the *is-a* test we applied to determine whether we should have `Circle` inherit from `Point`, we can apply a similar test for composition: *has-a* (figure 8.3).

Instead of inheriting behavior from a type, we can define a property of that type. This technique still gives us the state that the contained type stores but as a component part of our type rather than an inherited part of our type.

> **COMPOSITION AND THE HAS-A RELATIONSHIP** Composition establishes a *has-a* relationship between a container type and the contained type. If our type is `Circle`, and our contained class is `Point`, the relationship is "`Circle` has a `Point`" (which defines its center). This is the semantic meaning of composition and a good test to apply to two types to determine whether we should use composition.

A major benefit of composition is that all the state coming from component properties (such as the coordinates of the center of a `Circle`) is encapsulated in those components (such as the center property of type `Point`), so our type is much cleaner.

An instance `circle` of our `Circle` type has a `circle.id` property, which it inherits from `Shape`, but the x and y center coordinates from its center point are in `center`: `circle.center.x` and `circle.center.y`. If we want, we can make `center` private, and in that case external code wouldn't be able to access it. We cannot do that with an inherited property: if `Shape` declares `id` as public, `Circle` cannot hide it.

We'll go over a few applications of composition next, but in general, this method is the preferred way of making state and behavior available to a class, as opposed to inheriting it. Unless there is a clear *is-a* relationship between two types, composition is a good default.

8.3.2 *Composite classes*

We'll start with another simple, straightforward example because again, this is a concept you are likely familiar with. It shows up everywhere in object-oriented programming (and outside it).

A company has many constituent parts: various departments, an operating budget, a CEO, and so on. All these parts are properties of Company. We covered an aspect of such types in chapter 3, when we talked about product types. If, for a moment, we simply look at the set of possible states a company can be in, it's the product of the state each department is in, the state the budget is in, the state the CEO is in, and so on. The additional twist is that we can encapsulate parts of this state by making it private and enhance the composite class with additional methods that can access the privates in their implementation (something that an external function wouldn't be able to do).

We can't simply get the CEO of the company and ask them a question, for example. We can try sending a message to the CEO by contacting the company through official channels, and the CEO might or might not get back to us, as the next listing shows.

Listing 8.8 Ask the CEO

```
class CEO {                          ◁——   A CEO is very busy and
    isBusy(): boolean {                     can answer questions.
        /* ... */
    }

    answer(question: string): string {
        /* ... */
    }
}

class Department {
    /* ... */
}

class Budget {
    /* ... */
}
                                          A company has a CEO, a set of
class Company {                    ◁——    departments, and a budget.
    private ceo: CEO = new CEO();
    private departments: Department[] = [];
    private budget: Budget = new Budget();          If we want to contact
                                                    the CEO, we do it
    askCEO(question: string): string | undefined {  ◁── through the company.
        if (!this.ceo.isBusy()) {
            return this.ceo.answer(question);        If the CEO is not busy,
        }                                            they will answer us.
    }
}
```

The ability to hide class members and provide controlled access to them is one of the key extra distinctions that encapsulation brings to the table compared with plain old product types such as tuples and records.

Value types and reference types

You might also have heard of *value types* and *reference types*, or about differences between *struct* and *class* types and so on. Although there is a lot of nuance to cover there, unfortunately, little of it is general enough. Different programming languages implement these types differently, so it's more a matter of understanding how your language handles the nuances.

In general, when we assign an instance of a value type to a variable or pass it as an argument to a function, its content gets copied in memory, effectively creating a distinct instance. On the other hand, when we assign an instance of a reference type, the full state doesn't get copied—just a reference to it. Both the old and new variables point to the same object and can alter its state.

The reason why we are not covering this topic in depth here is that it might get very confusing because of the way each language implements these concepts. In C#, for example, a struct looks a lot like a class, but it is a value type; assigning it causes its state to be copied. On the other hand, Java does not support proper value types outside the primitive numerical types that come out of the box: everything is a reference type. C++, again, is different: a struct in C++ simply means that members are public by default and private by default in classes. In C++, everything is by value, unless we explicitly declare a value as pointer (*) or reference (&). Some functional languages work with immutable data, in which the distinction between value and reference doesn't exist, as everything is moved around.

Although the difference between value and reference types matters (we don't want to copy large amounts of data, as it affects performance; we'd rather copy than share because it's safer to have a single owner of the state), you should understand how your programming language expresses and handles these nuances.

Next, let's look at another, maybe not-so-obvious application of composition: the very useful adapter pattern.

8.3.3   *Implementing the adapter pattern*

The adapter pattern can make two classes compatible without requiring us to modify either of the two classes. An adapter is used very much like a physical adapter. We might have a laptop with only USB ports and want to connect it to a wired network, for example, which we would do with an Ethernet cable. An Ethernet-to-USB adapter manages the translation between the two incompatible components, USB and Ethernet, and ensures that they work together.

As an example, let's say we use an external geometry library that provides some important operations we need, but it doesn't fit our object model. It expects a circle to be defined in terms of an `ICircle` interface that declares two methods to get the x and y coordinates of the center, `getCenterX()` and `getCenterY()`, and another method, `getDiameter()`, to get the diameter of the circle, as shown in the following code.

```
Listing 8.9   Geometry library

namespace GeometryLibrary {

    export interface ICircle {          ◁─┐  The Geometry library
        getCenterX(): number;               │  expects circles to adhere
        getCenterY(): number;               │  to a certain contract.
        getDiameter(): number;
    }

    /* Operations on ICircle omitted */  ◁─┐  We won't go over the exact
                                              │  operations because they're not
}                                             │  important for our example.
```

Our `Circle` is defined in terms of a center `Point` and a radius. Assuming that we have a large codebase, and this circle is just a small piece of it, we probably don't want to refactor everything just to be compatible with this library. The good news is that there is an easier solution: we can implement a `CircleAdapter` class, which wraps a `Circle`, implements the expected interface, and handles the logic of converting from our `Circle` to what the library expects.

```
Listing 8.10   CircleAdapter

                                                    CircleAdapter implements
                                                    the ICircle interface that
                                                    the library expects.

class CircleAdapter implements GeometryLibrary.ICircle {   ◁──────────┘
    private circle: Circle;              ◁─┐  CircleAdapter wraps
                                              │  a Circle instance.
    constructor(circle: Circle) {
        this.circle = circle
    }

    getCenterX(): number {
        return this.circle.center.x;     ◁─┐
    }                                         │  getCenterX() and getCenterY()
                                              │  get the corresponding x and y
    getCenterY(): number {                    │  coordinates from Circle.
        return this.circle.center.y;     ◁─┘
    }

    getDiameter(): number {
        return this.circle.radius * 2;   ◁─┐  getDiameter() gets the radius
    }                                         │  and multiplies it by 2.
}                                             │  (Diameter is twice the radius.)
```

Now, whenever we need to use the geometry library with a `Circle` instance, we create a `CircleAdapter` for it and pass that to the geometry library. The adapter pattern is extremely useful for dealing with code that we cannot modify, such as code that comes

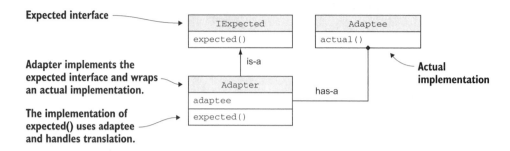

Figure 8.4 We have an `IExpected` interface and an `Adaptee` actual implementation that are incompatible. The `Adapter` makes them compatible by providing an implementation of `IExpected` and handling translation between what `IExpected` declares and what the `Adaptee` provides.

from external libraries outside our control. This is, in fact, the general structure of the adapter pattern as shown in figure 8.4.

The adapter can hide the actual implementation it translates from by marking it as private. This is an interesting application of composition: instead of bringing together several components, we wrap a single component but provide the "glue" it needs to be consumed as another type.

With interfaces, inheritance, and composition out of the way, we've covered the most common elements of object-oriented programming. Next, we'll look at a slightly more advanced (and more controversial!) concept: mix-ins.

8.3.4   *Exercises*

1   How would you model a `FileTransfer` class that uses a `Connection` to transfer files over the network?

a   `FileTransfer` extends `Connection` (inherits connection behavior from the `Connection` type).

b   `FileTransfer` implements `IConnection` (implements an interface that declares connection behavior).

c   `FileTransfer` wraps a `Connection` (class member provides connection functionality).

d   `Connection` extends abstract `FileTransfer` (connection extends the abstract FileTransfer class and provides the additional behavior required).

2   Implement an `Airplane` with two wings and an engine on each wing, given an `Engine` class. Try to model this by using composition.

8.4   *Extending data and behavior*

Another way to bring in additional data or behavior to a type is not quite inheritance, though unfortunately, it is mostly implemented as such in the languages that support it.

Let's go back to our simplistic animal example: a Cat is a Pet is an Animal. Let's introduce a WildAnimal type in our hierarchy and a Wolf child type of that. Wild animals can roam(), and a wolf can also hunt. Hunting consists of three separate methods: track(), stalk(), and pounce() (figure 8.5).

If we want, we can even implement an IHunter interface with the standard track(), stalk(), and pounce() methods.

What if we add a Tiger type to the mix? A Tiger can also hunt, and assuming that hunting behavior is similar across predators, we don't want to duplicate the code across our Wolf and Tiger types. One option is to introduce a common type in the hierarchy: a Hunter type, which is the child of WildAnimal and the parent of Wolf and Tiger (figure 8.6).

This approach works until we realize that a Cat also hunts. How do we make all this hunter behavior available to Cat without completely rejiggering our type hierarchy?

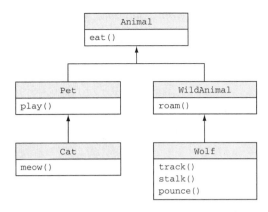

Figure 8.5 Extended animal hierarchy with WildAnimal and Wolf. Wild animals can roam(), and a wolf can hunt with its track(), stalk(), and pounce() methods.

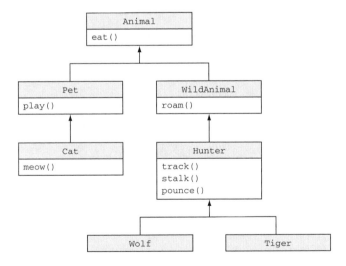

Figure 8.6 The Hunter type is the parent of Wolf and Tiger, and provides hunting behavior.

8.4.1   *Extending behavior with composition*

One way to go about it is to define an `IHunter` interface and a `HuntingBehavior` class that encapsulates the common hunting behavior, as shown in listing 8.11. Then we can have all three of our types—`Cat`, `Wolf`, and `Tiger`—wrap a `Hunting-Behavior` instance and forward the implementation of the interface to it (figure 8.7).

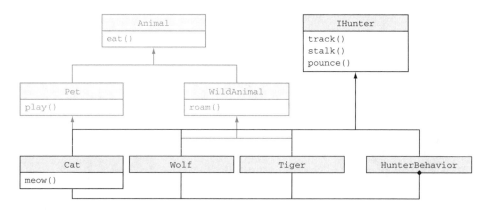

Figure 8.7   `Cat`, `Wolf`, and `Tiger` **wrap an instance of** `HunterBehavior` **and implement the** `IHunter` **interface. They forward all calls to the wrapped object.** `HunterBehavior` **provides an implementation of** `IHunter` **that all animals implementing** `IHunter` **can use as a component.** `HunterBehavior` **is no longer part of the** `Animal` **hierarchy.**

Listing 8.11   Hunting behavior

```
interface IHunter {                         ◁───┐ Common IHunter
    track(): void;                               │ interface
    stalk(): void;
    pounce(): void;
}

class HuntingBehavior implements IHunter {  ◁───┐ Hunting behavior common
    pray: Animal | undefined;                    │ to all hunting animals

    track(): void {
        /* ... */
    }

    stalk(): void {
        /* ... */
    }

    pounce(): void {
        /* ... */
    }
}
```

```
class Cat extends Pet implements IHunter {
    private huntingBehavior: HuntingBehavior = new HuntingBehavior();    ◁──┐

    track(): void {                                                Cat wraps an instance
        this.huntingBehavior.track();    ◁──┐                      of HuntingBehavior.
    }

    stalk(): void {                                    All methods of IHunter
        this.huntingBehavior.track();    ◁──┤          interface are simply
    }                                                  forwarded to
                                                       huntingBehavior.
    pounce(): void {
        this.huntingBehavior.track();    ◁──┘
    }

    meow(): void {
        /* ... */
    }
}
```

This approach works, but we end up with several classes that implement IHunter by wrapping HuntingBehavior. Adding a new hunting animal to our hierarchy now comes with a bunch of boilerplate that we have to copy/paste from another type. Even worse, an addition to the IHunter interface causes a cascade of changes in our code base, as we have to update each individual animal with hunting behavior, even though the only thing that really changes is the HuntingBehavior itself.

Is there a better way of implementing this? The answer is both yes and no.

8.4.2 *Extending behavior with mix-ins*

An easier way to have all hunting animals share this behavior is to mix it into each type. Unfortunately, the way to mix in behavior is usually achieved with multiple inheritance. This fact is unfortunate because it is at odds with what we covered at the beginning of the chapter with the *is-a* rule of thumb. We haven't even covered all the perils of multiple inheritance (and we won't, but look up *the diamond inheritance problem* if you are curious).

We can look at this from the multiple-inheritance point of view, creating a Hunter class that implements the hunting behavior and have all hunting animals derive from it. Then a Cat is both an Animal and a Hunter.

On the other hand, mix-ins aren't the same as inheritance. We can create a HunterBehavior class that implements the hunting behavior and have all hunting animals *include* this behavior.

> **MIX-INS AND THE INCLUDES RELATIONSHIP** Mix-ins establish an *includes* relationship between a type and its mixed-in type. If our class is Cat, and our mixed-in class is HunterBehavior, the relationship is "Cat includes HunterBehavior." This is the semantic meaning of mix-ins and is different from the *is-a* relationship of inheritance (figure 8.8).

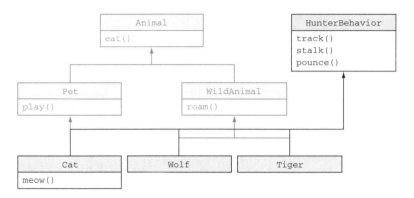

Figure 8.8 `Cat`, `Wolf`, and `Tiger` mix in `HunterBehavior`, which removes a bunch of boilerplate: the classes no longer need to wrap a `HunterBehavior` object and forward calls. They can simply include the behavior.

The reason why mix-ins are nuanced and controversial is that many languages don't support them altogether to keep things simple, and in most languages that do support them, mixing in another type is indistinguishable from inheritance. This makes sense, as after we mix in a class such as `HunterBehavior`, our `Cat` class automatically becomes a subtype of that class. We can pass in a `Cat` instance whenever we need `HunterBehavior.`, but the *is-a* test fails: a `Cat` is not `HunterBehavior`.

Mix-ins are very useful for reducing boilerplate code. They allow us to put together an object by mixing in different behaviors and to reuse common behavior across multiple types. They are best used to implement *cross-cutting concerns*: aspects of a program that affect other concerns and can't be easily decomposed. Think of things like reference counting, caching, persistence, and so on.

We'll quickly go over a TypeScript example, but the syntax is very specific to the language. Don't worry if it looks complicated; the underlying principle is the important part.

8.4.3   *Mix-in in TypeScript*

One way to mix two types is to use an `extend()` function that takes two instances of two different types and copies all members of the second instance to the first one, as shown in listing 8.12. We can do this in TypeScript because of the dynamic nature of the underlying JavaScript language. In JavaScript, we can add and remove members of an object at run time. `extend()` is generic, so it can work with instances of any two types.

Listing 8.12   **Extending an instance with the members of another one**

```
function extend<First, Second>(first: First, second: Second):
    First & Second {
    const result: unknown = {};
```
                                              The function return type
                                              is a combination of the First
                                              and Second types.

```
    for (const prop in first) {
        if (first.hasOwnProperty(prop)) {
            (<First>result)[prop] = first[prop];
        }
    }
    for (const prop in second) {
        if (second.hasOwnProperty(prop)) {
            (<Second>result)[prop] = second[prop];
        }
    }
    return <First & Second>result;
}
```

First, we iterate over all members of the first object and copy them to the result.

Next, we do the same for the members of the second type.

This is the first time we encounter the & syntax: First & Second defines a type that has all the members of First and all the members of Second. This is called an *intersection type* in TypeScript. Don't worry too much about this particular implementation; what's important is the concept of combining two types into a type that contains both their members.

Most languages don't make it so easy to add new members to an object at run time, but it is possible in JavaScript—thus, also in TypeScript. As a compile-time alternative, in C++ we can use multiple-inheritance to declare a type as a combination of two other types.

Now that we have our extend() method, we can update our animal example as follows in listing 8.13. Instead of Cat, we define a MeowingPet as a child of Pet, which is an animal that can meow() but not quite a Cat yet, as it doesn't have hunting behavior. Next, we can define a Cat as the intersection of MeowingPet & Hunting-Behavior. Whenever we want to create a new instance of Cat, we create a new instance of MeowingPet and extend() it with a new instance of HuntingBehavior.

Listing 8.13 Mixing in behavior

```
class MeowingPet extends Pet {
    meow(): void {
        /* ... */
    }
}

class HunterBehavior {
    track(): void {
        /* ... */
    }

    stalk(): void {
        /* ... */
    }

    pounce(): void {
        /* ... */
    }
}
```

Instead of Cat, we have a MeowingPet that is not quite a Cat, as it can't hunt.

HunterBehavior is the same as in our previous examples.

```
type Cat = MeowingPet & HunterBehavior;   ◁─┐  Cat becomes an intersection type of
                                              MeowingPet and HunterBehavior.

const fluffy: Cat = extend(new MeowingPet(), new HunterBehavior());   ◁─┐
```

> **Cat becomes an intersection type of MeowingPet and HunterBehavior.**

> **We can create an instance of Cat by extending a MeowingPet with HunterBehavior.**

We can wrap the call to `extend()` in a `makeCat()` function, which makes it easier to create `Cat` objects. Unlike with inheritance, by using mix-ins, we define different types for different aspects of behavior; then we put them together into a complete type. We usually have some properties and methods that are very specific to one particular type—in our case, the `meow()` method—and some properties and methods that cross-cut across multiple types, such as the hunting behavior of multiple animals.

Now that we've covered interfaces, inheritance, composition, and mix-ins—the main elements of OOP—let's look at a few alternatives to purely object-oriented code.

8.4.4 *Exercise*

1 How would you model shipping letters and packages that could also have tracking (through an `updateStatus()` method)?

8.5 *Alternatives to purely object-oriented code*

Object-oriented programming is extremely useful. The ability to create components with public interfaces while hiding the implementation details and have them interact with one another is key to managing complexity and dividing and conquering complex domains.

That being said, there are more ways to design software, as we've seen with some of the examples in earlier chapters that showed different takes on design patterns, such as strategy, decorator, and visitor. In some cases, the alternatives offer better decoupling, componentization, and reusability.

The reason why the alternatives are not as popular is that many languages started as purely object-oriented, without support for things like function types and generics. Although most of them evolved to support these things, many programmers are still learning almost exclusively the purely object-oriented methods of the earlier days. Let's quickly go over a few available alternatives.

8.5.1 *Sum types*

We covered sum types in chapter 3, when we looked at a way to implement the visitor pattern by using a `Variant` and a `visit()` function. Following is a quick refresher on how the code looked like with OOP and without it.

We'll pick another scenario this time: a simple UI framework. The UI consists of a tree of `Panel`, `Label`, and `Button` objects. In one scenario, a `Renderer` will draw these elements on the screen. In a second scenario, an `XmlSerializer` will serialize the UI tree as XML that so we can save it and reload it later.

Remember that we could add a method to render and a method to serialize on each of the UI elements, but that technique is not ideal: whenever we want to add another scenario, we have to touch all the classes that make up the UI. These classes also end up knowing way too much about the environment in which they are used. Instead, we can use a visitor pattern that will decouple the scenarios from the UI widgets and keep them oblivious to how they will be used in our application, as shown in the following listing.

Listing 8.14 Visitor with OOP

```
interface IVisitor {
    visitPanel(panel: Panel): void;
    visitLabel(label: Label): void;
    visitButton(button: Button): void;
}

class Renderer implements IVisitor {
    visitPanel(panel: Panel) { /* ... */ }
    visitLabel(label: Label) { /* ... */ }
    visitButton(button: Button) { /* ... */ }
}

class XmlSerializer implements IVisitor {
    visitPanel(panel: Panel) { /* ... */ }
    visitLabel(label: Label) { /* ... */ }
    visitButton(button: Button) { /* ... */ }
}

interface IUIWidget {
    accept(visitor: IVisitor): void;
}

class Panel implements IUIWidget {
    /* Panel members omitted */
    accept(visitor: IVisitor) {
        visitor.visitPanel(this);
    }
}

class Label implements IUIWidget {
    /* Label members omitted */
    accept(visitor: IVisitor) {
        visitor.visitLabel(this);
    }
}

class Button implements IUIWidget {
    /* Button members omitted */
    accept(visitor: IVisitor) {
        visitor.visitButton(this);
    }
}
```

In the OOP implementation, we need `IVisitor` and `IUIWidget` interfaces to glue the system together. All UI widgets need to know about `IVisitor` to make things work, even though that shouldn't be necessary.

The alternative implementation—using a `Variant`—removes the need for interfaces, and document items don't need to know that visitors exist.

Listing 8.15   Visitor with `Variant`

```
class Renderer {
    renderPanel(panel: Panel) { /* ... */ }
    renderLabel(label: Label) { /* ... */ }
    renderButton(button: Button) { /* ... */ }
}

class XmlSerializer {
    serializePanel(panel: Panel) { /* ... */ }
    serializeLabel(label: Label) { /* ... */ }
    serializeButton(button: Button) { /* ... */ }
}

class Panel {
    /* Panel members omitted */
}

class Label {
    /* Label members omitted */
}

class Button {
    /* Button members omitted */
}

let widget: Variant<Panel, Label, Button> =
    Variant.make1(new Panel());

let serializer: XmlSerializer = new XmlSerializer();

visit(widget,
    (panel: Panel) => serializer.serializePanel(panel),
    (label: Label) => serializer.serializeLabel(label),
    (button: Button) => serializer.serializeButton(button)
);
```

> The Variant type we defined in chapter 3 can store types that are not related.

> visit() glues the system together, matching the UI widget with the serializer method.

Note that we are showing the `Variant` and `visit()` being used, but technically, the equivalent of the OOP example is just the first five class definitions. Notice that no interfaces are needed.

In general, if we want to pass around objects of different types in the same manner or put them in a common collection, they don't necessarily need to implement the same interface or have a common parent. Instead, we can use a sum type, which enables the same behavior without enforcing any relationship between the types.

8.5.2   *Functional programming*

Before OOP languages supported function types, we had to wrap any piece of behavior in a class. As we saw in chapter 5, a typical strategy pattern implementation required an interface for the behavior and several classes to implement the interface.

Let's review the figures from chapter 5, which described the two alternative implementations for the strategy pattern (figure 8.9).

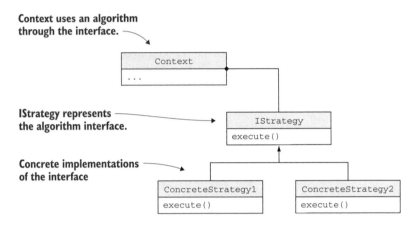

Figure 8.9   Object-oriented strategy pattern. Different versions of an algorithm are implemented in `ConcreteStrategy1` and `ConcreteStrategy2`.

This can be simplified a lot if we can just pass the algorithm implementation as a function. Instead of an interface, we use a function type; instead of classes, we use functions (figure 8.10).

Functional programming also avoids maintaining state: a function can take a set of arguments, perform some computation, and return the result without changing any state.

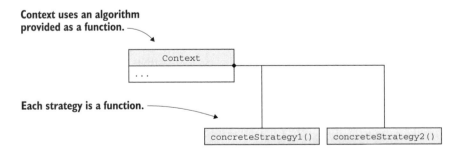

Figure 8.10   Functional strategy pattern. Different versions of an algorithm are implemented as functions.

Let's revisit our binary expression example in listing 8.16 and see how a functional implementation would look. If we define an expression as something that evaluates to a number, we can replace our `IExpression` with a function type `Expression` that takes no arguments and returns a number. Instead of a `SumExpression`, we can implement a factory function `makeSumExpression()` that, given two numbers, returns a closure that can add them up. Remember that a closure captures state—in this case, the a and b arguments. The same is true for multiplication.

> **Listing 8.16   Functional expressions**

```
type Expression = () => number;        ◁──┐  The Expression function
                                           │  type replaces IExpression.
function makeSumExpression(a: number, b: number): Expression {
    return () => a + b;                    ◁──┐  makeSumExpression() returns
}                                              │  the closure () => a + b.

function makeMulExpression(a: number, b: number): Expression {
    return () => a * b;        ◁──┐  makeMulExpression() returns the
}                                  │  closure () => a * b.
```

We no longer need `BinaryExpression`; that class used to hold state, but now state is wrapped in the closures.

If our `IExpression` were more complex, declaring multiple methods, the object-oriented approach might have worked better. But keep an eye out for simple cases in which you can achieve the same behavior with much less code by using a functional approach.

8.5.3   *Generic programming*

The other alternative to purely object-oriented programming is generic programming. We've used generics in many code examples thus far but haven't covered them in depth yet. We'll do that in the next two chapters, and we'll see different ways to abstract and reuse code.

The takeaway from this section shouldn't be to avoid object-oriented programming; it is an important tool that we can use to solve a broad range of problems. The takeaway is that there are alternatives that we should keep in mind. We should pick the approach that makes our code as safe, as clear, and as loosely coupled as possible.

Summary

- We use interfaces to specify contracts. Interfaces can be extended and combined.
- The *is-a* rule of thumb is a good test for when we should use inheritance.
- We use inheritance to represent hierarchies or to implement parameterized behavior by using abstract or overridden methods.

- The *has-a* rule of thumb is a good test for when we should use composition.
- We use composition to encapsulate multiple parts into a single type.
- The adapter pattern is an example in which we leverage encapsulation and composition to adapt a type to a different interface without modifying it.
- We use mix-ins to add behavior into a type.
- Sum types, functional programming, and generic programming are alternatives to pure OOP that we should keep in mind. They don't replace OOP; rather, they are better in some cases.

We touched only briefly on generics in this chapter, as the next two chapters will focus exclusively on that topic. Read on!

Answers to exercises

DEFINING CONTRACTS WITH INTERFACES

1 c—From the point of view of the index() function, this is clearly a contract, so expecting an INamed interface is the approach.

2 We can define this interface simply by combining the two other interfaces:

```
interface IterableIterator<T> extends Iterable<T>, Iterator<T> {
}
```

INHERITING DATA AND BEHAVIOR

1 d—Even by just seeing the class name, we can tell that none of the three examples describe an *is-a* relationship, so none of them look like a good use of inheritance.

2 A possible implementation using inheritance:

```
abstract class UnaryExpression implements IExpression {
    readonly a: number;

    constructor(a: number) {
        this.a = a;
    }

    abstract eval(): number;
}

class UnaryMinusExpression extends UnaryExpression {
    eval(): number {
        return -this.a;
    }
}
```

COMPOSING DATA AND BEHAVIOR

1 c—This scenario is a good one for using composition. Connection should be a member of FileTransfer, as it is needed by FileTransfer, but neither type should directly extend the other.

2 A possible implementation using composition:

```
class Wing {
    readonly engine: Engine = new Engine();
}

class Airplane {
    readonly leftWing: Wing = new Wing();
    readonly rightWing: Wing = new Wing();
}
```

EXTENDING DATA AND BEHAVIOR

1 One way to model this is to provide tracking behavior in a `Tracking` class and then mix it in with `Letter` and `Package` classes to add tracking behavior to them. In TypeScript, this can be done with a method like `extend()`:

```
class Letter { /*...*/ }
class Package { /*...*/ }

class Tracking {
    setStatus(status: Status) { /*...*/ }
}

type LetterWithTracking = Letter & Tracking;
type PackageWithTracking = Package & Tracking;
```

Generic data structures

We'll start our discussion of generic types by covering a common case in which they should be used: making independent, reusable components. We'll look at a couple of scenarios in which we would benefit from an identity function (a function that simply returns its argument) and see a generic implementation of such a function. We'll also review the `Optional<T>` type we built in chapter 3 as another simple but powerful generic type.

Next, we'll talk about data structures. Data structures give shape to our data without having to be aware of what the data is. Making these structures generic allows us to reuse the shape for all sorts of values, significantly reducing the amount of code we need to write. We'll start with a binary tree of numbers and a linked list of strings, and derive a generic binary tree and linked list from them.

Generic data structures don't solve all our problems: we still need to traverse them. We'll see how we can use iterators to provide a common interface for traversing any data structure. This also helps us reduce the amount of code we need, as we don't have to provide different versions of functions for each data structure, but a single version that works with iterators. Again, we'll use generators, which we introduced in chapter 6. These resumable functions yield values, and we can use them to implement iterators over our data structures.

Finally, we'll talk about chaining functions into processing pipelines and running them over potentially infinite streams of data.

9.1 *Decoupling concerns*

Let's introduce generics with a simple example: we have a function, `getNumbers()`, that gives us an array of numbers but allows us to apply a transformation to them before returning them. This is done with a `transform()` argument that takes a number and returns a number. Callers can pass in such a `transform()` function, and `getNumbers()` will apply it before returning its result, as shown in the next listing.

Listing 9.1 `getNumbers()`

```
type TransformFunction = (value: number) => number;

function getNumbers(
    transform: TransformFunction): number[] {
    /* ... */
}
```

The type of a function that takes a number and returns a number

Callers provide a transform() that gets applied to each number before being returned in the result array.

What if the callers don't need to apply any transformation? A good default for this `transform()` would be a function that doesn't do anything—one that simply returns its result, as shown in the following listing.

Listing 9.2 Default `transform()`

```
type TransformFunction = (value: number) => number;

function doNothing(value: number): number {
    return value;
}

function getNumbers(
    transform: TransformFunction = doNothing): number[] {
    /* ... */
}
```

doNothing() simply returns its argument without applying any transformation.

getNumbers() uses doNothing() as a default, so callers can skip providing an argument if they don't need any transformation applied.

Let's look at another example. Assume that we have an array of `Widget` objects and a way to create an `AssembledWidget` object out of a `Widget` object. An `assemble-Widgets()` function handles an array of `Widget` objects and returns an array of

`AssembledWidget` objects. Because we don't want to assemble more than needed, `assembleWidgets()` takes as argument a `pluck()` function, which, given an array of `Widget` objects, returns a subset of this array, as shown in the following code. This allows callers to tell the function which widgets really need assembling, so the rest can be ignored.

Listing 9.3   `assembleWidgets()`

The type of a function that takes an array of widgets and returns a subset of that array

```
type PluckFunction = (widgets: Widget[]) => Widget[];

function assembleWidgets(
    pluck: PluckFunction): AssembledWidget[] {
    /* ... */
}
```

Callers provide pluck(), which assembleWidgets() calls to select the widgets that need assembly.

What would be a good default for this `pluck()` function? We can say that if the caller doesn't supply a `pluck()` function, we transform the whole list of widgets. Let's call this default `pluckAll()` and have it simply return its argument in the next listing.

Listing 9.4   Default `pluck()`

```
type PluckFunction = (widgets: Widget[]) => Widget[];

function pluckAll(widgets: Widget[]): Widget[] {
    return widgets;
}

function assembleWidgets(
    pluck: PluckFunction = pluckAll): AssembledWidget[] {
    /* ... */
}
```

pluckAll() simply returns the whole array it gets.

We use pluckAll() as a default value for the argument if the user doesn't provide a pluck() themselves.

Looking at our two examples side by side, we can see that `doNothing()` and `pluckAll()` are very similar: they both take an argument and return it without doing any processing, as the following listing shows.

Listing 9.5   `doNothing()` and `pluckAll()`

```
function doNothing(value: number): number {
    return value;
}

function pluckAll(widgets: Widget[]): Widget[] {
    return widgets;
}
```

The difference between them is the type of the value they take and return: `doNothing()` uses a number, and `pluckAll()` uses an array of `Widget` objects. Both functions are *identity functions*. In algebra, an identity function is a function `f(x) = x`.

9.1.1 A reusable identity function

It's not great that we had to create two separate functions that are so similar. This approach doesn't scale well. Can we simplify this process by writing a reusable identity function? The answer is yes.

   Let's start with a naïve approach and say that because identity is the same for any type, we simply use `any`. This would give us an `identity()` function that takes a value of type `any` and returns a value of type `any`, as shown in the next listing.

Listing 9.6 Naïve identity

```
function identity(value: any): any {
    return value;
}
```

The problem with this implementation is that when we start using `any`, we bypass the type checker and lose type safety, as shown in the following listing. We can pass the result of calling `identity()` with a string to a function that expects a number, and the code will compile just fine, but it will fail at run time.

Listing 9.7 Unsafe use of `any`

```
function square(x: number): number {
    return x * x;
}

square(identity("Hello!"));
```
⊲ **This compiles and fails at run time because any bypasses the normal type checks.**

There is a safer way to do this: parameterize what is different between the functions, namely the type of their argument. This parameter will be a type parameter.

> **TYPE PARAMETER** A *type parameter* is an identifier for a generic type name. Type parameters are used as placeholders for specific types that the client specifies when creating an instance of the generic type.

In the next listing, our generic identity will use a type parameter `T`, which will be `number` in the first case and `Widget[]` in the second case.

Listing 9.8 Generic identity

```
function identity<T>(value: T): T {
    return value;
}
```
⊲ **Generic identity function with a type parameter T**

```
function getNumbers(
    transform: TransformFunction = identity): number[] {
    /* ... */
}
function assembleWidgets(
    pluck: PluckFunction = identity): AssembledWidget[] {
    /* ... */
}
```

We can use identity() instead of
doNothing(). T becomes number in this case.

We can use identity() instead of pluckAll().
T becomes Widget[] in this case.

The compiler is smart enough to figure out what T should be without our having to spell it out. We no longer need doNothing() and pluckAll(), and we can reuse this with any other type if we need an identity function. Now when the type is determined, such as when the getNumbers() case T is number, the compiler can perform type checking, and we no longer end up in a situation like attempting to square() a string, as shown in the next listing.

Listing 9.9 Type safety

```
function identity<T>(value: T): T {
    return value;
}

square(identity("Hello!"));
```

This no longer
compiles.

We could come up with this implementation because the mechanics of the identity function are the same regardless of the type the function is used with. We effectively decoupled the identity logic from the problem domain of getNumbers() and assembleWidgets() because the identity logic and the problem domain are *orthogonal*, or independent.

9.1.2 *The optional type*

As another example, take a look at the Optional implementation we provided in chapter 3. Remember that an optional type contains a value of some type T or doesn't contain anything.

Listing 9.10 Optional type

```
class Optional<T> {
    private value: T | undefined;
    private assigned: boolean;

    constructor(value?: T) {
        if (value) {
            this.value = value;
            this.assigned = true;
        } else {
            this.value = undefined;
            this.assigned = false;
        }
    }
}
```

Optional wraps a
generic type T.

value is an optional argument
because TypeScript doesn't
support constructor overloads.

```
hasValue(): boolean {
    return this.assigned;
}

getValue(): T {
    if (!this.assigned) throw Error();

    return <T>this.value;
}
```

> If a value is not assigned,
> attempting to get a value
> throws an exception.

The logic of handling the absence of a value is, again, independent of the actual type of the value. We have a generic `Optional` type that can store any other type, as it will handle anything in the same way. You can think of `Optional` as being in a completely different dimension from `T`, as any changes we make to `Optional` do not affect `T`, and any changes made to `T` do not affect `Optional`. This isolation is an extremely powerful feature of generic programming.

9.1.3   *Generic types*

We just saw two uses of generics: a generic function and a generic class. Now let's step back and look at what makes generic types special. We started the book by looking at basic types and ways to combine them. We have types such as `boolean` and `number`, and types such as `boolean | number`. We have function types such as `() => number`. As we can see, none of these types has any type parameter. A number is a number. A function that returns a number is a function that returns a number.

When we introduce generics, this situation changes. We have a generic function `(value: T) => T`, with a type parameter `T`. We create specific functions when we specify an actual type for `T`. If we use `Widget[]`, for example, we end up with a function type `(value: Widget[]) => Widget[]`. This is the first time when we can plug in types and get different type definitions (figure 9.1).

> **GENERIC TYPES**   A *generic type* is a generic function, class, interface, and so on that is parameterized over one or more types. Generic types allow us to write general code that works with different types, enabling a high level of code reuse.

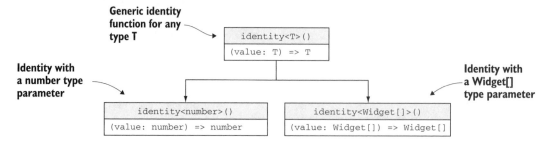

Figure 9.1   Generic identity with a type parameter `T` and two instances: `identity<number>()` with the concrete type `(value: number) => number` and `identity<Widget[]>()` with the concrete type `(value: Widget[]) => Widget[]`

As we saw in the previous examples, and as we'll see throughout this chapter and the next, being able to use generics makes our code much better componentized. We can use these generic components as building blocks and combine them to achieve the desired behavior while having minimal dependency between them. Moving beyond our simple `identity<T>()` and `Optional<T>` examples, let's look at data structures.

9.1.4 Exercises

1 Implement a generic `Box<T>` type that simply wraps a value of type `T`.
2 Implement a generic `unbox<T>()` function that takes a `Box<T>` and returns the boxed value.

9.2 Generic data layout

Let's start with a couple of nongeneric examples: a binary tree of numbers, shown in listing 9.11, and a linked list of strings shown in listing 9.12. I'm sure that you are familiar with these simple data structures. We will implement the tree as one or more nodes, each node storing a number value and references to its left and right children. These refences can be to nodes or `undefined` in case there is no child node.

Listing 9.11 Binary tree of numbers

```
class NumberBinaryTreeNode {
    value: number;
    left: NumberBinaryTreeNode | undefined;
    right: NumberBinaryTreeNode | undefined;

    constructor(value: number) {
        this.value = value;
    }
}
```

We will similarly implement the linked list as one or more nodes, each storing a `string` and a reference to the next node, or `undefined` if there is no next node, as the next listing shows.

Listing 9.12 Linked list of strings

```
class StringLinkedListNode {
    value: string;
    next: StringLinkedListNode | undefined;

    constructor(value: string) {
        this.value = value;
    }
}
```

Now what if we need, in another part of our project, a binary tree of strings? We can implement a `StringBinaryTreeNode` that is identical to `NumberBinaryTreeNode` and replace the type of value from `number` to `string`. This is tempting, as we can just copy/paste the code and replace a couple of things, but copy/pasting is never a good option. Imagine that our class also has a bunch of methods. If we copied/pasted those methods and then found a bug in one of the versions, we'd likely miss fixing the bug in the copied/pasted version. We're sure you see where this is going: we can use generics instead of duplication!

9.2.1 Generic data structures

We can implement a generic `BinaryTreeNode<T>` that works for any type, as shown in the next listing.

Listing 9.13 Generic binary tree

```
class BinaryTreeNode<T> {
    value: T;
    left: BinaryTreeNode<T> | undefined;
    right: BinaryTreeNode<T> | undefined;

    constructor(value: T) {
        this.value = value;
    }
}
```

A **BinaryTreeNode<T>** stores a value of type T.

In fact, we shouldn't wait for the new requirement to have a binary tree of strings to come in: our original `NumberBinaryTreeNode` implementation has an unnecessary coupling between the binary tree data structure and the type `number`. Similarly, we can replace our `StringLinkedListNode` with a generic `LinkedListNode<T>`, shown in the following listing.

Listing 9.14 Generic linked list

```
class LinkedListNode<T> {
    value: T;
    next: LinkedListNode<T> | undefined;

    constructor(value: T) {
        this.value = value;
    }
}
```

Do keep in mind that most languages have libraries that already provide most of the data structures you need (lists, queues, stacks, sets, dictionaries, and so on). We're going over implementations to better understand generics, but the best thing to do is not to write code at all. If we can choose a generic data structure from a library, we should do that.

9.2.2 What is a data structure?

Let's get a bit philosophical and ask "What is the nature of a data structure?" A data structure consists of three parts:

- *The data itself*—the `number` and `string` values in our trees and lists in the preceding example. Data structures contain data.

- *The shape of the data*—In our binary tree, the data is laid out in hierarchical fashion, with one element having at most two children. In our list, the data is laid out sequentially, one element coming after the previous one.
- *A set of shape-preserving operations*—Our data structure might provide this set of operations for adding or removing an element, for example. We did not provide any such operations in the preceding examples, but it's easy to imagine how after removing an element from the middle of a linked list, for example, we would still want to end up with a linked list.

There are two separate concerns here. One is the data—the type of the data and the actual value that an instance of the data structure holds. The other is the shape of the data and the shape-preserving operations. Generic data structures like the ones we saw at the beginning of this section help us decouple these concerns. A generic data structure handles the layout of the data, its shape, and any shape-preserving operations. A binary tree is a binary tree regardless of whether it contains strings or numbers. We can componentize our code by moving the responsibility for data layout to generic data structures that are independent of the actual data content.

Assuming that we have all these data structures, let's look at how we can traverse them and view their content.

9.2.3 Exercises

1 Implement a `Stack<T>` data structure representing a stack (last-in-first-out) with the common `push()`, `pop()`, and `peek()` methods.
2 Implement a `Pair<T, U>` data structure with `first` and `second` members of the two types.

9.3 *Traversing any data structure*

Let's say we want to traverse our binary tree in order and print the value of all its elements, as shown in listing 9.15. As a quick reminder, an in-order traversal is the recursive traversal left–parent–right (figure 9.2).

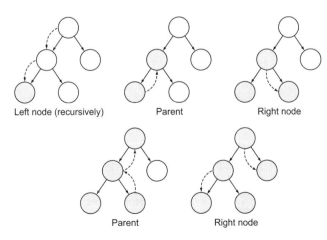

Left node (recursively)   Parent   Right node

Parent   Right node

Figure 9.2 In-order traversal. Recursively go left until we reach the leftmost node, go to its parent, and then go to the right node. Next, we go back to the parent of the parent and then go to its right node. The order is always *left*; then, when that subtree is all visited, *parent*; and then *right*.

Listing 9.15 Print in order

```
class BinaryTreeNode<T> {                        ◁─────┐ This is the same generic binary
    value: T;                                            tree we defined before.
    left: BinaryTreeNode<T> | undefined;
    right: BinaryTreeNode<T> | undefined;

    constructor(value: T) {
        this.value = value;
    }
}

function printInOrder<T>(root: BinaryTreeNode<T>): void {
    if (root.left != undefined) {                ◁─────┐ We recursively go to the
        printInOrder(root.left);                         left child if one exists.
    }
                                    ┌─ Then we print the
    console.log(root.value);     ◁──┘ value of this node.

    if (root.right != undefined) {               ◁─────┐ Finally, we recursively go to
        printInOrder(root.right);                        the right child if one exists.
    }
}
```

As an example, let's create a tree with a few nodes and see what `printInOrder()` returns in the following code.

Listing 9.16 `printInOrder()` example

```
let root: BinaryTreeNode<number> = new BinaryTreeNode(1);
root.left = new BinaryTreeNode(2);
root.left.right = new BinaryTreeNode(3);
root.right = new BinaryTreeNode(4);

printInOrder(root);
```

This code creates the tree shown in figure 9.3.

Traversing it in order will print

```
2
3
1
4
```

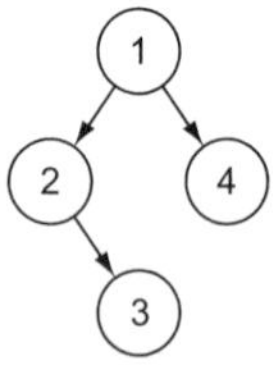

Figure 9.3 Binary tree example

What if we also want to print all the values of a linked list of strings? We can implement a `printList()` function that traverses a list from head to tail and prints each element, as the next listing shows.

Listing 9.17 Print linked list

```
class LinkedListNode<T> {                        ◁─────┐ The generic linked list
    value: T;                                            implementation we saw before
    next: LinkedListNode<T> | undefined;
```

```
    constructor(value: T) {
        this.value = value;
    }
}

function printLinkedList<T>(head: LinkedListNode<T>): void {
    let current: LinkedListNode<T> | undefined = head;

    while (current) {
        console.log(current.value);
        current = current.next;
    }
}
```

We start from
the head
of the list.

We repeat as long as
we still have a node.

Print the node value, and
advance to the next node.

Taking a concrete example, we can initialize a list of strings and print it by using
`printLinkedList()`, shown in the following listing.

Listing 9.18 `printLinkedList()` **example**

```
let head: LinkedListNode<string> = new LinkedListNode("Hello");
head.next = new LinkedListNode("World");
head.next.next = new LinkedListNode("!!!");

printLinkedList(head);
```

This code creates the list shown in figure 9.4.

Figure 9.4 **Linked list example**

Running the code will print

```
Hello
World
!!!
```

This works, but maybe there is a better way.

9.3.1 *Using iterators*

What if we could further split the code apart based on responsibilities? Our `print-InOrder()` and `printLinkedList()` functions perform two tasks: traverse a data structure and print its contents. Even worse, the second task overlaps; both functions print values.

We can make another generalization. Let's move traversal to its own component. Let's start with our binary tree. We need a way to go over every item in the tree in order and return the value of each node. We can call this traversal *iteration*; we are iterating over the data structure.

ITERATOR   An *iterator* is an object that enables traversal of a data structure. It provides a standard interface that hides the actual shape of the data structure from the clients.

Let's implement our iterators. We'll start by defining an `IteratorResult<T>` as a type that contains two properties: a `value` property of type `T` and a `done` property of type `boolean` that simply tells us whether we've reached the end, as shown in the following listing.

Listing 9.19   Iterator result

```
type IteratorResult<T> = {
    done: boolean;
    value: T;
}
```

In the next listing, define an iterator interface `Iterator<T>` that declares a single `next()` method. This method returns an `IteratorResult<T>`.

Listing 9.20   Iterator interface

```
interface Iterator<T> {
    next(): IteratorResult<T>;
}
```

Now we can implement a `BinaryTreeNodeIterator<T>` as a class implementing `Iterator<T>`, as shown in listing 9.21. We're doing an in-order traversal with the private method `inOrder()` and pushing all node values to a queue. The `next()` method dequeues the values by using the array `shift()` method and returns `IteratorResult<T>` values until there are no more values to return (figure 9.5).

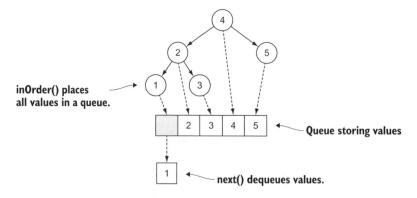

Figure 9.5   `inOrder()` traverses the binary tree in order and adds all values to a queue. `next()` dequeues values and returns them during traversal.

Listing 9.21 Binary tree iterator

```
class BinaryTreeIterator<T> implements Iterator<T> {
    private values: T[];
    private root: BinaryTreeNode<T>;

    constructor(root: BinaryTreeNode<T>) {
        this.values = [];
        this.root = root;

        this.inOrder(root);
    }

    next(): IteratorResult<T> {
        const result: T | undefined = this.values.shift();

        if (!result) {
            return { done: true, value: this.root.value };
        }

        return { done: false, value: result };
    }

    private inOrder(node: BinaryTreeNode<T>): void {
        if (node.left != undefined) {
            this.inOrder(node.left);
        }

        this.values.push(node.value);

        if (node.right != undefined) {
            this.inOrder(node.right);
        }
    }
}
```

Queue of values

Constructor performs an in-order traversal to populate the queue of values.

Each call to next() dequeues a value by calling shift().

If result is undefined, we set done as true and return some default value.

inOrder() performs the in-order traversal.

We add the value of each node to the value queue.

This implementation is not the most efficient, as we need a queue with the same number of elements as the number of nodes in the tree. We can do a more efficient traversal that requires less memory, but the logic gets more complex. Let's use this for now as an example, as we'll soon see a better and simpler way to do this.

Let's also implement the LinkedListIterator<T> to traverse our linked list in the next listing.

Listing 9.22 Linked list iterator

```
class LinkedListIterator<T> implements Iterator<T> {
    private head: LinkedListNode<T>;
    private current: LinkedListNode<T> | undefined;

    constructor(head: LinkedListNode<T>) {
        this.head = head;
        this.current = head;
    }
```

```
next(): IteratorResult<T> {
    if (!this.current) {
        return { done: true, value: this.head.value };
    }

    const result: T = this.current.value;
    this.current = this.current.next;
    return { done: false, value: result };
}
}
```

If we've reached the end of the list and current is undefined, set done to true and return some dummy value (which should never be used).

result stores the value of the current node.

We advance the current node to the next node in the list.

Return the stored result.

With the plumbing out of the way, let's see why these iterators are useful. If we want to print the values of all the nodes in a binary tree and all the strings in a linked list of strings, we no longer need separate functions. We can use a single common function that takes an iterator argument, which uses it to retrieve the values to print, as shown in the following code.

Listing 9.23 `print()` using iterator

print() is a generic function that takes an iterator as argument.

```
function print<T>(iterator: Iterator<T>): void {
    let result: IteratorResult<T> = iterator.next();

    while (!result.done) {
        console.log(result.value);
        result = iterator.next();
    }
}
```

We initialize with next(), pulling the first value.

Although result doesn't return done as true, we can print the value and advance the iterator.

Because `print()` works with iterators, we can pass to it either a `BinaryTree-Iterator<T>` or a `LinkedListIterator<T>`. In fact, we can use it to print any data structure as long as we have an iterator that can traverse that data structure.

With iterators, we can reuse a lot more code. If we need a way to determine whether a certain value exists in a data structure, for example, we don't need to implement a separate function for each data structure; we can simply implement a `contains()` function that takes an iterator and a value to look for, as shown in the next listing, and then we can use it with any iterator that implements the `Iterator<T>` interface (figure 9.6).

Listing 9.24 `contains()` using iterator

```
function contains<T>(value: T, iterator: Iterator<T>): boolean {
    let result: IteratorResult<T> = iterator.next();

    while (!result.done) {
        if (result.value == value) return true;
```

```
        result = iterator.next();
    }

    return false;
}
```

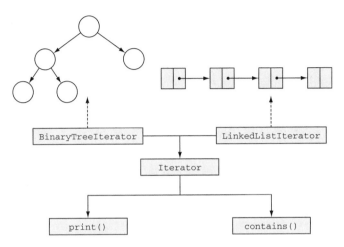

Figure 9.6 `BinaryTreeIterator` **implements binary tree traversal.**
`LinkedListIterator` **implements linked list traversal. Both**
implement the `Iterator` **contract.** `print()` **and** `contains()` **take**
an `Iterator` **as argument, so we can mix and match the functions**
with different data structures.

Iterators are the glue that connects data structures and algorithms, enabling this decoupling. With this approach, we can mix and match different data structures with different functions if the interface between them is `Iterator<T>`.

Note that a data structure may have different traversals. We've focused on an in-order traversal of a binary tree, but there are also pre-order and post-order traversals. We can implement all these traversals as iterators over the same binary tree. A one-to-one correspondence doesn't have to exist between traversal strategies and data structures.

9.3.2 *Streamlining iteration code*

Iterators are so useful that most mainstream languages provide library support for them and, in many cases, even special syntax. We briefly touched on this topic in chapter 6, when we looked at generators, and we'll expand on it here.

We didn't really have to define the `IteratorResult<T>` and `Iterator<T>` types; TypeScript has them predefined. In C#, the equivalent interface is `IEnumerator<T>`, which similarly enables traversal of data structures. The Java equivalent is also named `Iterator<T>`. The C++ library works with several kinds of iterators. We'll talk more about these categories in chapter 10, when we talk about iterator categories. The key takeaway here is that this pattern is so useful that it has out-of-the-box support.

Whereas iterators implement the code to traverse a data structure, another interface lets us mark a type as something that can be iterated over: the `Iterable<T>` interface, defined as follows.

```
interface Iterable<T> {
    [Symbol.iterator](): Iterator<T>;
}
```

The `[Symbol.iterator]` is a bit of TypeScript-specific syntax. It just means a special name, very much like the symbol trick we used to implement nominal subtyping throughout the book. The `Iterable<T>` interface declares a method named `[Symbol.iterator]()` that returns an `Iterator<T>`.

Let's update our `LinkedListNode<T>` type and make it iterable in the next listing.

```
class LinkedListNode<T> implements Iterable<T> {
    value: T;
    next: LinkedListNode<T> | undefined;

    constructor(value: T) {
        this.value = value;
    }

    [Symbol.iterator](): Iterator<T> {
        return new LinkedListIterator<T>(this);
    }
}
```

We implement the Iterable<T> interface by creating a new instance of LinkedListIterator on this list.

We can also mark our binary tree as iterable by providing a similar `[Symbol.iterator]()` method that creates a `BinaryTreeIterator<T>`.

Iterables allow us to use the `for ... of` syntax in TypeScript. This syntax is special syntax for iterating over all elements of an iterable and makes our code much cleaner. Most mainstream languages have an equivalent. C# has `IEnumerable<T>`, `IEnumerator<T>`, and `foreach` loops. Java has `Iterable<T>`, `Iterator<T>`, and `for :` loops.

Let's quickly review the `print()` and `contains()` implementations in the next listing and then update them to use iterables and `for ... of` instead.

```
function print<T>(iterator: Iterator<T>): void {
    let result: IteratorResult<T> = iterator.next();

    while (!result.done) {
        console.log(result.value);
        result = iterator.next();
```

```
    }
}

function contains<T>(value: T, iterator: Iterator<T>): boolean {
    let result: IteratorResult<T> = iterator.next();

    while (!result.done) {
        if (result.value == value) return true;

        result = iterator.next();
    }

    return false;
}
```

We'll update the functions to take an `Iterable<T>` argument instead of an `Iterator<T>` in the next listing. An `Iterator<T>` can always be obtained from an `Iterable<T>` by calling the `[Symbol.iterator]()` method.

Listing 9.28 `print()` and `contains()` **with Iterable argument**

```
function print<T>(iterable: Iterable<T>): void {
    for (const item of iterable) {          ⊲⎯⎯    print() uses a for...of
        console.log(item);                              loop to print each
    }                                                   element to the console.
}

function contains<T>(value: T, iterable: Iterable<T>): boolean {
    for (const item of iterable) {          ⊲⎯⎯    contains() uses a for...of
        if (item == value) return true;                 loop to compare each
    }                                                   element to the given value.

    return false;
}
```

As we can see, the code is much more succinct. Instead of iterating over our data structures manually, using an `Iterator<T>` and `next()`, we can do it with a one-liner that uses `for...of`.

Now let's see how we can simplify our iterator code. We said that our in-order binary tree traversal is inefficient, as it queues all the nodes before returning them. A more efficient solution would traverse the tree without queuing all nodes, but the implementation would get a bit more complex. Following is the implementation we've used so far.

Listing 9.29 Binary tree iterator

```
class BinaryTreeIterator<T> implements Iterator<T> {
    private values: T[];
    private root: BinaryTreeNode<T>;

    constructor(root: BinaryTreeNode<T>) {
        this.values = [];
        this.root = root;
```

```
        this.inOrder(root);
    }

    next(): IteratorResult<T> {
        const result: T | undefined = this.values.shift();

        if (!result) {
            return { done: true, value: this.root.value };
        }

        return { done: false, value: result };
    }

    private inOrder(node: BinaryTreeNode<T>): void {
        if (node.left != undefined) {
            this.inOrder(node.left);
        }

        this.values.push(node.value);

        if (node.right != undefined) {
            this.inOrder(node.right);
        }
    }
}
```

What we can do is replace this code with a generator. (We briefly talked about generators in chapter 6.) A generator is a resumable function that returns using a `yield` statement and, when called again, resumes execution from where it left off. Generators in TypeScript return an `IterableIterator<T>`, which is simply a combination of the two interfaces we've learned about: `Iterable<T>` and `Iterator<T>`. An object that implements both can be iterated over "manually" with `next()` but can also be used in a `for...of` statement.

Let's reimplement our binary tree traversal as a generator in listing 9.30. With generators, we can implement traversal recursively and keep yielding values until we've gone over the whole data structure (figure 9.7).

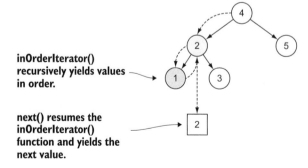

inOrderIterator()
recursively yields values
in order.

next() resumes the
inOrderIterator()
function and yields the
next value.

Figure 9.7   `inOrderIterator()` is a generator, so it returns an `IterableIterator<T>`. Like `inOrder()`, this function recursively traverses the tree, but instead of queuing items, it yields them. Calling `next()` on the returned iterator resumes the generator and yields the next value.

Listing 9.30   Binary tree iterator using generator

```
function* inOrderIterator<T>(root: BinaryTreeNode<T>):
    IterableIterator<T> {
    if (root.left) {
        for (const value of inOrderIterator(root.left)) {
            yield value;
        }
    }

    yield root.value;

    if (root.right) {
        for (const value of inOrderIterator(root.right)) {
            yield value;
        }
    }
}
```

⊲ **function* defines this function as a generator, so it can yield and resume.**

⊲ **First, traverse the left subtree and yield all returned values.**

⊲ **Then yield the current value.**

⊲ **Then traverse the right subtree and yield all returned values.**

This implementation is much more succinct. Note that `inOrderIterator()` is recursive. At each level, values are yielded "up" until they propagate to the original caller.

Similarly, we can traverse our linked list with a generator, simplifying the logic. Our original implementation looked like the following listing.

Listing 9.31   Linked list iterator

```
class LinkedListIterator<T> implements Iterator<T> {
    private head: LinkedListNode<T>;
    private current: LinkedListNode<T> | undefined;

    constructor(head: LinkedListNode<T>) {
        this.head = head;
        this.current = head;
    }

    next(): IteratorResult<T> {
        if (!this.current) {
            return { done: true, value: this.head.value };
        }

        const result: T = this.current.value;
        this.current = this.current.next;
        return { done: false, value: result };
    }
}
```

We can replace this with another generator that yields values as it traverses the list, as shown in the following listing.

Listing 9.32   Linked list iterator using generator

```
function* linkedListIterator<T>(head: LinkedListNode<T>):
    IterableIterator<T> {
    let current: LinkedListNode<T> | undefined = head;
```

```
    while (current) {
        yield current.value;
        current = current.next;
    }
}
```

> We yield each value as
> we traverse the linked list.

The compiler translates this into an iterator that provides `IteratorResult<T>` values from each `yield`. When the function reaches the end and exits (without yielding a value), a final `IteratorResult<T>` with `done` set to `true` is returned.

The final step is plugging these generators into the data structures themselves as implementations of `[Symbol.iterator]()`. Let's see what our final version of the linked list looks like.

Listing 9.33   Iterable linked list using generator

```
class LinkedListNode<T> implements Iterable<T> {
    value: T;
    next: LinkedListNode<T> | undefined;

    constructor(value: T) {
        this.value = value;
    }

    [Symbol.iterator](): Iterator<T> {
        return linkedListIterator(this);
    }
}
```

> **[Symbol.iterator]() simply
> returns the result of
> linkedListIterator().**

This works because the generator returns an `IterableIterator<T>`. Sometimes we want an `Iterable<T>` so we can embed a call to the generator inside a `for...of` loop (for example, `for (const value of linkedListIterator(...))`. Sometimes we want an `Iterator<T>` instead, as in the preceding example, so we can use a `for...of` loop on an instance of the data structure itself.

9.3.3   *Iterators recap*

We started with a couple of generic data structures that took care of the shape of the data, regardless of what that data was. We saw that this abstraction is powerful. But if we write code to traverse each data structure whenever we want to apply an operation over it, such as `print()` or `contains()`, we end up with multiple versions of each function.

Enter `Iterator<T>`, an interface that decouples the shape of the data from the functions by providing a unified traversal interface using `next()`. This interface allows us to write a single version of `print()` and a single version of `contains()`, both operating on iterators.

Iterating by calling `next()` and checking `done` is still cumbersome, though. Turns out `Iterable<T>` is an interface that declares a `[Symbol.iterator]()` method. We can use this method to get an iterator. Better yet, we can put an `Iterable<T>` in a for...of statement. Not only is this syntax cleaner, but we also never have to deal with the iterator explicitly, as on each iteration of the loop, we get the actual element.

Finally, we saw that we can simplify the traversal code if we use a generator that yields values as it traverses the data structure. Generators return an `Iterable-Iterator<T>`, so we can use them both directly inside `for...of` loops or to implement a data structure's `Iterable<T>` interface.

As mentioned earlier, most mainstream programming languages have an equivalent special type that enables a `for` loop that traverses over elements. As for generators, although Java lacks a built-in `yield` statement, C# supports them, using a syntax very similar to TypeScript's.

In general, when defining a data structure, make sure that it implements `Iterable<T>`. Avoid writing functions that embed traversal of one particular data structure; rather, have them work with iterators so that the same logic can be reused with different data structures. Consider `yield` when implementing the traversal logic, as it usually makes code cleaner and more concise.

A better IteratorResult<T>

It's unfortunate that we have to use `IteratorResult<T>` as the return type of `next()`. This is how the interface is defined out of the box in TypeScript. It goes against the principle we outlined in chapter 3 to return result or error from a function as opposed to both. `IteratorResult<T>` contains a `boolean` property `done` and a `value` property of type `T`. When the iterator has traversed the whole list, it returns `done` as `true` but also needs to return something for `value`. This `value` must be some default, as it is mandatory, but the data structure was fully traversed. Calling code is never meant to use `value` if `done` is `true`. Unfortunately, there is no way to enforce this rule.

A better contract would be a sum type such as `Optional<T>` or `T | undefined`. This will return `T`s as long as values are available and then nothing when traversal is finished.

9.3.4 Exercises

1 Implement a pre-order traversal for a generic binary tree. Pre-order traversal is parent first, followed by left subtree and then right subtree. Try implementing it with a generator.
2 Implement a function that iterates over an array backward (from back to front).

9.4 Streaming data

In this last section, we will look at a very interesting aspect of iterators: the fact that they don't necessarily have to be finite. In the next listing, let's implement a function that generates an infinite stream of random numbers. We'll call it `generateRandom-Numbers()` and have it yield these numbers from an infinite loop.

Listing 9.34   Inifinite stream of random numbers

```
function* generateRandomNumbers(): IterableIterator<number> {
    while (true) {                                          ⟵── Loop forever.
        yield Math.random();        ⟵── Yields a random
    }                                      number at each step.
}
```

We can call this function to get an `IterableIterator<T>` and then call `next()` on it a few times to get random numbers, as shown in the following listing.

Listing 9.35   Consuming values from the stream

```
let iter: IterableIterator<number> = generateRandomNumbers();

console.log(iter.next().value);
console.log(iter.next().value);
console.log(iter.next().value);
```

There are many examples of infinite streams of data in real life: reading characters from the keyboard, receiving data over a network connection, collecting sensor data, and so on. We can process such data by using pipelines.

9.4.1 *Processing pipelines*

The components of processing pipelines are functions that take an iterator as argument, do some processing, and return an iterator. Such functions can be chained together to process data as it arrives. This pattern is common in functional programming languages and the basis of reactive programming.

As an example, let's implement a `square()` function that squares all numbers of its input iterator. We can do this easily with a generator that takes an `Iterable<number>` argument and yields squares of its values, as shown in listing 9.36. Note that we don't need an `IterableIterator<number>` as input—just an `Iterable<number>`—but passing one in will work, as an `IterableIterator<number>` also satisfies the `Iterable<number>` interface.

Listing 9.36   `square()`

```
function* square(iter: Iterable<number>):
    IterableIterator<number> {                 The function takes an
    for (const value of iter) {                Iterable<number> and returns
        yield value ** 2;                      an IterableIterator<number>.
    }
}
```

A common function in processing pipeline is `take()`, a function that takes the first n elements of its input iterator and returns them, discarding the rest, as shown in the following code.

Listing 9.37 take()

```
function* take<T>(iter: Iterable<T>, n: number):
    IterableIterator<T> {
    for (const value of iter) {
        if (n-- <= 0) return;          ◁──┐ We decrement n and stop
                                           │ when we've yielded n values.
        yield value;          ◁──┐ Yield
    }                             │ one value.
}
```

Now let's create a pipeline in listing 9.38 that squares numbers from an infinite stream and takes the first five results, which we print to the console (figure 9.8).

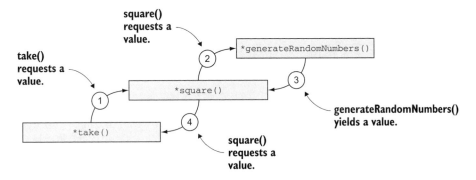

Figure 9.8 Pipeline and call sequence. take() requests a value from square()'s iterator. square() requests a value from generateRandomNumber()'s iterator. generateRandomNumbers() yields a value to square(). square() yields a value to take().

Listing 9.38 Pipeline

```
const values: IterableIterator<number> =
    take(square(generateRandomNumbers()), 5);     ◁──┐ take() takes five values from
                                                      │ square, which takes values from
for (const value of values) {                         │ generateRandomNumbers().
    console.log(value);
}
```

Iterators are the key to creating this type of pipeline, as they enable one-by-one processing of values. It's also important to understand that these pipelines are evaluated lazily. In our example in this listing, values is an IterableIterator<number>. Even though it is created by calling our pipeline, none of the code is executed yet. Only when we start consuming values in the for...of loop do values start flowing through.

In one iteration of the loop, next() is called on the values iterator, which invokes take(). take() needs a value, so it in turn calls square(). Similarly, square() needs

a value to square, so it calls generateRandomNumbers(). generateRandom-
Numbers() yields a random value to square(), which squares it and yields it to
take(). take() yields it to the loop, where it is printed to the console.

Because pipelines are evaluated lazily, we can work with infinite generators, such as
generateRandomNumbers(). We'll cover algorithms in more depth in chapter 10.

9.4.2   Exercises

1   drop() is another common function. This function is the opposite of take(),
    as it discards the first n elements of an iterator and returns the rest. Implement
    drop().
2   Create a pipeline that, given an iterator, returns the sixth, seventh, eighth,
    ninth, and tenth elements. Hint: this can be done with a combination of
    drop() and take().

Summary

- Generics are useful for separating independent concerns.
- Generic data structures are responsible for the shape of the data, regardless of
  what that data is.
- Iterators provide a common interface for traversing data structures.
- Iterator<T> represents an iterator, whereas Iterable<T> represents some-
  thing that can be iterated over.
- Iterators can be implemented by using generators.
- Most programming languages have iterators and special syntax to loop over
  them.
- Iterators don't have to be finite: they can produce values forever.
- Using functions that take and return iterators, we can build processing pipelines.

Now that we've covered generic data structures, chapter 10 looks at the other main
ingredients of programing: algorithms.

Answers to exercises

DECOUPLING CONCERNS

1   A possible implementation:

```
class Box<T> {
    readonly value: T;

    constructor(value: T) {
        this.value = value;
    }
}
```

2   A possible implementation:

```
function unbox<T>(boxed: Box<T>): T {
    return boxed.value;
}
```

GENERIC DATA LAYOUT

1 A possible implementation backed by an array (in JavaScript, arrays come with
pop() and push() out of the box):

```
class Stack<T> {
    private values: T[] = [];

    public push(value: T) {
        this.values.push(value);
    }

    public pop(): T {
        if (this.values.length == 0) throw Error();

        return this.values.pop();
    }

    public peek(): T {
        if (this.values.length == 0) throw Error();

        return this.values[this.values.length - 1];
    }
}
```

2 A possible implementation:

```
class Pair<T, U> {
    readonly first: T;
    readonly second: U;

    constructor(first: T, second: U) {
        this.first = first;
        this.second = second;
    }
}
```

TRAVERSING ANY DATA STRUCTURE

1 This implementation is very similar to the in-order one; we just yield
root.value before we yield the left subtree:

```
function* preOrderIterator<T>(root: BinaryTreeNode<T>):
    IterableIterator<T> {
    yield root.value;

    if (root.left) {
        for (const value of preOrderIterator(root.left)) {
            yield value;
        }
    }

    if (root.right) {
        for (const value of preOrderIterator(root.right)) {
            yield value;
        }
    }
}
```

2 This implementation does use a `for` loop to traverse the array backward so callers don't have to.

```
function* backwardsArrayIterator<T>(array: T[]): IterableIterator<T> {
    for (let i = array.length - 1; i >= 0; i--) {
        yield array[i];
    }
}
```

STREAMING DATA

1 A possible implementation:

```
function* drop<T>(iter: Iterable<T>, n: number):
    IterableIterator<T> {
    for (const value of iter) {
        if (n-- > 0) continue;

        yield value;
    }
}
```

2 We can define `count()`, a counter that yields numbers starting from 1 and keeps going. Taking the stream of value it produces, we `drop()` the first five and then `take()` the next five:

```
function* count(): IterableIterator<number> {
    let n: number = 0;

    while (true) {
        n++;
        yield n;
    }
}

for (let value of take(drop(count(), 5), 5)) {
    console.log(value);
}
```

Generic algorithms
and iterators

This chapter covers

- Using `map()`, `filter()`, and `reduce()` beyond arrays
- Using a set of common algorithms to solve a wide range of problems
- Ensuring that a generic type supports a required contract
- Enabling various algorithms with different iterator categories
- Implementing adaptive algorithms

This chapter is all about generic algorithms—reusable algorithms that work on various data types and data structures.

We looked at one version each of `map()`, `filter()`, and `reduce()` in chapter 5, when we discussed higher-order functions. Those functions operated on arrays, but as we saw in the previous chapters, iterators provide a nice abstraction over any data structure. We'll start by implementing generic versions of these three algorithms that work with iterators, so we can apply them to binary trees, lists, arrays, and any other iterable data structures.

map(), filter(), and reduce() are not unique. We'll talk about other generic algorithms and algorithm libraries that are available to most modern programming languages. We'll see why we should replace most loops with calls to library algorithms. We'll also briefly talk about fluent APIs and what a user-friendly interface for algorithms looks like.

Next, we'll go over type parameter constraints; generic data structures and algorithms can specify certain features they need available on their parameter types. This type of specialization allows for generic data structures and algorithms that don't work everywhere; they are somewhat less general.

We'll zoom in on iterators and talk about all the different categories of iterators. More specialized iterators enable more efficient algorithms. The trade-off is that not all data structures can support specialized iterators.

Finally, we'll take a quick look at adaptive algorithms. Such algorithms provide more general, less efficient implementations for iterators with fewer capabilities and more efficient, less general implementations for iterators with more capabilities.

10.1 *Better map(), filter(), reduce()*

In chapter 5, we talked about map(), filter(), and reduce(), and looked at a possible implementation of each of them. These algorithms are higher-order functions, as they each take another function as an argument and apply it over a sequence.

map() applies the function to each element of the sequence and returns the results. filter() applies a filtering function to each element and returns only the elements for which that function returns true. reduce() combines all the values in the sequence, using the given function, and returns a single value as the result.

Our implementation in chapter 5 used a generic type parameter T, and the sequences were represented as arrays of T.

10.1.1 *map()*

Let's take a look at how we implemented map(). We used two type parameters: T and U. The function takes an array of T values as the first argument and a function from T to U as the second argument. It returns an array of U values, as shown in the next listing.

> **Listing 10.1** map()

map() takes an array of items of type T and a function from T to U, and returns an array of Us.

```
function map<T, U>(items: T[], func: (item: T) => U): U[] {
    let result: U[] = [];

    for (const item of items) {
        result.push(func(item));
    }

    return result;
}
```

Start with an empty array of Us.

For each item, push the result of func(item) to the array of Us.

Return the array of Us.

Now that we know about iterators and generators, let's see in the next listing how we can implement `map()` to work on any `Iterable<T>`, not only arrays.

Listing 10.2 `map()` with iterator

```
function* map<T, U>(iter: Iterable<T>, func: (item: T) => U):
    IterableIterator<U> {
    for (const value of iter) {
        yield func(value);
    }
}
```

> map() is now a generator that takes an Iterable<T> as the first argument.

> map() returns an IterableIterator<U>.

> The given function is applied to each value retrieved from the iterator, and the result is yielded.

Whereas the original implementation was restricted to arrays, this one works with any data structure that provides an iterator. Not only that, but it is also more concise.

10.1.2 *filter()*

Let's do the same for `filter()`. Our original implementation expected an array of type `T` and a predicate. As a reminder, a *predicate* is a function that takes one argument of some type and returns a `boolean`. We say that a value satisfies the predicate if the function returns `true` for that value.

Listing 10.3 `filter()`

```
function filter<T>(items: T[], pred: (item: T) => boolean): T[] {
    let result: T[] = [];

    for (const item of items) {
        if (pred(item)) {
            result.push(item);
        }
    }

    return result;
}
```

> filter() takes an array of Ts and a predicate (a function from T to boolean).

> If the predicate returns true, the item is added to the result array; otherwise, it's skipped.

Just as we did with map(), we are going to use an `Iterable<T>` instead of an array and implement this iterable as a generator that yields values that satisfy the predicate, as shown in the following listing.

Listing 10.4 `filter()` with iterator

```
function* filter<T>(iter: Iterable<T>, pred: (item: T) => boolean):
    IterableIterator<T> {
    for (const value of iter) {
        if (pred(value)) {
```

> filter() returns an IterableIterator<T>.

> filter() is now a generator that takes an Iterable<T> as the first argument.

```
        yield value;                    ◁──┐  If a value satisfies the
    }                                      │  predicate, it is yielded.
}                                          │
}
```

We again end up with a shorter implementation that works with more than arrays. Finally, let's update `reduce()`.

10.1.3   *reduce()*

Our original implementation of `reduce()` expected an array of T, an initial value of type T (in case the array is empty), and an operation `op()`. The operation is a function that takes two values of type T and returns a value of type T. `reduce()` applies the operation to the initial value and the first element of the array, stores the result, applies the operation to the result and the next element of the array, and so on.

Listing 10.5   `reduce()`

```
function reduce<T>(items: T[], init: T, op: (x: T, y: T) => T): T {      ◁──┐
    let result: T = init;                                                   reduce() takes an array of Ts, an
                                                                            initial value, and an operation
    for (const item of items) {                                            combining two Ts into one.
        result = op(result, item);   ◁──┐
    }                                    Each item in the array is
                                         combined with the running
    return result;                       total, using the given operation.
}
```

We can rewrite this to use an `Iterable<T>` instead so that it works with any sequence, as shown in the following code. In this case, we don't need a generator. Unlike the previous two functions, `reduce()` does not return a sequence of elements, but a single value.

Listing 10.6   `reduce()` with iterator

```
function reduce<T>(iter: Iterable<T>, init: T,      ◁──┐  Instead of an array of T,
    op: (x: T, y: T) => T): T {                          reduce() takes an Iterable<T>
    let result: T = init;                               as its first argument.

    for (const value of iter) {
        result = op(result, value);
    }

    return result;
}
```

The rest of the implementation is unchanged.

10.1.4   *filter()/reduce() pipeline*

Let's see how we can combine these algorithms into a pipeline that takes only the even numbers from a binary tree and sums them up. We'll use our `BinaryTreeNode<T>`

from chapter 9, with its in-order traversal, and chain this with an even number filter and a `reduce()` using addition as the operation.

Listing 10.7 `filter()/reduce()` **pipeline**

```
let root: BinaryTreeNode<number> = new BinaryTreeNode(1);
root.left = new BinaryTreeNode(2);
root.left.right = new BinaryTreeNode(3);
root.right = new BinaryTreeNode(4);

const result: number =
    reduce(
        filter(
            inOrderIterator(root),
            (value) => value % 2 == 0),
        0, (x, y) => x + y);

console.log(result);
```

The same example binary tree we used in the previous chapter

We get an IterableIterator<number> that traverses the tree in order.

We filter using a lambda that returns true only if a number is even.

We reduce from an initial value of 0 with a lambda that sums two numbers.

This example should reinforce how powerful generics are. Instead of having to implement a new function to traverse the binary tree and sum up even numbers, we simply put together a processing pipeline customized for this scenario.

10.1.5 Exercises

1 Build a pipeline that processes an iterable of type `string` by concatenating all nonempty strings.
2 Build a pipeline that processes an iterable of type `number` by selecting all odd numbers and squaring them.

10.2 Common algorithms

We looked at `map()`, `filter()`, and `reduce()`, and also mentioned `take()` in chapter 9. Many other algorithms are commonly used in pipelines. Let's list a few of them. We will not look at the implementations—just describe what arguments besides the iterable they expect and how they process the data. We'll also mention some synonyms under which the algorithm might appear:

- `map()` takes a sequence of `T` values and a function `(value: T) => U`, and returns a sequence of `U` values, applying the function to all the elements in the sequence. It is also known as `fmap()`, `select()`.
- `filter()` takes a sequence of `T` values and a predicate `(value: T) => boolean`, and returns a sequence of `T` values containing all the items for which the predicate returns `true`. It is also known as `where()`.
- `reduce()` takes a sequence of `T` values, an initial value of type `T`, and an operation that combines two `T` values into one `(x: T, y: T) => T`. It returns a single value `T` after combining all the elements in the sequence using the operation. It is also known as `fold()`, `collect()`, `accumulate()`, `aggregate()`.

- `any()` takes a sequence of T values and a predicate `(value: T) => boolean`. It returns `true` if any one of the elements of the sequence satisfies the predicate.
- `all()` takes a sequence of T values and a predicate `(value: T) => boolean`. It returns `true` if all the elements of the sequence satisfy the predicate.
- `none()` takes a sequence of T values and a predicate `(value: T) => boolean`. It returns `true` if none of the elements of the sequence satisfies the predicate.
- `take()` takes a sequence of T values and a number n. It returns a sequence consisting of the first n elements of the original sequence. It is also known as `limit()`.
- `drop()` takes a sequence of T values and a number n. It returns a sequence consisting of all the elements of the original sequence except the first n. The first n elements are dropped. It is also known as `skip()`.
- `zip()` takes a sequence of T values and a sequence of U values. It returns a sequence containing pairs of T and U values, effectively zipping together the two sequences.

There are many more algorithms for sorting, reversing, splitting, and concatenating sequences. The good news is that because these algorithms are so useful and generally applicable, we don't need to implement them. Most languages have libraries that provide these algorithms and more. JavaScript has the `underscore.js` package and the `lodash` package, both of which provide a plethora of such algorithms. (At the time of writing, these libraries don't support iterators—only the JavaScript built-in array and object types.) In Java, they are in the `java.util.stream` package. In C#, they are in the `System.Linq` namespace. In C++, they are in the `<algorithm>` standard library header.

10.2.1 Algorithms instead of loops

You may be surprised that a good rule of thumb is to check, whenever you find yourself writing a loop, whether a library algorithm or a pipeline can do the job. Usually, we write loops to process a sequence, which is exactly what the algorithms we talked about do.

The reason to prefer library algorithms to custom code in loops is that there is less opportunity for mistakes. Library algorithms are tried and tested and implemented efficiently, and the code we end up with is easier to understand, as the operations are spelled out.

We've looked at a few implementations throughout this book to get a better understanding of how things work under the hood, but you'll rarely need to implement an algorithm yourself. If you do end up with a problem that the available algorithms can't solve, consider making a generic, reusable implementation of your solution rather than a one-off specific implementation.

10.2.2 *Implementing a fluent pipeline*

Most libraries also provide a fluent API to chain algorithms into a pipeline. Fluent APIs are APIs based on method chaining, making the code much easier to read. To see the difference between a fluent and a nonfluent API, let's take another look at the filter/reduce pipeline from section 10.1.4.

Listing 10.8   filter/reduce pipeline

```
let root: BinaryTreeNode<number> = new BinaryTreeNode(1);
root.left = new BinaryTreeNode(2);
root.left.right = new BinaryTreeNode(3);
root.right = new BinaryTreeNode(4);

const result: number =
    reduce(
        filter(
            inOrderBinaryTreeIterator(root),
            (value) => value % 2 == 0),
        0, (x, y) => x + y);

console.log(result);
```

Even though we apply `filter()` first and then pass the result to `reduce()`, if we read the code from left to right, we see `reduce()` before `filter()`. It's also a bit hard to make sense of which arguments go with which function in the pipeline. Fluent APIs make the code much easier to read.

Currently, all our algorithms take an iterable as the first argument and return an iterator. We can use object-oriented programming to improve our API. We can put all our algorithms in a class that wraps an iterable. Then we can call any of the iterables without explicitly providing an iterable as the first argument; the iterable is a member of the class. Let's do this for `map()`, `filter()`, and `reduce()` by grouping them into a new `FluentIterable<T>` class wrapping an iterable, as shown in the next listing.

Listing 10.9   Fluent iterable

```
class FluentIterable<T> {          │ FluentIterable<T>
    iter: Iterable<T>;             │ wraps an Iterable<T>.

    constructor(iter: Iterable<T>) {
        this.iter = iter;
    }

    *map<U>(func: (item: T) => U): IterableIterator<U> {    ◁─┐
        for (const value of this.iter) {        map(), filter(), and reduce() are similar to
            yield func(value);                      the previous implementations, but
        }                                        instead of taking an iterable as the first
    }                                            argument, they use the this.iter iterable.

    *filter(pred: (item: T) => boolean): IterableIterator<T> {    ◁─┘
        for (const value of this.iter) {
```

```
        if (pred(value)) {
            yield value;
        }
    }
}

reduce(init: T, op: (x: T, y: T) => T): T {
    let result: T = init;

    for (const value of this.iter) {
        result = op(result, value);
    }

    return result;
}
}
```

> map(), filter(), and reduce() are similar to the previous implementations, but instead of taking an iterable as the first argument, they use the this.iter iterable.

We can create a `FluentIterable<T>` out of an `Iterable<T>`, so we can rewrite our `filter()`/`reduce()` pipeline into a more fluent form. We create a `Fluent-Iterable<T>`, call `filter()` on it, create a new `FluentIterable<T>` from its result, and call `reduce()` on it, as the following listing shows.

Listing 10.10 Fluent filter/reduce pipeline

```
let root: BinaryTreeNode<number> = new BinaryTreeNode(1);
root.left = new BinaryTreeNode(2);
root.left.right = new BinaryTreeNode(3);
root.right = new BinaryTreeNode(4);

const result: number =
    new FluentIterable(
        new FluentIterable(
            inOrderIterator(root)
        ).filter((value) => value % 2 == 0)
    ).reduce(0, (x, y) => x + y);

console.log(result);
```

> We get an iterable over the binary tree from inOrderIterator and use it to initialize a FluentIterable.

> We call filter() on the FluentIterable and then create another FluentIterable from the result.

> Finally, we call reduce() on the FluentIterable to get the final result.

Now `filter()` appears before `reduce()`, and it's very clear that arguments go to that function. The only problem is that we need to create a new `Fluent-Iterable<T>` after each function call. We can improve our API by having our `map()` and `filter()` functions return a `FluentIterable<T>` instead of the default `IterableIterator<T>`. Note that we don't need to change `reduce()`, because `reduce()` returns a single value of type T, not an iterable.

Because we're using generators, we can't simply change the return type. Generators exist to provide convenient syntax for functions, but they always return an `IterableIterator<T>`. Instead, we can move the implementations to a couple of private methods—`mapImpl()` and `filterImpl()`—and handle the conversion from

`IterableIterator<T>` to `FluentIterable<T>` in the public `map()` and `reduce()` methods, as shown in the following listing.

Listing 10.11 Better fluent iterable

```
class FluentIterable<T> {
    iter: Iterable<T>;

    constructor(iter: Iterable<T>) {
        this.iter = iter;
    }

    map<U>(func: (item: T) => U): FluentIterable<U> {
        return new FluentIterable(this.mapImpl(func));
    }

    private *mapImpl<U>(func: (item: T) => U): IterableIterator<U> {
        for (const value of this.iter) {
            yield func(value);
        }
    }

    filter<U>(pred: (item: T) => boolean): FluentIterable<T> {
        return new FluentIterable(this.filterImpl(pred));
    }

    private *filterImpl(pred: (item: T) => boolean): IterableIterator<T> {
        for (const value of this.iter) {
            if (pred(value)) {
                yield value;
            }
        }
    }

    reduce(init: T, op: (x: T, y: T) => T): T {
        let result: T = init;

        for (const value of this.iter) {
            result = op(result, value);
        }

        return result;
    }
}
```

- map() forwards its argument to mapImpl() and converts the result to a FluentIterable.
- mapImpl() is the original map() implementation with a generator.
- Like map(), filter() forwards its argument to filterImpl() and converts the result to a FluentIterable.
- filterImpl() is the original filter() implementation with a generator.
- reduce() stays unchanged because it doesn't return an iterator.

With this updated implementation, we can more easily chain the algorithms, as each returns a `FluentIterable` that contains all the algorithms as methods, as shown in the next listing.

Listing 10.12 Better fluent filter/reduce pipeline

```
let root: BinaryTreeNode<number> = new BinaryTreeNode(1);
root.left = new BinaryTreeNode(2);
root.left.right = new BinaryTreeNode(3);
root.right = new BinaryTreeNode(4);
```

```
const result: number =
    new FluentIterable(inOrderIterator(root))
    .filter((value) => value % 2 == 0)
    .reduce(0, (x, y) => x + y);

console.log(result);
```

We need to explicitly new up a
FluentIterable only once, from the
original iterator over the tree.

filter() is a method of
FluentIterable and returns
a FluentIterable itself.

We can call reduce()
on the result of filter().

Now, in true fluent fashion, the code reads easily from left to right, and we can chain any number of algorithms that make up our pipeline with a very natural syntax. Most algorithm libraries take a similar approach, making it as easy as possible to chain multiple algorithms.

Depending on the programming language, one downside of a fluent API approach is that our `FluentIterable` ends up containing all the algorithms, so it is difficult to extend. If it is part of a library, calling code can't easily add a new algorithm without modifying the class. C# provides extension methods, which enable us to add methods to a class or interface without modifying its code. Not all languages have such features, though. That being said, in most situations, we should be using an existing algorithm library, not implementing a new one from scratch.

10.2.3 Exercises

1 Extend `FluentIterable` with `take()`, the algorithm that returns the first n elements from an iterator.
2 Extend `FluentIterable` with `drop()`, the algorithm that skips the first n elements of an iterator and returns the rest.

10.3 Constraining type parameters

We saw how a generic data structure gives shape to the data, regardless of what its specific type parameter T is. We also looked at a set of algorithms that uses iterators to process sequences of values of some type T, regardless of what that type is. Now let's look at a scenario in the following listing in which the type matters: we have a `renderAll()` generic function that takes an `Iterable<T>` as argument and calls the `render()` method on each element of the iterator.

Listing 10.13 renderAll sketch

```
function renderAll<T>(iter: Iterable<T>): void {
    for (const item of iter) {
        item.render();
    }
}
```

renderAll() takes an
Iterable<T> as argument.

We call render() on each item
returned by the iterator.

The function fails to compile, with the following error message:

```
Property 'render' does not exist on type 'T'.
```

We are attempting to call `render()` on a generic type `T`, but we have no guarantee that such a method exists on the type. For this type of scenario, we need a way to *constrain* the type `T` so that it can be instantiated only with types that have a `render()` method.

> **CONSTRAINTS ON TYPE PARAMETERS** Constraints inform the compiler about the capabilities that a type argument must have. Without any constraints, the type argument could be any type. As soon as we require certain members to be available on a generic type, we use constraints to restrict the set of allowed types to those that have the required members.

In our case, we can define an `IRenderable` interface that declares a `render()` method, as shown in the next listing. Then we can add a constraint on `T` by using the `extends` keyword to tell the compiler that we accept only type arguments that are `IRenderable`.

Listing 10.14 `renderAll` with constraint

```
interface IRenderable {          ◁──┐  IRenderable interface
    render(): void;                  │  requires implementers to
}                                    │  provide a render() method.

function renderAll<T extends IRenderable>(iter: Iterable<T>): void {   ◁──┐
    for (const item of iter) {                                            │
        item.render();                   T extends IRenderable and tells  │
    }                                    the compiler to accept only types │
}                                        that implement IRenderable as T.  │
```

10.3.1 Generic data structures with type constraints

Most generic data structures don't need to constrain their type parameters. We can store values of any type in a linked list, a tree, or an array. There are a few exceptions, though, such as a hash set.

A set data structure models a mathematical set, so it stores unique values, discarding duplicates. Set data structures usually provide methods to union, intersect, and subtract other sets. They also provide a way to check whether a given value is already part of the set. To check whether a value is already part of a set, we can compare it with every element of the set, but that approach is not the most efficient. Comparing with every element in the set requires us, in the worst case, to traverse the whole set. Such a traversal requires *linear time*, or $O(n)$. See the sidebar "Big O notation" on the next page for a refresher.

A more efficient implementation can hash each value and store it in a key-value data structure like a hash map or dictionary. Such data structures can retrieve a value in *constant time*, or $O(1)$, making them more efficient. A hash set wraps a hash map and can provide efficient membership checks. But it does come with a constraint: the type `T` needs to provide a hash function, which takes a value of type `T` and returns a number: its hash value.

Some languages ensure that all values can be hashed by providing a hash method on their top type. The Java top type, `Object`, has a `hashCode()` method, whereas the C# `Object` top type has a `GetHashCode()` method. But if a language doesn't have that, we need a type constraint to ensure that only hash-able types can be stored in the data structures. We could define an `IHashable` interface, for example, and make it a type constraint on the key type of our generic hash map or dictionary.

Big O notation

Big O notation provides an upper bound to the time and space required by a function to execute as its arguments tend toward a particular value n. We won't go too deep into this topic; instead we'll outline a few common upper bounds and explain what they mean.

Constant time, or O(1), means that a function's execution time does not depend on the number of items it has to process. The function `first()`, which takes the first element of a sequence, runs just as fast for a sequence of 2 or 2 million items, for example.

Logarithmic time, or O(log n), means that the function halves its input with each step, so it is very efficient even for large values of n. An example is binary search in a sorted sequence.

Linear time, or O(n), means that the function run time grows proportionally with its input. Looping over a sequence is O(n), such as determining whether all elements of a sequence satisfy some predicate.

Quadratic time, or $O(n^2)$, is much less efficient than linear, as the run time grows much faster than the size of the input. Two nested loops over a sequence have a run time of $O(n^2)$.

Linearithmic, or O(n log n), is not as efficient as linear but more efficient than quadratic. The most efficient comparison sort algorithms are O(n log n); we can't sort a sequence with a single loop, but we can do it faster than two nested loops.

Just as time complexity sets an upper bound on how the run time of a function increases with the size of its input, space complexity sets an upper bound on the amount of additional memory a function needs as the size of its input grows.

Constant space, or O(1), means that a function doesn't need more space as the size of the input grows. Our `max()` function, for example, requires some extra memory to store the running maximum and the iterator, but the amount of memory is constant regardless of how large the sequence is.

Linear space, or O(n), means that the amount of memory a function needs is proportional to the size of its input. An example of such a function is our original `inOrder()` binary tree traversal, which copied the values of all nodes into an array to provide an iterator over the tree.

10.3.2 *Generic algorithms with type constraints*

Algorithms tend to have more constraints on their types than data structures. If we want to sort a set of values, we need a way to compare those values. Similarly, if we want to determine the minimum or maximum element of a sequence, the elements of that sequence need to be comparable.

Let's look at a possible implementation of a max() generic algorithm in the next listing. First, we will declare an IComparable<T> interface and constrain our algorithm to use it. The interface declares a single compareTo() method.

Listing 10.15 `IComparable` **interface**

```
enum ComparisonResult {          ◁─┐   ComparisonResult represents
    LessThan,                          the result of a comparison.
    Equal,
    GreaterThan
}                                              IComparable declares a compareTo
                                               interface that compares the current
interface IComparable<T> {                     instance with another value of the same
    compareTo(value: T): ComparisonResult;  ◁─┘ type and returns a Comparison result.
}
```

Now let's implement a max() generic algorithm that expects an iterator over an IComparable set of values and returns the maximum element, as shown in listing 10.16. We will need to handle the case in which the iterator has no values, in which case max() will return undefined. For that reason, we won't use a for...of loop; rather, we will advance the iterator manually by using next().

Listing 10.16 `max()` **algorithm**

```
                                                           max() puts an
function max<T extends IComparable<T>>(iter: Iterable<T>)  IComparable<T>
    : T | undefined {                              ◁──────  constraint on the type T.
    let iterator: Iterator<T> = iter[Symbol.iterator]();  ◁──
                                                           We get an Iterator<T>
                                                           from the Iterable<T>
    let current: IteratorResult<T> = iterator.next();      argument.
We call
next()
once to      if (current.done) return undefined;      ◁──┐  In case there is no first
get to the                                                 value, we return undefined.
first value. let result: T = current.value;       ◁─┐
                                                      We initialize result to be the first
    while (true) {                                    value returned by the iterator.
        current = iterator.next();

When the       if (current.done) return result;
iterator is
done, we                                              Whenever the current value is
return the     if (current.value.compareTo(result) ==  greater than the currently stored
result.            ComparisonResult.GreaterThan) {     maximum, we update the result
                   result = current.value;       ◁──┘  with the current value.
        }
    }
}
```

Many algorithms, such as max(), require certain things from the types they operate on. An alternative is to make the comparison an argument to the function itself as opposed to a generic type constraint. Instead of IComparable<T>, max() can expect a second argument—a compare() function—from two arguments of type T to a ComparisonResult, as shown in the following code.

```
function max<T>(iter: Iterable<T>,
    compare: (x: T, y: T) => ComparisonResult)          compare() is a function that
    : T | undefined {                                    takes two Ts and returns a
    let iterator: Iterator<T> = iter[Symbol.iterator]();  ComparisonResult.

    let current: IteratorResult<T> = iterator.next();

    if (current.done) return undefined;

    let result: T = current.value;

    while (true) {
        current = iterator.next();

        if (current.done) return result;

        if (compare(current.value, result)
            == ComparisonResult.GreaterThan) {    Instead of the
            result = current.value;               IComparable.compareTo() method,
        }                                          we call the compare() argument.
    }
}
```

The advantage of this implementation is that the type T is no longer constrained, and we can plug in any comparison function. The disadvantage is that for types that have a natural order (numbers, temperatures, distances, and so on), we have to keep supplying a compare function explicitly. Good algorithm libraries usually provide both versions of an algorithm: one that uses a type's natural comparison and another for which callers can supply their own.

The more an algorithm knows about the methods and properties that a type T it operates on provides, the more it can leverage those in its implementation. Next, let's see how algorithms can use iterators to provide more efficient implementations.

10.3.3 Exercise

1 Implement a generic function clamp() that takes a value, a low, and a high. If the value is within the low-high range, it returns the values. If the value is less than low, it returns low. If the value is larger than high, it returns high. Use the IComparable interface defined in this section.

10.4　*Efficient reverse and other algorithms using iterators*

So far, we've looked at algorithms that process a sequence in a linear fashion. map(), filter(), reduce(), and max() all iterate over a sequence of values from start to finish. They all run in linear time (proportionate to the size of the sequence) and constant space. (Memory requirements are constant regardless of the size of the sequence.) Let's look at another algorithm: reverse().

This algorithm takes a sequence and reverses it, making the last element the first one, the second-to-last element the second one, and so on. One way to implement reverse() is to push all elements of its input into a stack and then pop them out, as shown in figure 10.1 and listing 10.18.

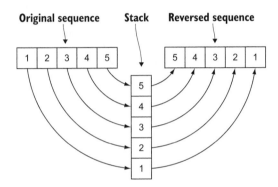

Figure 10.1　Reversing a sequence with a stack: elements from the original sequence get pushed on the stack and then popped to produce the reversed sequence.

Listing 10.18　reverse() with stack

```
function *reverse<T>(iter: Iterable<T>): IterableIterator<T> {     ◁   reverse() is a generator,
    let stack: T[] = [];                                          ◁        following the same pattern
                                                                              as our other algorithms.
    for (const value of iter) {                                       JavaScript arrays provide
        stack.push(value);              ◁   We push all values from     push() and pop() methods,
    }                                       the sequence on the stack.    so we use one as a stack.

    while (true) {
        let value: T | undefined = stack.pop();       ◁   We pop a value from the
                                                           stack; this is undefined if
        if (value == undefined) return;          ◁          the stack is empty.

        yield value;        ◁   Yield the value        If we emptied the stack,
    }                           and repeat.            return, as we are done.
}
```

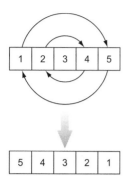

Figure 10.2   Reversing an array in place by swapping its elements

This implementation is straightforward but not the most efficient. Although it runs in linear time, it also requires linear space. The larger the input sequence, the more memory this algorithm will need to push all its elements onto the stack.

Let's set iterators aside for now and look at how we would implement an efficient reverse over an array, as shown in listing 10.19. We can do this in-place, swapping the elements of the array starting from both ends without requiring an additional stack (figure 10.2).

Listing 10.19   `reverse()` for array

```
function reverse<T>(values: T[]): void {        This version of reverse() expects
    let begin: number = 0;                      an array of Ts, not an Iterable.
    let end: number = values.length;            begin and end originally point to
                                                the beginning and end of the array.

    while (begin < end) {                       Repeat until the two
        const temp: T = values[begin];          meet or pass each other.
        values[begin] = values[end - 1];
        values[end - 1] = temp;                 Swap the value at begin with
                                                the value at end - 1. (Originally,
        begin++;      Increment the begin index end was one element after
        end--;        and decrement the end index. the last one in the array.)
    }
}
```

As we can see, this implementation is more efficient than the preceding one. It is still linear time, as we need to touch every element of the sequence (it is impossible to reverse a sequence without touching each element), but it requires constant space to run. Unlike the previous version, which needed a stack as large as its input, this one uses the temporary `temp` of type `T`, regardless of how large the input is.

Can we generalize this example and provide an efficient reverse algorithm for any data structure? We can, but we need to tweak our notion of iterators. `Iterator<T>`, `Iterable<T>`, and the combination of the two, `IterableIterator<T>`, are interfaces that TypeScript provides over the JavaScript ES6 standard. Now we'll go beyond that and look at some iterators that are not part of the language standard.

10.4.1 Iterator building blocks

JavaScript iterators allow us to retrieve values and advance until the sequence is exhausted. If we want to run an in-place algorithm, we need a few more capabilities. We also need to be able not only to read values at a given position, but also set them. In our `reverse()` case, we start from both ends of the sequence and end in the middle, which means that an iterator can't tell when it is done all by itself. We know that reverse() is done when begin and end pass each other, so we need a way to tell when two iterators are the same.

To support efficient algorithms, let's redefine our iterators as a set of interfaces, each describing additional capabilities. First, let's define an IReadable<T> that exposes a get() method returning a value of type T. We will use this method to read a value from an iterator. We'll also define an IIncrementable<T> that exposes an increment() method we can use to advance our iterator, as the following listing shows.

Listing 10.20 IReadable<T> and IIncrementable<T>

```
interface IReadable<T> {
    get(): T;                        ⊲──┐  IReadable declares a single
}                                        │  method, get(), that retrieves the
                                         │  current value T of an iterator.

interface IIncrementable<T> {
    increment(): void;               ⊲──┐  IIncrementable declares a single
}                                        │  method, increment(), that advances
                                         │  an iterator to the next element.
```

These two interfaces are almost enough to support our original linear traversal algorithms such as map(). The last thing missing is figuring out when we should stop. We know that an iterator can't tell by itself when it is done, as sometimes it doesn't need to traverse the whole sequence. We'll introduce the concept of equality: an iterator begin and an iterator end are equal when they point to the same element. This is much more flexible than the standard Iterator <T> implementation. We can initialize end to be one element *after* the last element of a sequence. Then we can advance begin until it is equal to end, in which case we'll know that we've traversed the whole sequence. But we can also move end back until it points to the first element of the sequence—something we couldn't have done with the standard Iterator<T>. (figure 10.3).

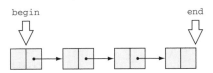

Figure 10.3 begin and end iterators define a range: begin points to the first element, and end points past the last element.

Let's define an IInputIterator<T> interface in the next listing as an interface that implements both IReadable<T> and IIncrementable<T>, plus an equals() method we can use to compare two iterators.

Listing 10.21 IInputIterator<T>

```
interface IInputIterator<T> extends IReadable<T>, IIncrementable<T> {
    equals(other: IInputIterator<T>): boolean;
}
```

The iterator itself can no longer determine when it has traversed the whole sequence. A sequence is now defined by two iterators—an iterator pointing to the start of the sequence and an iterator pointing to one past the last element of the sequence.

With these interfaces available, let's update our linked list iterator from chapter 9 in the next listing. Our linked list is implemented as the type `LinkedListNode<T>` with a `value` property and a `next` property that can be a `LinkedListNode<T>` or `undefined` for the last node in the list.

Listing 10.22   Linked list implementation

```
class LinkedListNode<T> {
    value: T;
    next: LinkedListNode<T> | undefined;

    constructor(value: T) {
        this.value = value;
    }
}
```

Let's see how we can model a pair of iterators over this linked list in the following listing. First, we'll need to implement a `LinkedListInputIterator<T>` that satisfies our new `IInputIterator<T>` interface for a linked list.

Listing 10.23   Linked list input iterator

```
class LinkedListInputIterator<T> implements IInputIterator<T> {
    private node: LinkedListNode<T> | undefined;

    constructor(node: LinkedListNode<T> | undefined) {
        this.node = node;
    }

    increment(): void {
        if (!this.node) throw Error();          ◁── If the current node is undefined,
                                                     throw an error; otherwise,
        this.node = this.node.next;                  advance to the next node.
    }

    get(): T {                                  ◁── If the current node is
        if (!this.node) throw Error();               undefined, throw an error;
                                                     otherwise, get its value.
        return this.node.value;
    }

    equals(other: IInputIterator<T>): boolean {                               ◁──┐
        return this.node == (<LinkedListInputIterator<T>>other).node;
    }
}
```

Iterators are considered to be equal if they wrap the same node. We can cast to **LinkedListInputIterator<T>** because callers shouldn't compare iterators of different types.

Now we can create a pair of iterators over a linked list by initializing `begin` to be the head of the list and `end` to be `undefined`, as shown in the following code.

Listing 10.24   Pair of iterators over linked list

```
const head: LinkedListNode<number> = new LinkedListNode(0);
head.next = new LinkedListNode(1);
head.next.next = new LinkedListNode(2);

let begin: IInputIterator<number> = new LinkedListInputIterator(head);
let end: IInputIterator<number> = new LinkedListInputIterator(undefined);
```

A list with a few nodes

begin is the head of the linked list passed as an argument.

end is undefined.

We call this an *input iterator* because we can read values from it by using the `get()` method.

> **INPUT ITERATORS**   An *input iterator* is an iterator that can traverse a sequence once and provide its values. It can't replay the values a second time, as the values may no longer be available. An input iterator doesn't have to traverse a persistent data structure; it can also provide values from a generator or some other source (figure 10.4).

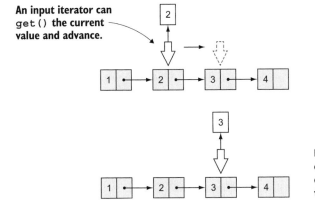

An input iterator can `get()` the current value and advance.

Figure 10.4   An input iterator can retrieve the value of the current element and advance to the next element.

Let's also define an output iterator as an iterator we can write to. For that, we'll declare an `IWritable<T>` interface with a `set()` method and have our `IOutput-Iterator<T>` be the combination of `IWritable<T>`, `IIncrementable<T>`, and an `equals()` method, as shown in the next listing.

Listing 10.25   `IWritable<T>` and `IOutputIterator<T>`

```
interface IWritable<T> {
    set(value: T): void;
}
```

```
interface IOutputIterator<T> extends IWritable<T>, IIncrementable<T> {
    equals(other: IOutputIterator<T>): boolean;
}
```

We can write values to this type of iterator, but we can't read them back.

> **OUTPUT ITERATORS** An *output iterator* is an iterator that can traverse a sequence and write values to it; it doesn't have to be able to read them back. An output iterator doesn't have to traverse a persistent data structure; it can also write values to other outputs.

Let's implement an output iterator that writes to the console. Writing to an output stream is the most common use case for an output iterator: that's when we can output data but can't read it back. We can write data (without being able to read it) to a network connection, standard output, standard error, and so on. In our case, advancing the iterator doesn't do anything, whereas setting a value calls `console.log()`, as shown in the next listing.

Listing 10.26   Console output iterator

```
class ConsoleOutputIterator<T> implements IOutputIterator<T> {
    set(value: T): void {
        console.log(value);          ⟵──┤ set() logs to the console.
    }
                                          increment() doesn't have to do
                                          anything because we're not traversing
    increment(): void { }         ⟵───── a data structure in this case.

    equals(other: IOutputIterator<T>): boolean {
        return false;             ⟵──┐ equals() can safely always return false,
    }                                  as writing to the console doesn't have
}                                      an end to compare against.
```

Now we have an interface that describes an input iterator and a concrete instance of an implementation over our linked list. We also have an interface that describes an output iterator and a concrete implementation that logs to the console. With these pieces in place, we can provide an alternative implementation of `map()` in listing 10.27.

This new version of `map()` will take as argument a pair of `begin` and `end` input iterators that define a sequence and an output iterator `out`, where it will write the results of mapping the given function over the sequence. Because we are no longer using standard JavaScript, we lose some of the syntactic sugar—no `yield` and no `for...of` loops.

Listing 10.27   `map()` with input and output iterators

```
function map<T, U>(
    begin: IInputIterator<T>, end: IInputIterator<T>,  ⟵──┤ begin and end iterators
    out: IOutputIterator<U>,                                define the input sequence.
    func: (value: T) => U): void {                    out is an output iterator for
                                                       the result of the function.
```

```
while (!begin.equals(end)) {
    out.set(func(begin.get()));

    begin.increment();
    out.increment();
}
}
```

Repeat until we traverse the whole sequence and begin becomes end.

Output the result of applying the function to the current element.

Increment both the input and the output iterators.

This version of map() is as general as the one based on the native Iterable-Iterator<T>: we can provide any IInputIterator<T>, one that traverses a linked list, one that traverses a tree in order, and so on. We can also provide any IOutput-Iterator<T>—one that writes to the console or one that writes to an array.

So far, this doesn't gain us much. We have an alternative implementation that can't leverage the special syntax that TypeScript provides. But these iterators are just the basic building blocks. We can define more-powerful iterators, and we'll look at these next.

10.4.2 A useful find()

Let's take another common algorithm: find(). This algorithm takes a sequence of values and a predicate, and returns the first element for which the predicate returns true. We can implement this by using the standard Iterable<T>, as the following listing shows.

Listing 10.28 find() with iterable

```
function find<T>(iter: Iterable<T>,
    pred: (value: T) => boolean): T | undefined {
    for (const value of iter) {
        if (pred(value)) {
            return value;
        }
    }

    return undefined;
}
```

This works, but it's not that useful. What if we want to change the value after we find it? If we are searching over a linked list of numbers for the first occurrence of 42 so that we can replace it with 0, it doesn't help us that find() returns 42. The result may as well be a boolean, as this function tells us only whether the value exists in the sequence.

What if, instead of returning the value itself, we get an iterator pointing to that value? The out-of-the-box JavaScript Iterator<T> is read-only. We've seen how to create an iterator through which we can also set values. For this scenario, we'll need a combination of readable and writable iterators. Let's define a forward iterator.

> **FORWARD ITERATORS** A *forward iterator* is an iterator that can be advanced, can read the value at its current position, and update that value. A forward iterator can also be cloned, so that advancing one copy of the iterator does not

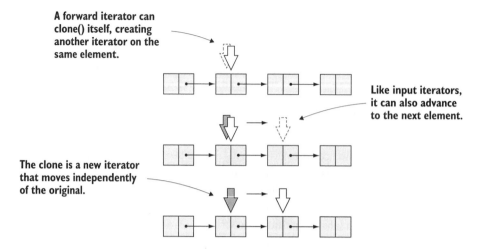

A forward iterator can clone() itself, creating another iterator on the same element.

Like input iterators, it can also advance to the next element.

The clone is a new iterator that moves independently of the original.

Figure 10.5   A forward iterator can read and write the value of the current element, advance to the next element, and create a clone of itself that enables multiple traversals. In this figure, we see how clone() **creates a copy of the iterator. As we advance the original, the clone doesn't move.**

advance the clone. This is important, as it allows us to traverse a sequence multiple times, unlike input and output iterators (figure 10.5).

Our IForwardIterator<T> interface shown in the next listing is a combination of IReadable<T>, IWritable<T>, IIncrementable<T>, and the equals() and clone() methods.

Listing 10.29   IForwardIterator<T>

```
interface IForwardIterator<T> extends
    IReadable<T>, IWritable<T>, IIncrementable<T> {
    equals(other: IForwardIterator<T>): boolean;
    clone(): IForwardIterator<T>;
}
```

As an example, let's implement the interface to iterate over our linked list in the following listing. We'll update our LinkedListIterator<T> to also provide the additional methods required by our new interface.

Listing 10.30   LinkedListIterator<T> implementing IForwardIterator<T>

```
class LinkedListIterator<T> implements IForwardIterator<T> {
    private node: LinkedListNode<T> | undefined;

    constructor(node: LinkedListNode<T> | undefined) {
        this.node = node;
    }

    increment(): void {
        if (!this.node) return;
```

This version of **LinkedListIterator<T>** implements the new **IForwardIterator<T>** interface.

```
        this.node = this.node.next;
    }

    get(): T {
        if (!this.node) throw Error();

        return this.node.value;
    }

    set(value: T): void {
        if (!this.node) throw Error();

        this.node.value = value;
    }

    equals(other: IForwardIterator<T>): boolean {
        return this.node == (<LinkedListIterator<T>>other).node;
    }

    clone(): IForwardIterator<T> {
        return new LinkedListIterator(this.node);
    }
}
```

set() is an additional method required by IWritable<T> that updates the value of a linked list node.

equals() now expects another IForwardIterator<T>.

clone() creates a new iterator pointing to the same node as this iterator.

Now let's look at a version of find() that takes a pair of begin and end iterators, and returns an iterator pointing to the first element satisfying the predicate, shown in the next listing. With this version, we can update the value when we find it.

Listing 10.31 find() with forward iterator

begin and end forward iterators define the sequence.

```
function find<T>(
    begin: IForwardIterator<T>, end: IForwardIterator<T>,
    pred: (value: T) => boolean): IForwardIterator<T> {
    while (!begin.equals(end)) {
        if (pred(begin.get())) {
            return begin;
        }

        begin.increment();
    }

    return end;
}
```

Repeat until we traverse the whole sequence.

The function returns a forward iterator pointing to the found element.

If we found the element we were looking for, return the iterator.

Increment iterator and advance to the next element in the sequence.

If we've reached the end, we haven't found an element. We return the end iterator.

Let's use a linked list of numbers, the iterator we just implemented to traverse a linked list, and apply this algorithm to find the first value equal to 42 and replace it with a 0, as shown in the following code.

Listing 10.32 Replacing 42 with 0 in a linked list

```
let head: LinkedListNode<number> = new LinkedListNode(1);
head.next = new LinkedListNode(2);
head.next.next = new LinkedListNode(42);
```

Create a linked list containing the sequence 1, 2, 42.

```
let begin: IForwardIterator<number> =
    new LinkedListIterator(head);
let end: IForwardIterator<number> =
    new LinkedListIterator(undefined);

let iter: IForwardIterator<number> =
    find(begin, end, (value: number) => value == 42);

if (!iter.equals(end)) {
    iter.set(0);
}
```

Initialize begin and end forward iterators for the linked list.

Call find and get an iterator to the first node with the value 42.

We need to ensure that we found a node with value 42; otherwise, we are past the end of the list.

If we did, we can update its value to 0.

Forward iterators are extremely powerful, as they can traverse a sequence any number of times and also modify it. This feature allows us to implement in-place algorithms that don't need to copy over a whole sequence of data to transform it. Finally, let's tackle the algorithm with which we started this section: reverse().

10.4.3 An efficient reverse()

As we saw in the array implementation, an in-place reverse() starts from both ends of the array and swaps elements, incrementing the front index and decrementing the back index until the two cross.

We can generalize the array implementation to work with any sequence, but we need one extra capability on our iterator: the ability to decrement its position. An iterator with this ability is called a *bidirectional iterator*.

> **BIDIRECTIONAL ITERATOR**   A *bidirectional iterator* has the same capabilities as a forward iterator; additionally, it can be decremented. In other words, a bidirectional iterator can traverse a sequence both forward and backward (figure 10.6).

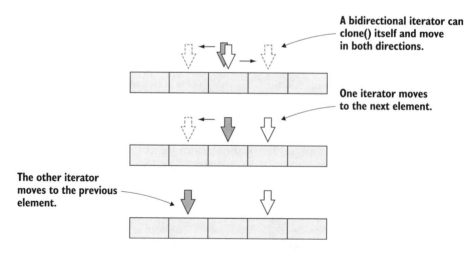

A bidirectional iterator can clone() itself and move in both directions.

One iterator moves to the next element.

The other iterator moves to the previous element.

Figure 10.6   A bidirectional iterator can read and write the value of the current element, clone itself, and step both forward and backward.

Let's define an IBidirectionalIterator<T> interface similar to IForward-Iterator<T> interface with an additional decrement() method. Note that not all data structures can support such an iterator, such as our linked list. Because a node has a reference only to its successor, we cannot move backward to the preceding node. But we can provide a bidirectional iterator over a doubly linked list, in which a node holds references to both its successor and its predecessor or an array. Let's implement an ArrayIterator<T> as an IBidirectionalIterator<T> in the next listing.

Listing 10.33 IBidirectionalIterator<T> and ArrayIterator<T>

```
interface IBidirectionalIterator<T> extends
    IReadable<T>, IWritable<T>, IIncrementable<T> {
    decrement(): void;
    equals(other: IBidirectionalIterator<T>): boolean;      ◁─┐   IBidirectioanlIterator<T>
    clone(): IBidirectionalIterator<T>;                        │   has an extra decrement()
}                                                              │   method compared with
                                                                   IForwardIterator<T>.
class ArrayIterator<T> implements IBidirectionalIterator<T> {
    private array: T[];
    private index: number;

    constructor(array: T[], index: number) {
        this.array = array;
        this.index = index;
    }

    get(): T {
        return this.array[this.index];
    }

    set(value: T): void {
        this.array[this.index] = value;
    }

    increment(): void {
        this.index++;
    }

    decrement(): void {
        this.index--;
    }

    equals(other: IBidirectionalIterator<T>): boolean {
        return this.index == (<ArrayIterator<T>>other).index;
    }

    clone(): IBidirectionalIterator<T> {
        return new ArrayIterator(this.array, this.index);
    }
}
```

Now let's implement reverse() in terms of a pair of begin and end bidirectional iterators. We will swap the values, increment begin, decrement end, and stop when the two iterators meet. We must make sure that the two iterators never pass each other, so as soon as we move one of them, we check whether they met.

Listing 10.34 `reverse()` with bidirectional iterator

```
                                                      Repeat until begin
                                                       and end meet.
function reverse<T>(
    begin: IBidirectionalIterator<T>, end: IBidirectionalIterator<T>
): void {
    while (!begin.equals(end)) {
        end.decrement();
        if (begin.equals(end)) return;

        const temp: T = begin.get();
        begin.set(end.get());
        end.set(temp);

        begin.increment();
    }
}
```

Repeat until begin and end meet.

Decrement end. Remember that end starts at one element past the end of the array, so we need to decrement it before using it.

Check again that decrementing end didn't get the two iterators pointing to the same element.

Swap the values.

Finally, increment start and then repeat. (The while loop condition checks again whether the two iterators met.)

Let's try it out on an array of numbers in the following listing.

Listing 10.35 Reversing an array of numbers

```
let array: number[] = [1, 2, 3, 4, 5];

let begin: IBidirectionalIterator<number>
    = new ArrayIterator(array, 0);
let end: IBidirectionalIterator<number>
    = new ArrayIterator(array, array.length);

reverse(begin, end);

console.log(array);
```

Initialize begin over the array at index 0.

Initialize end over the array at index length (one past the last element).

This will log [5, 4, 3, 2, 1].

Using bidirectional iterators, we can generalize an efficient, in-place `reverse()` to work on any data structure that we can traverse in two directions. We extended the original algorithm, which was limited to arrays to work with any `IBidirectional-Iterator<T>`. We can apply the same algorithm to reverse a doubly linked list and any other data structure over which we can move an iterator backward and forward.

Note that we can also reverse a singly linked list, of course, but such an algorithm does not generalize. When we reverse a singly linked list, we alter the structure, as we're flipping references to each next element to refer to the previous element instead. Such an algorithm is tightly coupled to the data structure it operates on and can't be generalized. By contrast, our generic `reverse()` that requires a bidirectional iterator works the same way for any data structure that can provide such an iterator.

10.4.4 *Efficient element retrieval*

There are algorithms that require more from their iterators than `increment()` and `decrement()`. A good example is sorting algorithms. An efficient, O(n log n) sort such as quicksort will have to jump around the data structure that it is sorting, accessing elements at arbitrary locations. For this purpose, a bidirectional iterator is not enough. We need a random-access iterator.

RANDOM-ACCESS ITERATORS A *random-access iterator* can jump forward and backward any given number of elements in constant time. Unlike a bidirectional iterator, which can be incremented or decremented one step at a time, a random-access iterator can move any number of elements (figure 10.7).

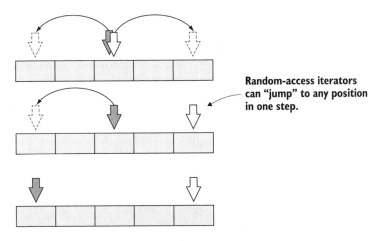

Random-access iterators can "jump" to any position in one step.

Figure 10.7   A random-access iterator can read and write the value of the current element, clone itself, and move backward or forward any number of steps.

Arrays are good examples of random-accessible data structures, in which we can index and quickly retrieve any element. By contrast, with a doubly linked list, we need to traverse through successor or predecessor references to reach an element. A doubly linked list cannot support a random-access iterator.

Let's define an `IRandomAccessIterator<T>` as an iterator that supports not only all the capabilities of `IBidirectionalIterator<T>`, but also a `move()` method that moves the iterator n elements. With random access iterators, it's also useful to tell how far apart two iterators are. We will add a `distance()` method that returns the difference between two iterators in the following listing.

Listing 10.36   `IRandomAccessIterator<T>`

```
interface IRandomAccessIterator<T>
    extends IReadable<T>, IWritable<T>, IIncrementable<T> {
    decrement(): void;
```

```
        equals(other: IRandomAccessIterator<T>): boolean;
        clone(): IRandomAccessIterator<T>;
        move(n: number): void;
        distance(other: IRandomAccessIterator<T>): number;
}
```

Let's update our `ArrayIterator<T>` in the next listing to implement `IRandom-AccessIterator<T>`.

```
class ArrayIterator<T> implements IRandomAccessIterator<T> {
    private array: T[];
    private index: number;

    constructor(array: T[], index: number) {
        this.array = array;
        this.index = index;
    }

    get(): T {
        return this.array[this.index];
    }

    set(value: T): void {
        this.array[this.index] = value;
    }

    increment(): void {
        this.index++;
    }

    decrement(): void {
        this.index--;
    }

    equals(other: IRandomAccessIterator<T>): boolean {
        return this.index == (<ArrayIterator<T>>other).index;
    }

    clone(): IRandomAccessIterator<T> {
        return new ArrayIterator(this.array, this.index);
    }

    move(n: number): void {                    move() advances the iterator
        this.index += n;                       n steps. (n can be negative to
    }                                          move backward.)

    distance(other: IRandomAccessIterator<T>): number {
        return this.index - (<ArrayIterator<T>>other).index;
    }
}                                              distance() determines
                                               the distance between
                                               two iterators
```

Let's take a very simple algorithm that benefits from a random-access iterator: `elementAt()`. This algorithm takes as arguments a `begin` and end iterator defining a sequence and a number n. It will return an iterator to the nth element of the sequence or the end iterator if n is larger than the length of the sequence.

We can implement this algorithm with an input iterator, but we would have to increment the iterator n times to reach the element. That is linear time complexity, or O(n). With a random-access iterator, we can do this in constant time, or O(1), as shown in the next listing.

Listing 10.38   Element at

```
function elementAtRandomAccessIterator<T>(
    begin: IRandomAccessIterator<T>, end: IRandomAccessIterator<T>,
    n: number): IRandomAccessIterator<T> {
    begin.move(n);                                    ⟵————————┐  Move begin n
                                                               │  elements forward.
    if (begin.distance(end) <= 0) return end;   ⟵——┐
                                                    │  If it is equal or larger than
    return begin;   ⟵——┐  Otherwise, return an    │  end, n is larger than the
}                       │  iterator to the element.   sequence, so return end.
```

Random-access iterators enable the most efficient algorithms, but fewer data structures can provide such iterators.

10.4.5 Iterator recap

We've looked at the various categories of iterators and how their different capabilities enable more efficient algorithms. We started with input and output iterators, which perform a one-pass traversal over a sequence. Input iterators allow us to read values, whereas output iterators allow us to set values.

This is all we need for algorithms such as `map()`, `filter()`, and `reduce()`, which process their input in linear fashion. Most programming languages provide algorithm libraries for only this type of iterator, including Java and C#, with their `Iterable<T>` and `IEnumerable<T>`.

Next, we saw that adding the ability to both read and write a value, and to create a copy of an iterator, enables other useful algorithms that can modify data in place. These new capabilities were supplied by a forward iterator.

In some cases, such as the `reverse()` example, moving only forward through a sequence is not enough. We need to move both ways. An iterator that can step both forward and backward is called a bidirectional iterator.

Finally, some algorithms perform better if they can jump around a sequence and access items at arbitrary locations without needing to traverse step by step. Sorting algorithms are good examples; so is the simple `elementAt()` that we just saw. To support such algorithms, we introduced the random-access iterator, which can move over multiple elements in one step.

These ideas are not new; the C++ standard library provides a set of efficient algorithms that use iterators with similar capabilities. Other languages limit themselves to a smaller set of algorithms or less-efficient implementations.

You may have noticed that the iterator-based algorithms were not fluent, as they took a pair of iterators as input and returned either `void` or an iterator. C++ is moving from iterators to ranges. We won't cover this topic deeply in this book, but at a high level, a *range* can be thought of as a pair of `begin`/`end` iterators. Updating the algorithms to take ranges as arguments and to return ranges sets the stage for a more fluent API in which we can chain operations on ranges. It is likely that at some point in the future, range-based algorithms will make their way into other languages. The ability to run efficient, in-place, generic algorithms over any data structure with a capable-enough iterator is extremely useful.

10.4.6 Exercises

1 What is the minimum iterator category required to support `drop()` that skips the first n elements of a range?

   a `InputIterator`

   b `ForwardIterator`

   c `BidirectionalIterator`

   d `RandomAccessIterator`

2 What is the minimum iterator category required to support a binary search algorithm (with O(log n))? As a reminder, binary search checks the middle element of a range. If it's larger than the value searched for, it splits the range in halves and looks at the first half. If not, it looks at the second half of the range and then repeats. The idea is that the search space is halved at each step, so the complexity of the algorithm is O(log n).

   a `InputIterator`

   b `ForwardIterator`

   c `BidirectionalIterator`

   d `RandomAccessIterator`

10.5 Adaptive algorithms

The more we ask of an iterator, the fewer the data structures that can supply it. We saw that we can create a forward iterator over a singly linked list, a doubly linked list, or an array. If we want a bidirectional iterator, singly linked lists are out of the picture. We can get a bidirectional iterator over doubly linked lists and arrays but not singly linked lists. If we want a random-access iterator, we need to drop doubly linked lists.

We want generic algorithms to be as general as possible, and they require the least capable iterator that is good enough to support the algorithm. But as we just saw, less efficient versions of an algorithm don't require that much from their iterators. For some algorithms, we can provide multiple versions: a less-efficient version that works with a less-capable iterator and a more-efficient version that works with a more-capable iterator.

Let's revisit our `elementAt()` example. This algorithm will return the nth value in a sequence or the end of the sequence if n is larger than the length of the sequence. If we have a forward iterator, we can increment it n times and return the value. This has linear, or $O(n)$ complexity, as we need to perform more steps as n increases. On the other hand, if we have a random-access iterator, we can retrieve the element in constant, or $O(1)$, time.

Do we want to provide a more-general, less-efficient algorithm or a more-efficient algorithm that is limited to fewer data structures? The answer is that we don't have to choose: we can provide two versions of the algorithm, and depending on the type of iterator we get, we can leverage the most-efficient implementation.

Let's implement an `elementAtForwardIterator()` that retrieves the element in linear time and an `elementAtRandomAccessIterator()` that retrieves the element in constant time, as shown in the following listing.

Listing 10.39 `elementAt()` **with input and random-access iterators**

```
function elementAtForwardIterator<T>(
    begin: IForwardIterator<T>, end: IForwardIterator<T>,
    n: number): IForwardIterator<T> {
    while (!begin.equals(end) && n > 0) {
        begin.increment();
        n--;
    }

    return begin;
}

function elementAtRandomAccessIterator<T>(
    begin: IRandomAccessIterator<T>, end: IRandomAccessIterator<T>,
    n: number): IRandomAccessIterator<T> {
    begin.move(n);

    if (begin.distance(end) <= 0) return end;

    return begin;
}
```

While n is greater than 0 and we haven't reached the end of the sequence, move the iterator to the next element and decrement n.

Return begin. This will be either the nth element or the end of the sequence.

This is the elementAt() implementation from the preceding section.

Now we can implement an `elementAt()` that picks the algorithm to apply based on the capabilities of the iterators it receives as arguments, as shown in listing 10.40. Note that TypeScript doesn't support function overloading, so we need to use a function that determines the type of the iterator. In other languages, such as C# and Java, we can simply provide methods that have the same name but take different arguments.

Listing 10.40 **Adaptive** `elementAt()`

```
function isRandomAccessIterator<T>(
    iter: IForwardIterator<T>): iter is IRandomAccessIterator<T> {
    return "distance" in iter;
}

function elementAt<T>(
    begin: IForwardIterator<T>, end: IForwardIterator<T>,
```

We consider iter to be a random-access iterator if it has a distance method.

If iterators are random-access, we call the efficient elementAtRandomAccessIterator() function.

```
n: number): IForwardIterator<T> {
if (isRandomAccessIterator(begin) && isRandomAccessIterator(end)) {
    return elementAtRandomAccessIterator(begin, end, n);
} else {
    return elementAtForwardIterator(begin, end, n);
}
}
```

If not, we fall back to the less-efficient elementAtForwardIterator() function.

A good algorithm works with what it has; it adapts to a less-capable iterator with a less-efficient implementation while enabling the most-efficient implementation for more-capable iterators.

10.5.1 *Exercise*

1   Implement nthLast(), a function that returns an iterator to the nth-last element of a range (or end if the range is too small). If n is 1, we return an iterator pointing to the last element; if n is 2, we return an iterator pointing to the second to last element, and so on. If n is 0, we return the end iterator pointing one past the last element of the range.

2   Hint: we can implement this with a ForwardIterator with two passes. The first pass counts the elements of the range. In the second pass, because we know the size of the range, we know when to stop to be n items from the end.

Summary

- Generic algorithms operate on iterators, so they can be reused across different data structures.
- Whenever you write a loop, consider whether a library algorithm or a composition of algorithms can achieve the same result.
- Fluent APIs provide a nice interface for chaining algorithms.
- Type constraints allow algorithms to require certain capabilities from the types they operate on.
- Input iterators can read values and can be advanced. We read from a stream, like standard input, with an input iterator. After we read a value, we can't reread; we can only move forward.
- Output iterators can be written to and can be advanced. We write to a stream, like standard output, with an output iterator. After we write a value, we can't read it back.
- Forward iterators can read values and be written to, advanced, and cloned. A linked list is a good example of a data structure that can support a forward iterator. We can move to the next element and hold multiple references to the

current element, but we can't move to the previous element unless we save a reference to it when we are initially on it.

- Bidirectional iterators have all the features of forward iterators but can also move backward. A doubly linked list is an example of a data structure that supports a bidirectional iterator. We can move to both the next and the previous element as needed.
- Random-access iterators can freely move to any position in a sequence. An array is a data structure that supports a random-access iterator. We can jump in one step to any element.
- Most mainstream languages provide algorithm libraries for input iterators.
- More-capable iterators enable more-efficient algorithms.
- Adaptive algorithms provide multiple implementations: the more capable the iterators, the more efficient the algorithm.

In chapter 11, we'll step it up to the next level of abstraction—higher kinded types—and explain what a monad is and what we can do with it.

Answers to exercises

BETTER MAP(), FILTER(), REDUCE()

1 A possible implementation using `reduce()` and `filter()`:

```
function concatenateNonEmpty(iter: Iterable<string>): string {
    return reduce(
        filter(
            iter,
            (value) => value.length > 0),
        "", (str1: string, str2: string) => str1 + str2);
}
```

2 A possible implementation using `map()` and `filter()`:

```
function squareOdds(iter: Iterable<number>): IterableIterator<number> {
    return map(
        filter(
            iter,
            (value) => value % 2 == 1),
        (x) => x * x
    );
}
```

COMMON ALGORITHMS

1 A possible implementation:

```
class FluentIterable<T> {
    /* ... */

    take(n: number): FluentIterable<T> {
        return new FluentIterable (this.takeImpl(n));
    }
```

```
            private *takeImpl(n: number): IterableIterator<T> {
                for (const value of this.iter) {
                    if (n-- <= 0) return;

                    yield value;
                }
            }
        }
```

2 A possible implementation:

```
class FluentIterable<T> {
    /* ... */

    drop(n: number): FluentIterable<T> {
        return new FluentIterable(this.dropImpl(n));
    }

    private *dropImpl(n: number): IterableIterator<T> {
        for (const value of this.iter) {
            if (n-- > 0) continue;

            yield value;
        }
    }
}
```

CONSTRAINING TYPE PARAMETERS

1 A possible solution using a generic type constraint to ensure that T is
   IComparable:

```
function clamp<T extends IComparable<T>>(value: T, low: T, high: T): T {
    if (value.compareTo(low) == ComparisonResult.LessThan) {
        return low;
    }

    if (value.compareTo(high) == ComparisonResult.GreaterThan) {
        return high;
    }

    return value;
}
```

EFFICIENT REVERSE AND OTHER ALGORITHMS USING ITERATORS

1 a—drop() can be used even on potentially infinite streams of data. Being able
   simply to advance is sufficient.

2 d—Binary search needs to be able to jump to the middle of the range at each
   step to be efficient. A bidirectional iterator would still have to step element by
   element to reach the half of the range, which would not make it O(log n).
   (Step by step is O(n) or linear.)

ADAPTIVE ALGORITHMS

1 An adaptive algorithm will decrement from the back if it receives bidirectional
   iterators and use the two-pass approach when it receives forward iterators. Here
   is a possible implementation:

```
function nthLastForwardIterator<T>(
    begin: IForwardIterator<T>, end: IForwardIterator<T>, n: number)
    : IForwardIterator<T> {
    let length: number = 0;
    let begin2: IForwardIterator<T> = begin.clone();

    // Determine the length of the range
    while (!begin.equals(end)) {
        begin.increment();
        length++;
    }

    if (length < n) return end;

    let curr: number = 0;

    // Advance until the current element is the nth from the back
    while (!begin2.equals(end) && curr < length - n) {
        begin2.increment();
        curr++;
    }

    return begin2;
}

function nthLastBidirectionalIterator<T>(
    begin: IBidirectionalIterator<T>, end: IBidirectionalIterator<T>,
n: number)
    : IBidirectionalIterator<T> {
    let curr: IBidirectionalIterator<T> = end.clone();

    while (n > 0 && !curr.equals(begin)) {
        curr.decrement();
        n--;
    }

    // Range is too small if we reached begin before decrementing n
times
    if (n > 0) return end;

    return curr;
}

function isBidirectionalIterator<T>(
    iter: IForwardIterator<T>): iter is IBidirectionalIterator<T> {
    return "decrement" in iter;
}
```

```
function nthLast<T>(
    begin: IForwardIterator<T>, end: IForwardIterator<T>, n: number)
    : IForwardIterator<T> {
    if (isBidirectionalIterator(begin) && isBidirectionalIterator(end))
{
        return nthLastBidirectionalIterator(begin, end, n);
    } else {
        return nthLastForwardIterator(begin, end, n);
    }
}
```

Higher kinded types and beyond

This chapter covers

- Applying `map()` to various other types
- Encapsulating error propagation
- Understanding monads and their applications
- Finding resources for further study

Throughout the book, we've looked at various versions of a very common algorithm, `map()`, and in chapter 10 we saw how iterators provide an abstraction that allows us to reuse it across various data structures. In this chapter, we'll see how we can extend this algorithm beyond iterators and provide an even more general version. This powerful algorithm allows us to mix and match generic types and functions, and can help by providing a uniform way to handle errors.

After we go over a few examples, we'll provide a definition for this broadly applicable family of functions, known as functors. We'll also explain what higher kinded types are and how they help us define such generic functions. We'll look at the limitations we run into with languages that lack support for higher kinded types.

Next, we'll look at monads. The term shows up in multiple places, and although it might sound intimidating, the concept is straightforward. We'll explain what a monad is and go over multiple applications, from better error propagation to asynchronous code and sequence flattening.

We will wrap up with a section that discusses some of the topics we learned about in this book and a couple of other kinds of types we did not cover: dependent types and linear types. We won't go into details here; rather, we'll provide a quick summary and list some resources in case you want to learn more. We recommend several books to learn more about each of these topics, as well as programming languages that provide support for some of these features.

11.1 *An even more general map*

In chapter 10, we updated our map() implementation from chapter 5, which worked only on arrays, to a generic implementation that worked on iterators, shown in listing 11.1. We talked about how iterators abstract data structure traversal, so our new version of map() can apply a function to elements in any data structure (figure 11.1).

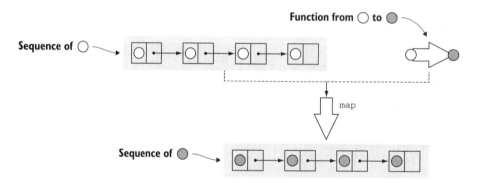

Figure 11.1   map() **takes an iterator over a sequence, in this case a list of circles, and a function that transforms a circle.** map() **applies the function to each element in the sequence and produces a new sequence with the transformed elements.**

Listing 11.1   Generic map()

```
function* map<T, U>(iter: Iterable<T>, func: (item: T) => U):
    IterableIterator<U> {
    for (const value of iter) {
        yield func(value);
    }
}
```

This implementation works on iterators, but we should be able to apply a function of the form (item: T) => U to other types too. Let's take, as an example, the Optional<T> type we defined in chapter 3, shown in the next listing.

Listing 11.2   Optional type

```
class Optional<T> {
    private value: T | undefined;
    private assigned: boolean;

    constructor(value?: T) {
        if (value) {
            this.value = value;
            this.assigned = true;
        } else {
            this.value = undefined;
            this.assigned = false;
        }
    }

    hasValue(): boolean {
        return this.assigned;
    }

    getValue(): T {
        if (!this.assigned) throw Error();

        return <T>this.value;
    }
}
```

It feels natural to be able to map a function `(value: T) => U` over an `Optional<T>`. If the optional contains a value of type `T`, mapping the function over it should return an `Optional<U>` containing the result of applying the function. On the other hand, if the optional doesn't contain a value, mapping would result in an empty `Optional<U>` (figure 11.2).

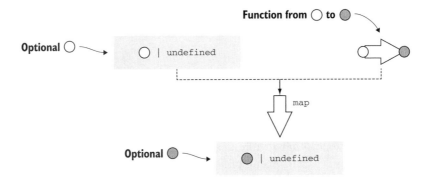

Figure 11.2   Mapping a function over an optional value. If the optional is empty, `map()` returns an empty optional; otherwise, it applies the function to the value and returns an optional containing the result.

Let's sketch out an implementation. We'll put this function in a namespace. Because TypeScript doesn't support function overloading, to have multiple functions with the same name, we need to put them in different namespaces so the compiler can determine the function we are calling.

Listing 11.3 Optional `map()`

export simply makes the function visible outside the namespace.

```
namespace Optional {
    export function map<T, U>(
        optional: Optional<T>, func: (value: T) => U): Optional<U> {
        if (optional.hasValue()) {
            return new Optional<U>(func(optional.getValue()));
        } else {
            return new Optional<U>();
        }
    }
}
```

If the optional has a value, we extract it, pass it to func(), and use its result to initialize an Optional<U>.

If the optional is empty, we create a new empty Optional<U>.

We can do something very similar with the TypeScript sum type T or undefined. Remember, Optional<T> is a DIY version of such a type that works even in languages that don't support sum types natively, but TypeScript does. Let's see how we can map over a "native" optional type T | undefined.

Mapping a function (value: T) => U over T | undefined should apply the function and return its result if we have a value of type T, or return undefined if we start with undefined.

Listing 11.4 Sum type `map()`

```
namespace SumType {
    export function map<T, U>(
        value: T | undefined, func: (value: T) => U): U | undefined {
        if (value == undefined) {
            return undefined;
        } else {
            return func(value);
        }
    }
}
```

These types can't be iterated over, but it still makes sense for a map() function to exist for them. Let's define another simple generic type, Box<T>, shown in the following listing. This type simply wraps a value of type T.

Listing 11.5 Box type

```
class Box<T> {
    value: T;
```

Box<T> simply wraps a value of type T.

```
constructor(value: T) {
    this.value = value;
}
}
```

Can we map a function (value: T) => U over this type? We can. As you might have guessed, map() for Box<T> would return a Box<U>: it will take the value T out of Box<T>, apply the function to it, and put the result back into a Box<U>, as shown in figure 11.3 and listing 11.6..

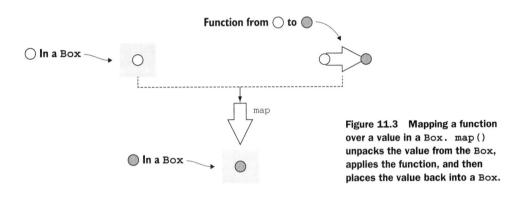

Figure 11.3 Mapping a function over a value in a Box. map() unpacks the value from the Box, applies the function, and then places the value back into a Box.

Listing 11.6 Box map()

```
namespace Box {
    export function map<T, U>(
        box: Box<T>, func: (value: T) => U): Box<U> {
        return new Box<U>(func(box.value));
    }
}
```
map() over Box<T> extracts the values, calls func() on it, and puts the result into a Box<U>.

We can map functions over many generic types. Why is this capability useful? It's useful because map(), like iterators, provides another way to decouple types that store data from functions that operate on that data.

11.1.1 *Processing results or propagating errors*

As a concrete example, let's take a couple of functions that process a numerical value. We'll implement a simple square(), a function that takes a number as an argument and returns its square. We'll also implement stringify(), a function that takes a number as an argument and returns its string representation, as shown in the next listing.

Listing 11.7 square() and stringify()

```
function square(value: number): number {
    return value ** 2;
}
```

```
function stringify(value: number): string {
    return value.toString();
}
```

Now let's say that we have a readNumber() function, which reads a numeric value from a file, as shown in listing 11.8. Because we are dealing with input, we might run into some problems. What if the file doesn't exist or can't be opened, for example? In that case, readNumber() will return undefined. We won't look at the implementation of this function; the important thing for our example is its return type.

Listing 11.8   readNumber() return type

```
function readNumber(): number | undefined {
    /* Implementation omitted */
}
```

If we want to read a number and process it by applying square() to it first and then stringify(), we need to ensure that we actually have a numerical value as opposed to undefined. A possible implementation is to convert from number | undefined to number, using if statements wherever needed, as the next listing shows.

Listing 11.9   Processing a number

```
function process(): string | undefined {
    let value: number | undefined = readNumber();

    if (value == undefined) return undefined;      ◁──┐  We need to check whether value
                                                       │  is undefined. In that case, we
    return stringify(square(value));      ◁─────────┐  │  immediately return undefined.
}                                                   │
                                        We process the value
                                        and return the result.
```

We have two functions that operate on numbers, but because our input can also be undefined, we need to handle that case explicitly. This is not particularly bad, but in general, the less branching our code has, the less complex it is. It is easier to understand and to maintain, and there are fewer opportunities for bugs. Another way to look at this is that process() itself simply propagates undefined; it doesn't do anything useful with it. It would be better if we could keep process() responsible for processing and let someone else handle error cases. How can we do this? With the map() we implemented for sum types, as shown in the following listing.

Listing 11.10   Processing with map()

```
namespace SumType {
    export function map<T, U>(                                        ◁──┐
        value: T | undefined, func: (value: T) => U): U | undefined {    │
        if (value == undefined) {                                        │
            return undefined;               This is the map() for sum types we
                                            implemented in listing 11.4.
```

```
        } else {
            return func(value);
        }
    }
}

function process(): string | undefined {
    let value: number | undefined = readNumber();

    let squaredValue: number | undefined =
        SumType.map(value, square);

    return SumType.map(squaredValue, stringify);
}
```

Instead of explicitly checking for undefined, we call map() to apply square() on the value. If it is undefined, map() will give us back undefined.

Just as with square(), we map() our stringify() function on the squaredValue. If it is undefined, map() will return undefined.

Now our `process()` implementation has no branching. The responsibility for unpacking `number | undefined` into a `number` and checking for `undefined` is handled by `map()`. `map()` is generic and can be used across many other types (such as `string | undefined`) and in many other processing functions.

In our case, because `square()` is guaranteed to return a number, we can create a small lambda that chains `square()` and `stringify()`, and pass that to `map()` in the next listing.

Listing 11.11 Processing with lambda

```
function process(): string | undefined {
    let value: number | undefined = readNumber();

    return SumType.map(value,
        (value: number) => stringify(square(value)));
}
```

Lambda that passes the result of square() to stringify()

This implementation is a functional implementation of `process()`, in that the error propagation is delegated to `map()`. We'll talk more about error handling in section 11.2, which discusses monads. For now, let's look at another application of `map()`.

11.1.2 Mix-and-match function application

Without the `map()` family of functions, if we have a `square()` function that squares a number, we would have to implement some additional logic to get a `number` from a `number | undefined` sum type. Similarly, we would have to implement some additional logic to get a value from a `Box<number>` and package it back in a `Box<number>`, as the following listing shows.

Listing 11.12 Unpacking values for `square()`

```
function squareSumType(value: number | undefined)
    : number | undefined {
    if (value == undefined) return undefined;
```

This function wraps the undefined check.

```
        return square(value);
}

function squareBox(box: Box<number>): Box<number> {
    return new Box(square(box.value));
}
```

> **This function unpacks the value from Box and then puts the result into another Box.**

So far, this isn't too bad. But what if we want something similar with `stringify()`? Again, we'll end up writing two functions that look a lot like the previous ones, as shown in the following code.

Listing 11.13   Unpacking values for `stringify()`

```
function stringifySumType(value: number | undefined)
    : string | undefined {
    if (value == undefined) return undefined;

    return stringify(value);
}

function stringifyBox(box: Box<number>): Box<string> {
    return new Box(stringify(box.value))
}
```

This starts to look like duplicate code, which is never good. If we have `map()` functions available for `number | undefined` and `Box`, they provide the abstraction to remove the duplicate code. We can pass either `square()` or `stringify()` to either `SumType.map()` or to `Box.map()` in the next listing; no additional code is needed.

Listing 11.14   Using `map()`

```
let x: number | undefined = 1;
let y: Box<number> = new Box(42);

console.log(SumType.map(x, stringify));
console.log(Box.map(y, stringify));

console.log(SumType.map(x, square));
console.log(Box.map(y, square));
```

Now let's define this family of `map()` functions.

11.1.3   *Functors and higher kinded types*

What we talked about in the preceding section are functors.

> **FUNCTORS** A *functor* is a generalization of functions that perform mapping operations. For any generic type like `Box<T>`, a `map()` operation that takes a `Box<T>` and a function from `T` to `U` and produces a `Box<U>` is a functor (figure 11.4).

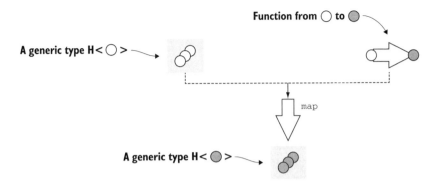

Figure 11.4 We have a generic type H that contains 0, 1, or more values of some type T and a function from T to U. In this case, T is an empty circle, and U is a full circle. The map() functor unpacks the T or Ts from the H<T> instance, applies the function, and then places the result back into an H<U>.

Functors are extremely powerful concepts, but most mainstream languages do not have a good way to express them because the general definition of a functor relies on higher kinded types.

HIGHER KINDED TYPES A generic type is a type that has a type parameter, such as a generic type T, or a type like Box<T> that has a type parameter T. A *higher kinded type*, just like a higher-order function, represents a type parameter with another type parameter. T<U> or Box<T<U>>, for example, have a type parameter T that in turn has a type parameter U.

Type constructors

In type systems, we can consider a *type constructor* to be a function that returns a type. This is not something that we would implement ourselves; this is how the type system looks at types internally.

Every type has a constructor. Some constructors are trivial. The constructor for the type number can be thought of as a function that takes no arguments and returns the type number. This would be () -> [number type].

Even a function, such as square(), that has the type (value: number) => number still has a type constructor with no arguments () -> [(value: number) => number type] because even though the function takes an argument, its type doesn't; it's always the same.

Things get more interesting when we get to generics. A generic type, such as T[], does need an actual type parameter to produce a concrete type. Its type constructor is (T) -> [T[] type]. When T is number, for example, we get an array of numbers number[] as our type, but when T is string, we get an array of strings type string[]. Such a constructor is also called a *kind*—that is, the kind of types T[].

(continued)

Higher kinded types, like higher-order functions, take things one level up. In this case, our type constructor can take another type constructor as an argument. Let's take the type `T<U>[]`, which is an array of some type `T` that also has a type argument `U`. Our first type constructor takes a `U` and produces a `T<U>`. We need to pass this to a second type constructor that produces `T<U>[]` from it `((U) -> [T<U> type]) -> [T<U>[] type]`.

Just as higher-order functions are functions that take other functions as argument, higher kinded types are kinds (parameterized type constructors) that take other kinds as arguments.

In theory, we can go any number of levels deep to something like `T<U<V<W>>>`, but in practice, things become less useful after the first `T<U>` level.

Because we don't have a good way to express higher kinded types in TypeScript, C#, or Java, we can't define a construct by using the type system to express a functor. Languages such as Haskell and Idris, which have more powerful type systems, make these definitions possible. In our case, though, because we can't enforce this capability through the type system, we can think of it as more of a pattern.

We can say that a functor is any type H with a type parameter T (`H<T>`) for which we have a function `map()` that takes an argument of type `H<T>` and a function from `T` to `U`, and returns a value of type `H<U>`.

Alternatively, if we want to be more object-oriented, we can make `map()` a member function and say that `H<T>` is a functor if it has a method `map()` that takes a function from `T` to `U` and returns a value of type `H<U>`. To see exactly where the type system is lacking, we can try to sketch out an interface for it. Let's call this interface `Functor` and have it declare `map()` in the next listing.

Listing 11.15   Sketch of `Functor` interface

```
interface Functor<T> {
    map<U>(func: (value: T) => U): Functor<U>;
}
```

We can update `Box<T>` to implement this interface in the following listing.

Listing 11.16   Box implementing the interface

```
class Box<T> implements Functor<T> {
    value: T;
```

```
constructor(value: T) {
    this.value = value;
}

map<U>(func: (value: T) => U): Box<U> {
    return new Box(func(this.value));
}
}
```

This code compiles; the only problem is that it isn't specific enough. Calling map() on Box<T> returns an instance of type Box<U>. But if we work with Functor interfaces, we see that the map() declaration specifies that it returns a Functor<U>, not a Box<U>. This isn't specific enough. We need a way to specify, when we declare the interface, exactly what the return type of map() will be (in this case, Box<U>).

We would like to be able to say, "This interface will be implemented by a type H with a type argument T." The following code shows how this declaration would look like if TypeScript supported higher kinded types. It obviously doesn't compile.

Listing 11.17 Functor interface

```
interface Functor<H<T>> {
    map<U>(func: (value: T) => U): H<U>;
}

class Box<T> implements Functor<Box<T>> {
    value: T;

    constructor(value: T) {
        this.value = value;
    }

    map<U>(func: (value: T) => U): Box<U> {
        return new Box(func(this.value));
    }
}
```

Lacking this, let's just think of our map() implementations as a pattern for applying functions to generic types or values in some box.

11.1.4 Functors for functions

Note that we also have functors over functions. Given a function with any number of arguments that returns a value of type T, we can map a function that takes a T and produces a U over it, ending up with a function that takes the same inputs as the original function and returns a value of type U. map() in this case is simply function composition as shown in figure 11.5.

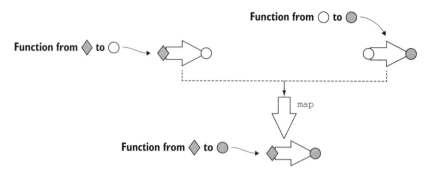

Figure 11.5 Mapping a function over another function composes the two functions. The result is a function that takes the same arguments as the original function and returns a value of the second function's return type. The two functions need to be compatible; the second function must expect an argument of the same type as the one returned by the original function.

As an example, let's take a function that takes two arguments of type T and produces a value of type T, and implement its corresponding map() in the next listing. This returns a function that takes two arguments of type T and returns a value of type U.

Listing 11.18   Function map()

```
namespace Function {                              map() takes a function (T, T) => T,
    export function map<T, U>(                     and a function T => U to map over it.
        f: (arg1: T, arg2: T) => T, func: (value: T) => U)
        : (arg1: T, arg2: T) => U {                        map() returns
        return (arg1: T, arg2: T) => func(f(arg1, arg2));  a function
    }                                                       (T, T) => U.
}
                               The implementation simply returns
                               a lambda that composes func() and f()
                               by calling func() on the result of f().
```

Let's map stringify() over an add() function that takes two numbers and returns their sum. The result is a function that takes two numbers and returns a string—the stringified result of adding the two numbers, as shown in the following listing.

Listing 11.19   Applying map() over a function

```
function add(x: number, y: number): number {      add() simply sums
    return x + y;                                   its arguments.
}

function stringify(value: number): string {     stringify() has the same
    return value.toString();                     implementation as before.
}
                               We map the stringify() function over add(). Then
                               we call the returned functions with the
                               arguments 40 and 2. The result is the string "42".

const result: string = Function.map(add, stringify)(40, 2);
```

After functors, we'll cover one final construct: the monad.

11.1.5 Exercise

1 We have an interface `IReader<T>` that defines a single method, `read(): T`. Implement a functor that maps a function `(value: T) => U` over an `IReader<T>` and returns an `IReader<U>`.

11.2 Monads

You have probably heard the term *monad*, as it's been getting a lot of attention lately. Monads are making their way into mainstream programming, so you should know one when you see it. Building on top of section 11.1, in this section we will explain what a monad is and how it is useful. We'll start with a few examples and then look at the general definition.

11.2.1 Result or error

In section 11.1, we had a `readNumber()` function that returned `number | undefined`. We used functors to sequence processing with `square()` and `stringify()`, so that if `readNumber()` returns `undefined`, no processing happens, and the `undefined` is propagated through the pipeline.

This type of sequencing works with functors as long as only the first function—in this case, `readNumber()`—can return an error. But what happens if any of the functions we want to chain can error out? Let's say that we want to open a file, read its content as a string, and then deserialize that string into a `Cat` object, as shown in listing 11.20.

We have an `openFile()` function that returns an `Error` or a `FileHandle`. Errors can occur if the file doesn't exist, if it is locked by another process, or if the user doesn't have permission to open it. If the operation succeeds, we get back a handle to the file.

We have a `readFile()` function that takes a `FileHandle` and returns either an `Error` or a `string`. Errors can occur if the file can't be read, perhaps due to being too large to fit in memory. If the file can be read, we get back a `string`.

Finally, `deserializeCat()` function takes a string and returns an `Error` or a `Cat` instance. Errors can occur if the string can't be deserialized into a `Cat` object, perhaps due to missing properties.

All these functions follow the "return result or error" pattern from chapter 3, which suggests returning either a valid result or an error from a function, but not both. The return type will be an `Either<Error, ...>`.

Listing 11.20 Functions returning result or error

**readFile() returns
an Error or a string.**

**openFile() returns an
Error or a FileHandle.**

```
declare function openFile(path: string): Either<Error, FileHandle>;

declare function readFile(handle: FileHandle): Either<Error, string>;
```

```
declare function deserializeCat(
    serializedCat: string): Either<Error, Cat>;
```

deserializeCat() returns an Error or a Cat.

We are omitting the implementations, as they are not important. Let's also quickly review the implementation of `Either` from chapter 3 in the next listing.

Listing 11.21   Either type

```
class Either<TLeft, TRight> {
    private readonly value: TLeft | TRight;
    private readonly left: boolean;

    private constructor(value: TLeft | TRight, left: boolean) {
        this.value = value;
        this.left = left;
    }

    isLeft(): boolean {
        return this.left;
    }

    getLeft(): TLeft {
        if (!this.isLeft()) throw new Error();

        return <TLeft>this.value;
    }

    isRight(): boolean {
        return !this.left;
    }

    getRight(): TRight {
        if (this.isRight()) throw new Error();

        return <TRight>this.value;
    }

    static makeLeft<TLeft, TRight>(value: TLeft) {
        return new Either<TLeft, TRight>(value, true);
    }

    static makeRight<TLeft, TRight>(value: TRight) {
        return new Either<TLeft, TRight>(value, false);
    }
}
```

The type wraps a value of either TLeft or TRight and a flag to keep track of that type is used.

Private constructor, as we need to make sure that the value and boolean flag are in sync

Attempting to get a TLeft when we have a TRight, or vice versa, throws an error.

Factory functions call the constructor and ensure that the boolean flag is consistent with the value.

Now let's see in the next listing how we could chain these functions together into a `readCatFromFile()` function that takes a file path as an argument and returns a `Cat` instance, or an `Error` if anything went wrong along the way.

Listing 11.22 Processing and explicitly checking for errors

**readCatFromFile()
returns either an Error
or a Cat instance.**

**First, we attempt to open
the file. We get back either
an Error or a FileHandle.**

**If we have a
FileHandle, we
attempt to read
the content
of the file.**

```
function readCatFromFile(path: string): Either<Error, Cat> {
    let handle: Either<Error, FileHandle> = openFile(path);

    if (handle.isLeft()) return Either.makeLeft(handle.getLeft());

    let content: Either<Error, string> = readFile(handle.getRight());

    if (content.isLeft()) return Either.makeLeft(content.getLeft());

    return deserializeCat(content.getRight());
}
```

**If we have an Error,
we return early. We call
Either.makeLeft(), as
we need to convert from
Either<Error, FileHandle>
to Either<Error, Cat>.
We unpack the Error from
Either<Error, FileHandle>
and pack it back into an
Either<Error, Cat>.**

**Similarly, we return early
if we encountered an
error reading the file.**

**Finally, if we have the content, we
call deserializeCat(). Because this
function has the same return
type as readCatFromFile(), we
simply return its result.**

This function is very similar to the first implementation of process() earlier in this chapter. There, we provided an updated implementation that removed all the branching and error checking from the function and delegated those tasks to map(). Let's see what a map() for Either<TLeft, TRight> would look like in listing 11.23. We will follow the convention "Right is right; left is error," which means that TLeft contains an error, so map() will just propagate it. map() will apply a given function only if the Either contains a TRight.

Listing 11.23 Either map()

**func() is only applied if the input Either
contains a value of type TRight, so its
argument must be of type TRight.**

**If the input contains a TLeft, we
unpack it from Either<TLeft,
TRight> and repack it into
Either<TLeft, URight>.**

```
namespace Either {
    export function map<TLeft, TRight, URight>(
        value: Either<TLeft, TRight>,
        func: (value: TRight) => URight): Either<TLeft, URight> {
        if (value.isLeft()) return Either.makeLeft(value.getLeft());

        return Either.makeRight(func(value.getRight()));
    }
}
```

**If the input contains a TRight, we unpack it,
apply func() to it, and pack the result it into an
Either<TLeft, URight>.**

There is a problem with using map(), though: the types of the functions it expects as arguments are incompatible with the functions we are using. With map(), after we call openFile() and get back an Either<Error, FileHandle>, we would need a function (value: FileHandle) => string to read its content. That function can't itself return an Error, like square() or stringify(). But in our case, readFile() can fail, so it doesn't return string; it returns Either<Error, string>. If we attempt to use it in our readCatFromFile(), we get a compilation error, as the next listing shows.

Listing 11.24   Incompatible types

```
function readCatFromFile(path: string): Either<Error, Cat> {
    let handle: Either<Error, FileHandle> = openFile(path);

    let content: Either<Error, string> = Either.map(handle, readFile);   ◁──┐

    /* ... */                                              **This fails to compile due**
}                                                          **to a type mismatch.**
```

The error message we get is

```
Type  'Either<Error,  Either<Error,  string>>'  is  not
assignable to type 'Either<Error, string>'.
```

Our functor falls short here. Functors can propagate an initial error through the processing pipeline, but if every step in the pipeline can fail, functors no longer work. In figure 11.6, the black square represents an Error, and the white and black circles represent two types, such as FileHandle and string.

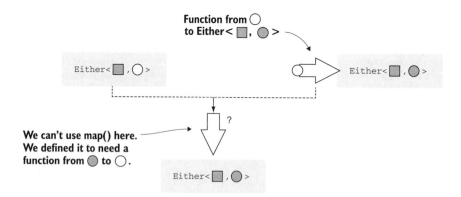

Figure 11.6   We can't use a functor in this case because the functor is defined to map a function from a white circle to a black circle. Unfortunately, our function returns a type already wrapped in an Either (an Either<black square, black circle>). We need an alternative to map() that can deal with this type of function.

`map()` from `Either<Error, FileHandle>` would need a function from File-Handle to `string` to produce an `Either<Error, string>`. Our `readFile()` function, on the other hand, is from `FileHandle` to `Either<Error, string>`.

This problem is easy to fix. We need a function similar to `map()` that goes from `T` to `Either<Error, U>`, as shown in the next listing. The standard name for such a function is `bind()`.

Listing 11.25 `Either bind()`

```
namespace Either {
    export function bind<TLeft, TRight, URight>(
        value: Either<TLeft, TRight>,
        func: (value: TRight) => Either<TLeft, URight>    ◁——  func() has a different type
    ): Either<TLeft, URight> {                                  from the func() in map().
        if (value.isLeft()) return Either.makeLeft(value.getLeft());

        return func(value.getRight());    ◁——  We can simply return the result
    }                                            of func(), as it has the same
}                                                type as the result of bind().
```

As we can see, the implementation is even simpler than the one for `map()`: after we unpack the value, we simply return the result of applying `func()` to it. Let's use `bind()` to implement our `readCatFromFile()` function in the next listing and get the desired branchless error propagation behavior.

Listing 11.26 Branchless `readCatFromFile()`

```
function readCatFromFile(path: string): Either<Error, Cat> {
    let handle: Either<Error, FileHandle> = openFile(path)

    let content: Either<Error, string> =                  Unlike map(), this code works.
        Either.bind(handle, readFile);        ◁——  Applying readFile() to handle gives
                                                    us back an Either<Error, string>.

    return Either.bind(content, deserializeCat);    ◁——  deserializeCat() has
}                                                         the same return type as
                                                          readCatFromFile(), so we simply
                                                          return the result of bind().
```

This version seamlessly chains together `openFile()`, `readFile()`, and `deserializeCat()` so that if any of the functions fails, the error gets propagated as the result of `readCatFromFile()`. Again, branching is encapsulated in the `bind()` implementation, so our processing function is linear.

11.2.2 *Difference between map() and bind()*

Before moving on to define monads, let's take another simplified example and contrast `map()` and `bind()`. We'll again use `Box<T>`, a generic type that simply wraps a value of type T. Although this type is not particularly useful, it is the simplest generic type we can have. We want to focus on how `map()` and `bind()` work with values of types T and U in some generic context, such as Box<T>, Box<U> (or T[], U[]; or Optional<T>, Optional<U>; or Either<Error, T>, Either<Error, U>, and so on).

For a Box<T>, a functor (map()) takes a Box<T> and a function from T to U and returns a Box<U>. The problem is that we have scenarios in which our functions are directly from T to Box<U>. This is what bind() is for. bind() takes a Box<T> and a function from T to Box<U> and returns the result of applying the function to the T inside Box<T> (figure 11.7).

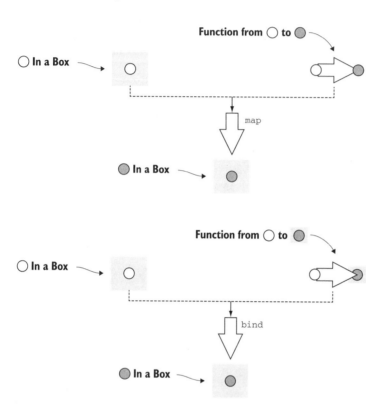

Figure 11.7 Contrasting map() and bind(). map() applies a function T => U over a Box<T> and returns a Box<U>. bind() applies a function T => Box<U> over a Box<T> and returns a Box<U>.

If we have a function stringify() that takes a number and returns its string representation, we can map() it on a Box<number> and get back a Box<string>, as shown in the following listing.

Listing 11.27 map() on Box

```
namespace Box {
    export function map<T, U>(
        box: Box<T>, func: (value: T) => U): Box<U> {
```

map() implementation for Box from earlier in this chapter.

```
        return new Box<U>(func(box.value));
    }
}
function stringify(value: number): string {     ◁──┐
    return value.toString();
}

const s: Box<string> = Box.map(new Box(42), stringify);   ◁──┐
```

stringify() implementation from earlier in this chapter takes a number and returns a string.

We can map stringify() on a Box<number> and get back a Box<string>.

If instead of `stringify()`, which goes from `number` to `string`, we have a `boxify()` function that goes from `number` directly to `Box<string>`, `map()` won't work. We'll need `bind()` instead, as shown in the next listing..

Listing 11.28 `bind()` on Box

```
namespace Box {
    export function bind<T, U>(
        box: Box<T>, func: (value: T) => Box<U>): Box<U> {   ◁──┐
        return func(box.value);
    }
}
function boxify(value: number): Box<string> {   ◁──┐
    return new Box(value.toString());
}

const b: Box<string> = Box.bind(new Box(42), boxify);   ◁──┐
```

bind() unpacks the value from Box and calls func() on it.

boxify() differs from stringify() in that it returns a Box<string> instead of a string.

We can bind boxify() on a Box<number> and get back a Box<string>.

The result of both `map()` and `bind()` is still a `Box<string>`. We still go from `Box<T>` to `Box<U>`; the difference is how we get there. In the `map()` case, we need a function from `T` to `U`. In the `bind()` case, we need a function from `T` to `Box<U>`.

11.2.3 *The monad pattern*

A monad consists of `bind()` and one more, simpler function. This other function takes a type `T` and wraps it into the generic type, such as `Box<T>`, `T[]`, `Optional<T>`, or `Either<Error, T>`. This function is usually called `return()` or `unit()`.

A monad allows structuring programs generically while encapsulating away boilerplate code needed by the program logic. With monads, a sequence of function calls can be expressed as a pipeline that abstracts away data management, control flow, or side effects.

Let's look at a few examples of monads. We can start with our simple `Box<T>` type and add `unit()` to it in the next listing to complete the monad.

Listing 11.29 Box monad

```
namespace Box {
    export function unit<T>(value: T): Box<T> {   ◁──┐
        return new Box(value);
    }
}
```

unit() simply calls Box's constructor to wrap the given value into an instance of Box<T>.

```
export function bind<T, U>(
    box: Box<T>, func: (value: T) => Box<U>): Box<U> {     ◁
    return func(box.value);
}
}
```
> bind() unpacks the value from Box and calls func() on it.

The implementation is very straightforward. Let's look at the `Optional<T>` monad functions in the following listing.

Listing 11.30   Optional monad

```
namespace Optional {
    export function unit<T>(value: T): Optional<T> {     ◁
        return new Optional(value);
    }
```
> unit() takes a value of type T and wraps it into an Optional<T>.

```
    export function bind<T, U>(
        optional: Optional<T>,
        func: (value: T) => Optional<U>): Optional<U> {
        if (!optional.hasValue()) return new Optional();     ◁

        return func(optional.getValue());     ◁
    }
}
```
> If the optional is empty, bind() returns an empty optional of type Optional<U>.

> If the optional contains a value, bind() returns the result of calling func() on it.

Very much as with functors, if a programming language can't express higher kinded types, we don't have a good way to specify a `Monad` interface. Instead, let's think of monads as a pattern.

> **MONAD PATTERN**   A monad is a generic type `H<T>` for which we have a function like `unit()` that takes a value of type `T` and returns a value of type `H<T>`, and a function like `bind()` that takes a value of type `H<T>` and a function from `T` to `H<U>`, and returns a value of type `H<U>`.

Bear in mind that because most languages use this pattern, without a way to specify an interface for the compiler to check, in many instances the two functions, `unit()` and `bind()`, may show up under different names. You may hear the term *monadic*, as in *monadic error handling*, which means that error handling follows the monad pattern.

Next, we'll look at another example. You may be surprised to see that this example showed up much earlier in this book, in chapter 6; we just didn't have a name for it yet.

11.2.4   The continuation monad

In chapter 6, we looked at ways to simplify asynchronous code. We ended up looking at promises. A *promise* represents the result of a computation that will happen sometime in the future. `Promise<T>` is the promise of a value of type T. We can schedule execution of asynchronous code by chaining promises, using the `then()` function.

Let's say we have a function that determines our location on the map. Because this function will work with the GPS, it may take longer to finish, so we make it asynchronous. It will return a promise of type `Promise<Location>`. Next, we have a function that, given a location, will contact a ride-sharing service to get us a `Car`, as the next listing shows.

Listing 11.31   Chaining promises

```
declare function getLocation(): Promise<Location>;
declare function hailRideshare(location: Location): Promise<Car>;

let car: Promise<Car> = getLocation().then(hailRideshare);
```

When getLocation() returns, hailRideshare() will be invoked with its result.

This should look very familiar to you at this point. `then()` is just how `Promise<T>` spells `bind()`!

As we saw in chapter 6, we can also create an instantly resolved promise by using `Promise.resolve()`. This takes a value and returns a resolved promise containing that value, which is the `Promise<T>` equivalent of `unit()`.

It turns out that chaining promises, an API available in virtually all mainstream programming languages, is monadic. It follows the same pattern that we saw in this section, but in a different domain. While dealing with error propagation, our monad encapsulated checking whether we have a value that we can continue operating on or have an error that we should propagate. With promises, the monad encapsulates the intricacies of scheduling and resuming execution. The pattern is the same, though.

11.2.5 *The list monad*

Another commonly used monad is the list monad. Let's look at an implementation over sequences: a `divisors()` function that takes a number n and returns an array containing all of its divisors except 1 and n itself, as shown in listing 11.32.

This straightforward implementation starts from 2 and goes up to half of n, and adds all numbers it finds that divide n without a remainder. There are more efficient ways to find all divisors of a number, but we'll stick to a simple algorithm in this case.

Listing 11.32   Divisors

```
function divisors(n: number): number[] {
    let result: number[] = [];

    for (let i = 2; i <= n / 2; i++) {
        if (n % i == 0) {
            result.push(i);
        }
    }

    return result;
}
```

Now let's say we want to take an array of numbers and return an array containing all their divisors. We don't need to worry about dupes. One way to do this is to provide a function that takes an array of input numbers, applies divisors() to each of them, and joins the results of all the calls to divisors() into a final result, as shown in the following code.

Listing 11.33 All divisors

```
function allDivisors(ns: number[]): number[] {
    let result: number[] = [];

    for (const n of ns) {
        result = result.concat(divisors(n));
    }

    return result;
}
```

It turns out that this pattern is common. Let's say that we have another function, anagrams(), that generates all permutations of a string and returns an array of strings. If we want to get the set of all anagrams of an array of strings, we would end up implementing a very similar function, as the next listing shows.

Listing 11.34 All anagrams

```
declare function anagram(input: string): string[];        ← anagram() implementation
                                                              omitted
function allAnagrams(inputs: string[]): string[] {        ←
    let result: string[] = [];                               allAnagrams() is very
                                                              similar to allDivisors().
    for (const input of inputs) {
        result = result.concat(anagram(input));
    }

    return result;
}
```

Now let's see whether we can replace allDivisors() and allAnagrams() with a generic function in the next listing. This function would take an array of Ts and a function from T to an array of Us, and return an array of Us.

Listing 11.35 List bind()

```
function bind<T, U>(inputs: T[], func: (value: T) => U[]): U[] {   ←
    let result: U[] = [];
                                          bind() takes an array of Ts, a function
    for (const input of inputs) {          that returns an array of Us given a T,
        result = result.concat(func(input));   ←   and returns an array of Us.
    }
                                          We apply func() to each input
    return result;                        T and concatenate the results.
}
```

```
function allDivisors(ns: number[]): number[] {
    return bind(ns, divisors);
}
```

allDivisors() can be expressed by binding divisors() to an array of numbers.

```
function allAnagrams(inputs: string[]): string[] {
    return bind(inputs, anagram);
}
```

allAnagrams() can be expressed by binding anagram() to an array of strings.

As you've probably guessed, this is the `bind()` implementation for the list monad. In the case of lists, `bind()` flattens the arrays returned by each call of the given function into a single array. While the error-propagating monad decides whether to propagate an error or apply a function and the continuation monad wraps scheduling, the list monad combines a set of results (a list of lists) into a single flat list. In this case, the box is a sequence of values (figure 11.8).

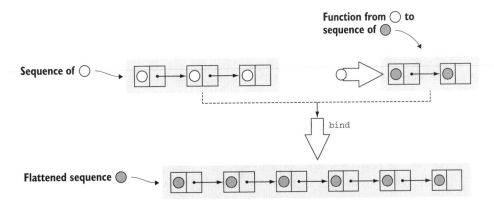

Figure 11.8 List monad: `bind()` takes a sequence of Ts (white circles, in this case) and a function T => sequence of Us (black circles, in this case). The result is a flattened list of Us (black circles).

The `unit()` implementation is trivial. Given a value of type T, it returns a list containing just that value. This monad generalizes to all kinds of lists: arrays, linked lists, and iterator ranges.

Category theory

Functors and monads come from category theory, a branch of mathematics that deals with structures consisting of objects and arrows between these objects. With these small building blocks, we can build up structures such as functors and monads. We won't go into its details now; we'll just say that multiple domains, like set theory and even type systems, can be expressed in category theory.

Haskell is a programming language that took a lot of inspiration from category theory, so its syntax and standard library make it easy to express concepts such as functors, monads, and other structures. Haskell fully supports higher kinded types.

(continued)

Perhaps because the building blocks of category theory are so simple, the abstractions we've been talking about are applicable across so many domains. We just saw that monads are useful in the context of error propagation, asynchronous code, and sequence processing.

Although most mainstream languages still treat monads as patterns instead of proper constructs, they are definitely useful structures that show up over and over in different contexts.

11.2.6 Other monads

A couple of other common monads, which are popular in functional programming languages with pure functions (functions that don't have side effects) and immutable data, are the state monad and the IO monad. We'll provide only a high-level overview of these monads, but if you decide to learn a functional programming language such as Haskell, you will likely encounter them early in your journey.

The state monad encapsulates a piece of state that it passes along with a value. This monad enables us to write pure functions that, given a current state, produce a value and an updated state. Chaining these together with `bind()` allows us to propagate and update state through a pipeline without explicitly storing it in a variable, enabling purely functional code to process and update state.

The IO monad encapsulates side effects. It allows us to implement pure functions that can still read user input or write to a file or terminal because the impure behavior is removed from the function and wrapped in the IO monad.

If you are interested in learning more, section 11.3 provides some resources for further study.

11.2.7 Exercise

1 Let's take the function type `Lazy<T>` defined as `() => T`, a function that takes no arguments and returns a value of type `T`. It's `Lazy` because it produces a `T`, but only when we ask it to. Implement `unit()`, `map()`, and `bind()` for this type.

11.3 Where to next?

We have covered a lot of ground, from primitive types and composition, to function types, subtyping, generics, and a sliver of higher kinded types. Still, we've barely scratched the surface of the world of type systems. In this final section, we'll look at a few topics you may be interested in learning more about and provide some starting points for each one.

11.3.1 Functional programming

Functional programming is a very different paradigm from object-oriented programming. Learning a functional programming language gives you another way to think about code. The more ways you have to approach a problem, the easier it is to break it down and solve it.

More and more features and patterns from functional programming are making their way into nonfunctional languages, which is a testament to their applicability. Lambdas and closures, immutable data structures, and reactive programming all come from the functional world.

The best way to get started is to pick up a functional programming language. I recommend Haskell as a starting language. It has a fairly simple syntax and a very powerful type system, and it stands on a solid theoretical foundation. A good, easy-to-read introductory book on the topic is *Learn You a Haskell for Great Good!* by Miran Lipovaca, published by No Starch Press.

11.3.2 Generic programming

As we saw in previous chapters, generic programming enables extremely powerful abstractions and code reusability. Generic programming became popular with the C++ standard template library and its mix-and-match collection of data structures and algorithms.

Generic programming has its roots in abstract algebra. Alexander Stepanov, who coined the term *generic programming* and implemented the original template library, wrote two books on the subject: *Elements of Programming* (coauthored with Paul McJones) and *From Mathematics to Generic Programming* (coauthored with Daniel E. Rose), both published by Addison-Wesley Professional.

Both books leverage some math, but I hope that fact won't discourage you. The elegance and beauty of the code are astonishing. The underlying theme is that with the right abstractions, we don't need to compromise: we can have code that is succinct, performant, easy to read, and elegant.

11.3.3 Higher kinded types and category theory

As we mentioned earlier, constructs such as functors come directly from category theory. Bartosz Milewski's *Category Theory for Programmers* (self-published) is a surprisingly easy-to-read introduction to this field.

We talked about functors and monads, but there is a lot more to higher kinded types. It will probably take a while for things to trickle down to more mainstream languages, but if you want to get ahead of the curve, Haskell is a good language with which to grasp these concepts.

Having the ability to specify higher-level abstractions such as monads enables us to write even-more-reusable code.

11.3.4 Dependent types

We didn't have space to cover dependent types in this book, but if you want to know more ways that a powerful type system makes code safer, this topic is another good one.

Very briefly, we saw how a type can dictate the values that a variable can take. We also looked at generics, in that a type can dictate what another type can be (type parameters). Dependent types flip this situation around: we have values that dictate types. The classic example is encoding the length of a list in the type system. A list of numbers with two elements ends up having a different type from a list of numbers with five elements, for example. Concatenating them gives us another type: a list with seven elements. You can imagine how encoding such information in the type system can guarantee, for example, that we never index out of bounds.

If you want to learn more about dependent types, I recommend *Type Driven Development with Idris* by Edwin Brady, published by Manning. Idris is a programming language with a syntax very similar to Haskell's, but it adds support for dependent types.

11.3.5 *Linear types*

In chapter 1, we briefly mentioned the deep connection between type systems and logic. Linear logic is a different take on classic logic that deals with resources. Unlike classic logic, in which a deduction, if true, is true forever, a linear logic proof consumes deductions.

This has a direct application in programming languages, in which using linear types in a type system encodes resource use tracking. Rust is a programming language that is steadily gaining in popularity; it uses linear types to ensure resource safety. Its borrow checker ensures that there is always a single owner of a resource. If we pass an object to a function, we transfer ownership of the resource, and the compiler no longer allows us to reference the resource until the function hands back the resource. This situation aims to eliminate concurrency issues, as well as the dreaded "use after free" and "double free" of C.

Rust is another good language to learn for its powerful generic support and unique safety features. *The Rust Programming Language* book is available for free on the Rust website and provides a good introduction to the language (https://doc.rust -lang.org/book).

Summary

- map() generalizes beyond iterators to other generic types.
- Functors encapsulate data unboxing with applications in composition and error propagation.
- With higher kinded types, we can express constructs such as functors by using generics that themselves have type parameters.
- Monads allow us to chain operations that return values in a Box.
- Error monads allow us to chain together operations that return result or failure, encapsulating the error-propagation logic.
- Promises are monads that encapsulate scheduling/asynchronous execution.
- The list monad applies a function that produces a sequence to a sequence of values and returns a flattened sequence.
- In languages that don't support higher kinded types, we can think of functors and monads as being patterns that we can apply to various problems.

- Haskell is a good language to learn for understanding functional programming and higher kinded types.
- Idris is a good language to learn for understanding dependent types and their applications.
- Rust is a good language to learn for understanding linear types and their applications.

I hope that you enjoyed this book, learned something you can use in your work, and gained some new perspectives. Happy, type-safe programming!

11.4 Answers to exercises

AN EVEN MORE GENERAL MAP

1 A possible implementation uses the object-oriented decorator pattern we recapped in chapter 5 to provide another type implementing IReader<U> that wraps an IReader<T> and, when read() is called, maps the given function over the original value:

```
interface IReader<T> {
    read(): T;
}

namespace IReader {
    class MappedReader<T, U> implements IReader<U> {
        reader: IReader<T>;
        func: (value: T) => U;

        constructor(reader: IReader<T>, func: (value: T) => U) {
            this.reader = reader;
            this.func = func;
        }

        read(): U {
            return this.func(this.reader.read());
        }
    }

    export function map<T, U>(reader: IReader<T>, func: (value: T) => U)
        : IReader<U> {
        return new MappedReader(reader, func);
    }
}
```

MONADS

1 A possible implementation follows. Notice the difference between map() and bind().

```
type Lazy<T> = () => T;

namespace Lazy {
    export function unit<T>(value: T): Lazy<T> {
        return () => value;
    }
}
```

```
export function map<T, U>(lazy: Lazy<T>, func: (value: T) => U)
    : Lazy<U> {
    return () => func(lazy());
}

export function bind<T, U>(lazy: Lazy<T>, func: (value: T) =>
Lazy<U>)
    : Lazy<U> {
    return func(lazy());
}
}
```

appendix A
TypeScript installation and source code

ONLINE

For simple code, such as trying out some code samples without dependencies, you can use the online TypeScript playground at https://www.typescriptlang.org/play.

LOCAL

To install locally, you first need Node.js and npm, the Node Package Manager. You can get them at https://www.npmjs.com/get-npm. When you have those, run `npm install -g typescript` to install the TypeScript compiler.

You can compile a single TypeScript file by passing it as an argument to the TypeScript compiler, such as `tsc helloworld.ts`. TypeScript compiles to JavaScript.

For projects that contain multiple files, a tsconfig.json file is used to configure the compiler. Running `tsc` with no arguments from a directory with a tsconfig.json file will compile the whole project according to the configuration.

SOURCE CODE

The code samples in this book are available at https://github.com/vladris/programming-with-types. Each chapter is in its own separate directory and has its own tsconfig.json.

Code was built with version 3.3 of TypeScript, targeting the ES6 standard, with `strict` settings.

Each sample file is stand-alone, so all types and functions required to run a code sample are inlined within each sample file. Each sample file uses a unique namespace to prevent naming conflicts, because some examples present different implementations of the same function or pattern.

To run a sample file, compile by using `tsc`; then run the compiled JavaScript file with Node. After compiling with `tsc helloworld.ts`, for example, run with `node helloworld.js`.

DIY

The book covers DIY implementations for variant and other types in TypeScript. For C# and Java versions of these types, check out the Maki type library: https://github.com/vladris/maki.

appendix B
TypeScript cheat sheet

This cheat sheet is not exhaustive. It covers the TypeScript syntax subset used in this book. For a full TypeScript reference, see http://www.typescriptlang.org/docs.

Table B.1 Primitive types

Type	Description
boolean	Can be true or false.
number	64-bit floating-point number.
string	UTF-16 Unicode string.
void	Type used as return type for functions that don't return meaningful values.
undefined	Can be only undefined. Represents, for example, a variable that was declared but not initialized.
null	Can be only null.
object	Represents an object or nonprimitive type.
unknown	Can represent any value. Type-safe, so it isn't implicitly converted to another type.
Any	Bypasses type checking. Type-unsafe and automatically converted to any other type.
Never	Cannot represent any value

Table B.2   Nonprimitive types *(continued)*

Example	Description
`string[]`	Array types are denoted by `[]` after the type name—in this case, an array of strings.
`[number, string]`	Tuples are declared as a list of types within `[]`—in this case, a `number` and a `string`, such as `[0, "hello"]`.
`(x: number, y: number) => number;`	Function types are declared as a list of arguments in `()`, then `=>`, then the return type.

`enum Direction {`
`    North,`
`    East,`
`    South,`
`    West,`
`}`
	Enumerations are declared with the keyword `enum`. In this case, a value can be one of the literals `North`, `East`, `South`, or `West`.

`type Point {`
`    X: number,`
`    Y: number`
`}`
	A type with `X` and `Y` properties of type `number`.

`interface IExpression {`
`    evaluate(): number;`
`}`
	An interface with an `evaluate()` method that returns a `number`.

`class Circle extends Shape`
`    implements IGeometry {`
`    // ...`
`}`
	`Circle` class extending the `Shape` base class and implementing the `IGeometry` interface.

`type Shape = Circle	Square;`	Union types are declared as an `|`-separated list of types. `Shape` is either a `Circle` or a `Square`.
`type SerializableExpression` `    = Serializable & Expression;`	Intersection types are declared as a `&`-separated list of types. `SerializableExpression` has both all members of `Serializable` and all members of `Expression`.

Table B.3   Declarations

Declaration	Description
`let x: number = 0;`	Declares a variable named `x` of type `number` with the initial value `0`.
`let x: number;`	Declares a variable named `x` of type `number`. Must be assigned a value before use.
`const x: number = 0;`	Declares a constant name `x` of type `number` with the value `0`. `x` can't be changed.

Table B.3 Declarations *(continued)*

Declaration	Description
```function add(x: number, y: number): number {\nreturn x + y;\n}```	Declares a function `add()` that takes two arguments, `x` and `y` of type `number`, and returns a `number`.
```(x: number, y: number) => x + y;```	A lambda (anonymous function) that takes two arguments and returns their sum.
```namespace Ns {\n export function func(): void {\n }\n}\n\nNs.func();```	Namespaces are declared with the `namespace` keyword. Declarations inside a namespace must be prefixed with `export` to be visible outside the namespace.
```class Example {\n a: number = 0;\n private b: number = 0;\n protected c: number = 0;\n readonly d: number;\n\n constructor(d: number) {\n this.d = d;\n }\n\n getD(): number {\n return this.d;\n }\n}\n\nlet instance: Example\n = new Example(5);```	All class members are `public` by default. Can also be `protected` (visible to derived classes) and `private` (visible only inside the class). Properties can also be `readonly`, in which case they can't be modified after they are assigned. Unless properties allow `undefined` as a value, they must be initialized either inline or with the constructor. The constructor of any class is `constructor()`. References to class members within the class must always be prefixed with `this`. Objects are instantiated with `new`, which invokes the constructor.
```declare const Sym: unique symbol;```	A `Symbol` guaranteed to be unique. No two constants declared as `unique symbol` can ever be equal.

Table B.4 Generics

Example	Description
```function identity<T>(value: T): T {\n return value;\n}\n\nlet str: string =\n identity<string>("Hello");```	A generic function has one or more type parameters between `<>`, before the argument list. `identity()` has one type argument `T`. It takes a value of type `T` and returns it. Specifying a concrete type between `<>` instantiates the generic function. `identity<string>()` is the `identity()` function where `T` is `string`.

Table B.4 Generics *(continued)*

Example	Description
| ```
class Box<T> {
    value: T;

    constructor(value: T) {
        this.value = value;
    }
}

let x: Box<number> = new Box(0);
``` | A generic class has one or more type parameters between <>, after the class name. Box has a property value of type T.<br>Specifying a concrete type between <> instantiates the generic class. Box<number> is the Box class where T is number. |
| ```
class Expr<T extends IExpression> {
    /* ... */
}
``` | A generic constraint is declared after the generic type parameter. In this example, T must support the IExpression interface. |

Table B.5 Type casts and type guards

Example	Description
| ```
let x: unknown = 0;

let y: number = <number>x;
``` | Specifying a type between <> before a value reinterprets the value as that type. x can be assigned to y only after being explicitly reinterpreted as number. |
| ```
type Point = {
    x: number;
    y: number;
}

function isPoint(p: unknown):
    p is Point {
 return
    ((<Point>p).x
            !== undefined) &&
     ((<Point>p).y
            !== undefined);
}

let p: unknown = { x: 10, y: 10 };

if (isPoint(p)) {
    // p is of type Point here
    p.x -= 10;
}
``` | A type predicate is a boolean that states that a variable is of a certain type. If we reinterpret p as a Point, and it has both an x and a y member (neither is undefined), p is a Point.<br>Within an if statement where a type predicate is true, the tested value is automatically reinterpreted as having that type. |

index